INFINITE AWARENESS

INFINITE AWARENESS

The Awakening of a Scientific Mind

Marjorie Hines Woollacott

Foreword by Pim van Lommel

ROWMAN & LITTLEFIELD
Lanham • Boulder • New York • London

Published by Rowman & Littlefield
A wholly owned subsidary of The Rowman & Littlefield Publishing Group,
Inc.
4501 Forbes Boulevard, Suite 200, Lanham, Maryland 20706
www.rowman.com

Unit A, Whitacre Mews, 26-34 Stannary Street, London SE11 4AB

British Library Cataloguing in Publication Information Available

Library of Congress Cataloging-in-Publication Data

Woollacott, Marjorie H., 1946-
Infinite awareness : the awakening of a scientific mind / Marjorie Woollacott ; foreword by Pim van
Lommel.
pages cm
Includes bibliographical references and index.
ISBN 978-1-4422-5033-8 (cloth : alk. paper) -- ISBN 978-1-4422-5034-5 (electronic)
1. Philosophy of mind. 2. Consciousness. 3. Religion and science. 4. Spiritual life. 5. Parapsychology. 6. Occultism. I. Title.
BD418.3.W66 2015
128'.2--dc23
2015014098

♾ ™ The paper used in this publication meets the minimum requirements of
American National Standard for Information Sciences Permanence of Paper
for Printed Library Materials, ANSI/NISO Z39.48-1992.

Printed in the United States of America

CONTENTS

FOREWORD

What happens to a neuroscientist who has a totally unexpected conscious experience with enhanced awareness during meditation, when the nervous system is quiet, and who realizes that this experience cannot be fully understood by current mainstream neuroscience? The inevitable result of this experience was that the neuroscientist, Marjorie Woollacott, had a great secret that could not be shared with her colleagues and that she started on a lifelong search, a scientific inquiry to understand and accept this unexpected and at first inexplicable experience.

Marjorie wanted to write this important, groundbreaking, and open-hearted book, which has the potential to change permanently our ideas about the interface between consciousness and the brain. She was disappointed that the transcendent level of awareness she experienced in meditation is something that most scientists do not acknowledge. And if neuroscientists should ever be willing to explore this kind of experience of enhanced consciousness and the feeling of unity with the universe, Marjorie was absolutely certain that they would have to include the first-person perspective. For most neuroscientists a subjective experience is not empirical evidence; they think a first-person account should never be trusted because it lacks so-called scientific objectivity. How could Marjorie resolve this problem? It was obvious that her own experiences of meditation challenged her own assumptions that materiality is the sole basis of the universe. They did not fit the current neuroscience model.

Through her practice of meditation, Marjorie had come to realize that the mind, while being influenced by the brain, is much more than just a function of the brain. At the same time, she was dismayed to consider that most of the eminent leaders in neuroscience maintain that consciousness is only a product of a functioning brain, that human beings have no free will, and that determinism—the idea that we are entirely controlled by our genetics and our neural circuitry—has been scientifically proven.

But there is no evidence whatsoever that determinism is a proven fact nor that only the brain produces the mind. For a traditional neuroscientist such phenomena as inspiration, intuition, emotions, and cognitive functioning are nothing more than neural activities in the brain. Marjorie was disheartened to find how few of her colleagues in neuroscience were willing even to question this materialist paradigm. It was her scientific curiosity that stimulated her to study her own experiences during meditation and the unusual conscious experiences of others, and to seek scientific theories to understand how and why these experiences could occur.

She found that, as unlikely as it seems, thousands of scientific studies about meditation are largely ignored by mainstream neuroscience. An important and intriguing finding from these studies is that meditation has an effect on the structure and function of the brain itself: an acute change found during meditation and a permanent change in brain activity induced by many years of meditation. These changes can only be explained by neuroplasticity, which means that changes in conscious awareness during meditation cause changes in the brain's synaptic connections. For Marjorie, these changes in the brain supported the idea that consciousness cannot be only a product of brain function but that, on the contrary, consciousness (or mind) must also have an existence apart from the body and that conscious awareness also comes from a source beyond the brain (the top-down perspective).

For Marjorie, some of the most compelling evidence that supports the idea that consciousness can exist without a functioning brain comes from the scientific literature on near-death experiences (NDEs) during cardiac arrest. Though NDEs seem to be fairly regularly occurring, they are, to many physicians, an inexplicable phenomenon and hence are often ignored. According to a recent random poll, about nine million people in the United States have had this extraordinary conscious experience.

As a cardiologist, I had the privilege to meet many patients who were willing to share accounts of their NDEs with me. In 1969, during my rotating internship, a patient was successfully resuscitated in the coronary care unit by electrical defibrillation, but the patient seemed to be very, very disappointed. He told me about going through a tunnel, seeing a light and also beautiful colors, and hearing music. At that time, I did not know that the same kind of experiences have been reported in many cultures, in many religions, and at all times in human history. The term "near-death experience" did not yet exist, nor had I ever heard of people having such a recollection from the period of their cardiac arrest. In fact, while studying for my degree, I had learned that such an experience is impossible: being unconscious means being unaware, and this applies to any patient suffering a cardiac arrest or in a coma. During cardiac arrest, the brain is not functioning at all; how could there be an experience? Yet I felt certain my patients had had the experience they were describing. For one thing, many of these patients underwent profound life changes afterward.

The important questions for me were these: *How is consciousness related to the integrity of brain function? How and why does an NDE occur? How does the content of an NDE come about? Why does a person's life change so radically after an NDE?* The answers I had to these questions seemed incomplete, incorrect, or unfounded.

This is why in 1988 we started a prospective study in survivors of cardiac arrest in ten Dutch hospitals to either corroborate or refute the existing theories on the cause and content of an NDE. This study was carried out among 344 patients with a proven life-threatening crisis: all these patients had been clinically dead, experiencing a period of unconsciousness caused by total lack of oxygen in the brain (anoxia) because of the arrest of circulation and breathing. In this situation, if no resuscitation is initiated within five to ten minutes, the brain cells will be irreversibly damaged and the patient will always die. During cardiac arrest there is no observable brain activity, with a flat-line EEG coming within fifteen seconds, and clinical findings in these unconscious patients show no body nor brainstem reflexes, as well as no breathing. Some patients, however, may report memories, with self-identity, with cognition, with emotion, and with the possibility of perception outside and above the lifeless body, and even with the experience of a conscious return into the body. We found in our study that 82 percent of the patients had no recollection of the period of their unconsciousness, whereas 18 percent reported an NDE. Why only 18 percent of patients reported an NDE was, and still is, a mystery. The degree or gravity of the lack of oxygen in the brain (anoxia) appeared to be irrelevant. So a physiological explanation for NDE in such cases could be excluded. The NDE seems to be an authentic experience that cannot be attributed to imagination, fear of death, hallucination, psychosis, the use of drugs, or oxygen deficiency. Also, people appear to be permanently changed by an NDE they have had during a cardiac arrest of only some minutes' duration.

Marjorie writes more about the results of this study in chapters 7 and 8 of this book. What I would like to speak of here are the changes that this study brought about in me, as a doctor and scientist. I was raised in an academic world where I was taught that for every observation, a reductionist and materialist (a so-called scientific) explanation was obvious. This made it impossible to accept that a clear consciousness could be experienced during a period of cardiac arrest or coma, or even briefly before, during, or after death. Until twenty-five years ago I accepted this view without question. Today, I feel "scientific" means asking questions with an open mind. Science itself should be the search to explain new mysteries, rather than sticking with old concepts and dogmas. He who has never changed his mind because he cannot accept new concepts has rarely learned something. I can assure the reader that I changed my mind—and learned quite a lot because of all those patients who were willing to share their near-death experiences with me. These patients greatly changed my views on the mind–brain relation and on the meaning of life and death. People with NDEs have been my greatest teachers.

According to several prospective studies on NDE in survivors of cardiac arrest, the current materialistic view of the relationship between the brain and consciousness held by most physicians, philosophers, and psychologists is too restricted for a proper understanding of this phenomenon. Research on NDE and on meditation questions the purely materialistic paradigm in science. Both kinds of conscious experiences could be seen as a glimpse into a higher or transpersonal aspect of our consciousness. During meditation the nervous system is quiet, but the mental functioning is active. The characteristics of NDEs are often seen in mystical experiences related to meditation traditions, including out-of-body experiences, enhanced mental functioning, and heightened perceptions. Some physicians who have had an NDE themselves discovered later that their experience could be duplicated by meditation.

As well as looking at scientific studies investigating near-death experiences during cardiac arrest, Marjorie Woollacott has looked at studies on meditation and reincarnation and about neuroplasticity, placebos, hypnosis, and distant healing. With all of this, she has come to the, I think inevitable, conclusion that the brain must have the function of facilitating, and not producing, the experience of consciousness. This means that consciousness is associated with, but not solely produced by, the brain. As Marjorie discusses, there are good reasons to assume that our consciousness does not always arise from our brain: there is evidence of enhanced and transpersonal consciousness; consciousness can sometimes be experienced separately from the body; and intention can change the function and structure of our body and brain. All of this should be a stimulus for further scientific study and debate. And, above all, we as scientists should question a purely materialist paradigm. I join Marjorie in the hope that in the near future modern science will embark on empirical research on the nature of consciousness. On this subject, science desperately needs a paradigm shift.

In this intriguing book, Marjorie is very open about her own evolution and her gradual growing insight that she and her fellow neuroscience teachers had been wrong in their ideas about how consciousness is related to brain function. Unfortunately, for years she was unable to share her new ideas with her colleagues. She felt divided, torn between the two perspectives in her life: mainstream neuroscience and meditation. By writing this book, she wanted to bring these two halves of her existence into resonance.

In *Infinite Awareness* Marjorie asks herself: *How was this awareness during meditation possible? Why did my life change so radically? And is there a neuroscientific explanation?* Many of these questions, and more, are answered in this book, which touched my heart with its honesty and with the author's obvious acceptance of the many consequences for her personal and professional life. She concludes that enhanced consciousness and infinite awareness are experienced beyond body and brain, and that the brain inevitably cannot be the sole producer of consciousness. Consciousness is what we are in essence.

I highly recommend this important book, which has the potential to break many scientific taboos. We should also realize, however, that the acceptance of new scientific ideas—in particular those ideas about the experience of enhanced consciousness that occurs independent of a normal functioning brain—requires us, as men and women of science, to open our minds and to abandon dogma.

—Pim van Lommel, cardiologist,
author of *Consciousness Beyond Life*

ACKNOWLEDGMENTS

This book would not have come into being without the assistance and nurturing support of many people.

The first was the encouragement of my poet/writer husband, Paul Hawkwood, when I mentioned my desire to go back to school to get a master's degree in a new field: Asian studies. I think Paul knew that, for my own well-being, I needed to take some time to explore the interface between my inner experiences as a meditator and my external life as a University of Oregon neuroscience professor, firmly established in material reality.

I entered the UO's Asian studies program and completed the research for and wrote my master's thesis with the help and guidance of three insightful professors. Mark Unno, my advisor, was a wonderful guide, reading many drafts of my thesis and directing me to writings that explored the shared ground of Asian philosophy and science in ways that were new to me. Veena Howard, my Sanskrit professor, helped me dive deeper into my understanding of texts I was studying and became a great friend with whom I discussed spirituality throughout these studies and in the years to follow, both in her office and over sweet moments of coffee and dinner together. And Jim Earl, a professor with a love of Indian literature, served a vital function on the thesis committee, as a friendly skeptic, challenging my evolving ideas as I attempted to integrate science and spirituality.

When Mark Unno asked if I would like to turn my thesis into a book, it was an exciting prospect, and a whole new area to explore. I am a entist and had written only about laboratory experiments, my own and my students'. A new group of people supported me in this endeavor. It was my great good fortune that Margaret Bendet, a friend and editor who is well versed in Asian spiritual traditions, was available to work with me. It was a great adventure to make monthly visits to her home on Whidbey Island and work with her to turn my thesis into an accessible account of my exploration of the science that offers evidence that consciousness is more than just a product of the brain. I am grateful to Margaret for her editorial creativity, her skill, and her friendship.

Throughout the writing of the book, my husband, who is a professor and meditator himself, has been very enthusiastic, patient, and lovingly supportive. And my friend and colleague Anne Shumway-Cook would often take walks with me, listening to my latest exciting discoveries and asking to hear drafts of the chapters as they began to unfold. The enthusiasm of these two was unfailing.

My special thanks go to Ed Kelly and his colleagues at the University of Virginia, for their wholehearted hospitality when I inquired about coming to visit so I could learn more about the research that went into their books *Irreducible Mind* and *Beyond Physicality*. Ed became a friend and a mentor throughout the rest of the publishing process, and I thank him again and again for his encouragement and assistance.

And finally, I thank my own meditation teachers, who ignited within me the new consciousness I explore in this book. Their inspiration, guidance, and teaching have comprised the constant substrate of my last four decades.

I

THE MAKING OF A RENEGADE

The year the Dalai Lama headlined the annual Society for Neuroscience conference, almost thirty-five thousand people attended, making it the largest gathering of neuroscientists ever. It may appear that many of these men and women of science were drawn to hear a venerable spiritual leader, but I'm certain that isn't the case. The view of most neuroscientists is that the sum of existence is the material world.

"So, what is a Buddhist monk doing taking such a deep interest in science," the Dalai Lama asked at a workshop he gave in the days before this huge conference.[1] He said that while the Eastern contemplative tradition and Western science have evolved from different roots, they share some striking commonalities: a philosophical outlook and methodology.

For philosophy, he said that both Buddhism and Western science view the emergence of the cosmos and of life "in terms of the complex interrelations of the natural laws of cause and effect."

For methodology, he said, "both favor empiricism." He meant by this that Buddhists no longer rest their view of reality on scriptural authority but also, like scientists, insist on "observed facts of experience." In this gracious appraisal, I think the Dalai Lama was giving science greater credit than it wants.[2]

His reception at the Society for Neuroscience conference was less than cordial. Before the first plenary session, there were news reports that more than six hundred neuroscientists (a small but statistically relevant percentage of the whole) had signed a petition attempting to prevent his lecture. The protestors were concerned, they wrote, that the Dalai Lama's appearance at this conference would misrepresent the scientific views of meditation, "a subject with largely unsubstantiated claims and compromised scientific rigor and objectivity."[3]

One petitioner said, "No opportunity should be given to anybody to use neuroscience for supporting transcendent views of the world."

"As the public face of neuroscience," another said, "we have a responsibility to at least see that research is replicated before it is promoted and highlighted. If we don't do that, we may as well be the Flat Earth Society."[4]

The battle between science and religion goes back at least as far as the Middle Ages, when it was the all-powerful Christian clerics who had the upper hand. The church tortured and executed blasphemers who even questioned the shape of the earth (flat), the center of the solar system (the earth), or the validity of the Bible. In the intervening years the position between these two adversaries has been reversed. Scientists are a placid lot and have never, as far as I know, exacted a blood revenge from their tormentors of yore, but academics have long memories. Representatives of various religious and spiritual traditions, like the Dalai Lama, have been knocking at the door of science for at least a century now, and that door, I observe, remains largely shut.

This point is underscored by something that came up with a former student at the neuroscience conference a year earlier, during a "poster session." In poster sessions, the scientists stand beside boards, or posters, each explaining one of their recent or ongoing research projects. The posters are grouped by topic and remain up for three hours. When you aren't explaining your own research projects, you walk around to see what others are doing. In this pleasant melee, a former University of Oregon neuroscience grad student, by then a professor at a school in California, stopped to say hello and mentioned in passing that one of his own students had recently finished a study that he didn't have time to help her write up and submit for publication.

Usually, the way such research happens is that a professor will require his graduate students to explore areas of interest to the teacher himself. Then he's happy to guide the experiments, help find a publisher, and add his name to the final research; the students are doing the experiments *for* him.

"This study is on meditation," the reluctant advisor explained.

He knew, of course, this former student of my favorite colleague, that unlike most neuroscientists, I was myself a meditator and had done research on the topic. "I'll work with her," I told him. "I'd be happy to."

Later, I contemplated just how difficult it is to find a neuroscientist who is even willing to put his name on meditation research, let alone give it his time. I, for empirical reasons, know the value of meditation. As the Dalai Lama indicated, I have done research within the scope of my own personal laboratory—my mind, my body, my life—and the results have led me to question the stance of the neuroscience traditionalists.

Neuroscientists typically assume that all mental activity is a product of the brain. Through my practice of meditation, I have come to think that the mind, while being influenced by the brain, is much more than a function of it. This is a long-standing debate: brain versus mind—physical apparatus and neural connections versus pure awareness, pure consciousness. Here, the word "pure" indicates that awareness, consciousness, can exist without neural activity, a hypothesis I address again and again in this book.

Many neuroscientists don't even consider the mind to be a factor that influences human behavior. To a traditionalist such phenomena as inspiration, contemplation, resolution, and certainly mental focus like meditation are nothing more than functions of the brain. He or she thinks that activity in the brain determines what, when, and indeed if a writer will write, a composer will compose, and any one of us will resolve to take a new stance in life, to evaluate our habits, to change our accustomed actions in order to reap a new outcome. The traditionalist says that such mental experience is no more than a function of neural activity in the brain.

This traditional neuroscientist would never imagine that he shares methods with the Dalai Lama, because to the scientist "experience" is not empirical evidence; it is subjective opinion, at times to be collected and analyzed but never to be trusted. Neural activity, physical markers, even behavior—these are measures we can trust.

Or not. As a neuroscientist, I find this traditional stance inadequate to account for the commonplace inner events I just named: inspiration, creativity, and shifts of attitude. As a meditator, I am acutely aware that most of my colleagues would discount as fanciful the meditation experiences I've been having for forty years now. It is for these reasons that I undertook to write this book.

Let me begin by describing my orientation to the study of neuroscience and how my own assumptions that materiality is the sole basis of the universe were first challenged.

INVESTIGATING THE MATERIAL WORLD

As long as I can remember, I have approached the world with a sense of exploration. I vividly remember when, at age five, I dissected a gopher my mother had killed for the crime of building tunnels across our front lawn. We lived on a farm, and my mother raised animals to feed our family, so I was accustomed to the idea of animals dying and their bodies being put to a use. We weren't going to eat the gopher, and when I saw his carcass, about six inches in length, lying in the grass, I wanted to see what was inside it. With a paring knife from the kitchen, I cut into the soft belly. What emerged could have been from another world: glistening little packages (I now call them organs) in varying sizes and shapes and colors. I had no idea how they fit together or what their functions might be, but I was entranced by what I found. I think it was then that my future vocation as a scientist was set. Clearly, I loved investigating the material world.

Twenty years after my first dissection, I was a doctoral student at the University of Southern California, sitting up late at night in a neuroscience laboratory with a *Navanax*, a primitive form of sea life often referred to as a sea slug. The *Navanax* is an exquisite animal, about the size of a gopher but taupe in color with gold and blue "feet" or "fins," the parapodia with which it swims. Through a process too complex to describe here, I had just cut into the back of the *Navanax*, inserted a glass tube microelectrode, and impaled two of its golden neurons. As I penetrated the cells, I could hear the electrical activity of the two neurons talking with each other—*brrrrrrt, brrrrrrrrrt, brrrt*—a concert of clicks on my audio monitor. These particular neurons were involved in the animal's feeding impulse, so as I listened, I could see the *Navanax*'s muscles contract in preparation for capturing its prey. I was watching the workings of the brain; I was hearing it talk, and I was as happy as I'd ever been in my life.

I felt as if I were eavesdropping on a secret conversation, finding clues as to how the enigma we call life is put together. I had learned to think of the brain as a mysterious organ that was somehow the source of all behaviors—but how? What was the process by which that happened? Now, at least I had *heard* it taking place. I was beginning to understand principles I could later apply to a complex brain. And, as a neurologist, this was my goal: understanding the human brain.

Moving forward several years more, I was a new neurology professor at the University of Oregon, running experiments to explore the brain's development. My subjects were the two- to fourteen-month-old offspring of, mainly, academics—people who were as interested in seeing how their children performed as I was. One subject I remember in particular was a nine-month-old girl we'll call Celeste, who was just beginning to master standing. This skill involves, most especially, the ability to balance, which is what my test monitored. Celeste was set on a small, motorized platform that also held a toy castle, which fascinated the infant and kept her attention, while I measured her ability to hold herself erect as I challenged her by moving the platform. I had attached sensors (EMGs) to her leg muscles, and the sensors were connected to a loudspeaker, so her mother and I could hear the muscles working. First, as she swayed backward, the tibialis and quadriceps muscles on the front side of the body were activated. Then, as she swayed forward, the calf and hamstrings muscles were activated. The sounds—again, *brrrrrrrt, brrrt, brrrrrrrt*—were the song of her nervous system and were beautiful to my ear.

Celeste came into the laboratory monthly, and over a period of about three months, I watched her muscles transform, from producing contractions that were chaotic and weak (firing randomly and at very low levels) to contractions that were coordinated and strong. It was as if her muscles operated with the skill and harmonious consistency of musicians in a well-practiced orchestra, each part moving in concert with the others. It was astonishing to me. How had her brain learned such behavior? How did her nervous system perfect her balancing skills in that way? And why did the cerebral palsy victim—a child of the same age who came into my laboratory to play on the same platform and with the same castle—not make the same strides in learning?

Such questions absorbed my mind for years. One day early in my career, however, I had an experience that didn't fit the neuroscience model.

A MINOR MIRACLE

As a postdoctoral fellow, I was given brief holidays, and the only practical way for me to spend Christmas with my parents in Sedona, Arizona, was to travel by air. Flying had always frightened me, I suppose because I could envision a crash landing with no hope of controlling the outcome. I didn't fly at all until I was in graduate school, and then I flew with white knuckles and only when I had to. One Christmas—operating on a strict timetable and coming from Eugene—I had to. While I was with my family, there was news that two planes had collided in the airspace over California, and everyone onboard died.

So, I was particularly nervous about my return flight. My elder sister walked me to the gate—this was before stringent airport security—and I confided my fears to her.

Cathie said, "I have something that will help you." I expected her to hand me a pill, but instead she gave me a mantra, *so-ham.* She instructed me to think *so* as I breathed in and *ham* as I breathed out. She said she'd received this mantra from her meditation teacher. It worked for her, so she felt it would work for me. "Try it," she said.

My sister and I had never moved through life on parallel tracks. She now lived in a communal house in Hawaii, explored alternative lifestyles with other free spirits, and met whatever spiritual master arrived on the prevailing trade winds. Over the holiday she had been talking about one of these teachers in particular, a swami from India. While I loved my sister, I didn't have a lot of respect for this latest turn in her life. My boyfriend always referred to her as Bubblehead, and I felt he might be right about that.

Walking down the ramp to the plane, however, I was terrified, and desperate. I started repeating Cathie's teacher's mantra—*so* on the in-breath, *ham* on the out-breath. What happened then was a minor miracle: with no faith whatsoever in the process I was engaging, I found that it worked. The physical tension I'd been experiencing all the way to the airport—a contraction in my chest and abdomen, almost as if my body were caught in a vise—relaxed, diminished, and, as I buckled my seat belt, disappeared altogether.

Throughout the entire trip I continued to repeat this mantra, feeling as light as if I myself were the one in flight. I watched the cloud forms out the window and wondered at their beauty. It occurred to me that, whatever else it is, flying is also magical.

But where had my anxiety gone? And why had it been replaced by delight—delight in the very activity that had always terrified me before? Could two syllables with no meaning for me do all of this?

When a mystery presents itself, I invariably investigate further. The next day, safe in my own cottage in the woods back in Eugene, I sat on my bed to repeat this mantra—*so . . . ham . . . so . . . ham . . . so . . . ham*—and I found myself, once again, deeply relaxed. This time I felt as if my body were sinking down, and coming to rest on a foundation that held it securely. It occurred to me that I had been holding myself in an adrenalized state of attention for quite some time. I poured effort into my life. I saw that I could allow myself to relax. I could be in my life. I could just *be*.

For about five minutes, that's what I did. When I came out of this inner space, I knew that I had been meditating. I understood that mantra repetition is a technique of meditation, that sitting and silently thinking a mantra is itself a form of meditation.

Even though I liked the feeling of my short meditation, the demands and commitments of academia superseded any interest I might have had in relaxing. I didn't think about meditation again for almost a year, when Cathie called to invite me to a weekend meditation workshop with her teacher. She and I were both on the East Coast, me teaching for a year at Virginia Polytechnic Institute and she on the staff of this meditation teacher. "Your birthday's coming up," she said. "Let me treat you."

I accepted, but when I spoke with my boyfriend about her invitation, he didn't want me to go. The whole Indian-guru thing sounded weird and cultish to him, and in the face of his opposition, I waffled. I called Cathie and told her it wasn't convenient. Afterward, though, I remembered the deep sweetness I had experienced with that mantra—with meditation! I realized I wanted to try meditation again, so I called Cathie back, and she got me one of the last seats for the workshop.

The swami and his entourage of about five hundred were staying in a rural hotel his organization had rented for the summer. The workshop, two days, was held in the ballroom. I remember the room as darkened, fragrant with incense, and quiet.

The first morning, it was announced that during the meditation session the swami would walk around the room and initiate every individual there. The initiation was described as a spiritual awakening, and it was to happen through the swami's touch. Obviously, the scientist in me was skeptical. Since I was there, however, I decided to put my skepticism aside for the weekend. Besides, I was curious to see what would happen.

For some time we chanted Sanskrit syllables repetitively, back and forth with a lead group of singers. This was another mantra, *om namah shivaya*. When the music stopped, I could hear the swami working his way down the aisles. I could hear a *swish-swish-swish* . . . the *swish* of what I didn't know, but I could tell the sound was coming closer. When he reached me, I felt the brush of feathers—peacock feathers I later learned—across the top of my head with a gentle *whoosh*. I was enveloped in the sweet scent of *hina*. Then, firmly, I felt the swami's thumb and fingers right between my eyes and on the bridge of my nose.

I was alert. My eyes were closed, but my senses were otherwise fully engaged, so that when in this moment I experienced a current of what felt like electricity enter from the swami's fingers into my body, I had a sense of utter certainty about the event. It isn't that I knew precisely what had happened. To this day, I can't explain it. But it seemed as if a tiny lightning bolt leapt from his fingers to a point between my eyes and down to the center of my chest. I could feel the exact point where the energy stopped. I knew it was my heart, not the physical heart but parallel to the physical heart and more like a *heart* than my physical heart had ever been. I say that because for the first time I could feel energy pulsating from my "new" heart, which seemed to be at my very core. The energy that came from my heart radiated outward, filling my whole being and beyond. This energy was like honey—it was sweet, and it moved in a leisurely and steady flow. If it had a color, it must have been golden. It felt like nectar; it felt like pure love pouring through me.

Words went through my mind, and they had nothing to do with scientific analysis: *I'm home, I'm home! My heart is my home!*

As I flew back to Virginia from that meditation workshop, I was looking in wonder at the photograph of my sister's teacher on the cover of his autobiography. I kept asking: *Who are you? What have you given me?* At some deep level inside of me I wanted more, and that part of me was determined to find a way for that to happen.

This was forty years ago.

A MATTER OF INTEGRITY

For me, what was most astonishing about that weekend workshop is what happened afterward. Without my effort or will or my even thinking about it, I made a 180-degree shift in my habits, beginning the morning after I returned. I woke up at 5:00 am, spontaneously, and I got up to meditate. This happened day after day after day and, in fact, has never ceased.

The most significant change was the direction of my attention. The nature of neuroscience research is to enter the world of your subjects, to explore their nervous systems in order to plumb mysteries hidden within them. Now, through meditation, I attempted to do the very same thing in my own field of consciousness. I did this knowing that just beneath the surface simmered a quiet ecstasy. I had tapped it once; I felt it was there, waiting for me.

Of course, I didn't talk like this with my colleagues—for the longest time, I referred to the swami as "my sister's meditation teacher"— because whenever a conversation at school hit a topic like meditation, energy healing, or, God forbid, spiritual teachers, my colleagues would look amused, disdainful, or alarmed. I didn't want to risk drawing these negative assessments to myself, so with most people at school I said nothing about my own experiences of meditation.

I recall talking with a friend about integrity shortly after that first workshop. I told her that, with meditation, I had a new understanding of the term. For me "integrity" meant having an experience of my own wholeness and of my connection with everyone around me.

By writing this book, I am seeking another level of integrity. I want to speak frankly, and openly, about my experiences as a meditator. I want to explore what these experiences have to say about the world we inhabit and the nature of the human mind. The experiences I and many others have had may not fit into the view of traditional neuroscience, but if—as I feel certain is the case—they did happen, then perhaps we need to remeasure the box we call neuroscience. Perhaps it's time for this box to expand.

In *Infinite Awareness*, we look at the nature of subjective experience, at competing theories of human consciousness, and at scientific studies on near-death experiences, various forms of energy healing, and experiences suggestive of reincarnation. The question at the center of these seemingly disparate topics is whether the consciousness, the awareness, that each of us experiences through the mind is primary—or can in certain instances *be* primary—or whether it is solely a product of the physical brain.

Many questions hinge on this one issue. Do I, as a human being, have free will? At all? Or are my seeming choices determined at a neural level, by the mechanics of the brain? When the brain dies, do I, as I know myself, disappear? Am I nothing more than a physical apparatus?

2

TO EXAMINE A QUIET MIND

The most efficient and effective way to explore any newly uncovered aspect of reality is thought to be scientific inquiry. Such investigation requires you, the researcher, to make systematic observations, to posit various theories (called alternative hypotheses), and to make predictions. Your predictions are tested and retested, by you and others. Once there is repeated evidence to support one of your theories, you have results that will stand up in the court of science.

This template is what's implied by the term *scientific inquiry*. This is the way I was trained in neuroscience and the way I conducted my doctoral studies and also my scientific research on physical rehabilitation. To me, it seemed the most logical way to approach my personal experiments with meditation.

From the very beginning, I wanted to approach meditation with intelligence, as a scientist. In the first meditation workshop I took from the teacher I will call "the swami," I learned that meditation is a way to quiet the mind. I wasn't sure I knew what it meant to quiet the mind. I'd always valued thinking. I was an academic, and from that perspective, it seemed the more thoughts I had, the better. Academics are judged on their ability to come up with brilliant arguments, to envision alternative solutions, to find creative explanations. Pursuing useful thoughts had been the goal of my professional life.

Yet my initial taste of meditation had been quite blissful. Obviously, there were benefits to a temporarily quiet mind. Besides, I wouldn't be meditating all day long.

From this perspective, I was willing to explore this idea of the quiet mind, and my first hypothesis was that one way to quiet the mind was to repeat a mantra. Specifically, I intended to repeat the mantra *om namah shivaya* silently; I would focus on the sound of the mantra rather than any sensory input and, ergo, my mind would be quiet.

That first morning I got up at five, sat on a cushion before a low table on which I had propped a photograph of my sister's meditation teacher—I still thought of this swami as "my sister's meditation teacher"—closed my eyes, and began to silently intone *om namah shivaya, om namah shivaya, om namah shivaya....*

Almost immediately I noticed that my mind was not at all quiet. By this I mean that my interior experience was not empty. Images came up, especially faces—faces of people I knew and also of people I wasn't aware of ever having seen before. There was no pattern to these faces, no rhythm, no meaning that I could discern. They were unfocused, mostly unrecognizable, but they were relentlessly present. How could *this* be a quiet mind?

And there was narrative as well. I heard a voice in my mind providing observations I recognized as my own. This voice went into monologues concerning events of the day before, recounting shards of conversation with my sister or boyfriend, echoing perceived criticisms from colleagues. This mental voice droned on and on. It was definitely not a quiet mind.

Then I realized I had stopped repeating the mantra. So, I began again—*om namah shivaya, om namah shivaya, om namah shivaya*—while images continued to dance through my mind.

I remembered something my sister's teacher had said in the meditation workshop I took with him: look for the space between the thoughts. In that moment, however, there didn't seem to *be* any space between these thoughts.

A MEDITATION PRACTICE

Now, I understand that this is an ordinary experience that comes to almost anyone learning to meditate. I think I found it less frustrating than do many beginning meditators because, as a neuroscientist, I was fascinated to see what I was encountering in my own mind. Whose faces were these? Were they from dream images? Were they people I had seen before with no reason to consciously remember the experience? Where had these images come from?

And, too, there is the achiever in me: the straight-A student who loves a challenge, the laurel wearer who is happy only when performing in the ninetieth percentile. The question became: How long could I keep repeating this string of syllables without forgetting my purpose? I was being my own best subject for experimentation.

So, in my search for a quiet mind, I continued to repeat *om namah shivaya*. This phrase translates roughly as "I honor Shiva," Shiva being one of the names of divinity in India. I did not, however, think about the meaning of the mantra; I was intent on the repetition itself. Before long, I noticed that I never had inner quiet when I was repeating the mantra; I had the sound of the mantra. The mantra was itself a thought!

What the mantra did do, however, was to replace all of the other thoughts I might have been having—thoughts in which I planned my next several hours or days or months, thoughts that suggested dialogues I could have with specific people, thoughts with emotions and expectations trailing from them. Unlike these other thoughts, the mantra carried no freight. The mantra was so light that it could, in time, fall away and leave my mind in silence. From this perspective, the observer—that's me—could see background input from the universe registering on my own consciousness.

In meditation I am in a darkened, quiet room with my eyes closed, and yet my senses are engaged. I see a sweep of nondescript grey with almost imperceptible patterning in it. I know this as the experience of looking at the back of my eyelids. I hear—or perhaps feel, or perhaps both hear and feel—my heartbeat. I hear the refrigerator humming. I hear a plane flying overhead. I feel pain in my left knee. Each of these perceptions comes into my awareness. They do not, however, interrupt the silence I am experiencing. I have no narrative.

I see that it's my own internal narrative that breaks the silence. Without the narrative, I am sitting peacefully. *This* is a quiet mind. So, after some time of practice, study, and reflection, my new hypothesis became that a quiet mind, a meditative mind, is a mind without thoughts.

There were, however, mornings when I would drop from the mantra into unconsciousness. I was aware of nothing. I would come out of this space of nonawareness and wonder what had happened. Where had "I" been? The way I felt in that moment was recognizable to me—it was exactly the way I felt when awakening from a nap: slightly groggy and refreshed. This, too, was a state without thoughts, but it was also without awareness, and I had to wonder if it qualified as meditation.

Continued observation demonstrated that on the mornings when I slept in my "meditation," I had usually stayed up late the night before or had been pushing particularly hard at work.

So, I came to another insight about the nature of meditation. I saw that there is a fine line between a quiet, alert state of consciousness— meditation—and an equally quiet state of dozing, when my mind became lax. I found that in meditation I needed to constantly calibrate my own state of alertness to keep myself from falling into a somnolent state. So my new hypothesis was that meditation is a state of awareness without thoughts.

Because it took effort to remain in this state of quiet awareness, I began to believe that the more effort I put into my meditation, the faster I would succeed—the faster my mind would become quiet. Again, this was not a valid hypothesis, but it took me quite a while to learn that. For years I put herculean effort into my repetition of the mantra, into watching my breath, into attempting to find the space between the breaths. I would look at the clock, I would repeat the mantra, I would have a thought come up, look at the clock, repeat the mantra, hear another thought, look at the clock, and on and on. It's an exhausting way to spend an hour.

Also, I found it difficult to be truly aware of what was happening in my inner space when I was putting so much naked effort into *doing* something. What awakened me to this problem was an instruction from a meditation teacher—not my own—who said that people from the Americas need to make different levels of effort. Those from the United States should make a 25 percent effort to focus; those from the Spanish- and Portuguese-speaking countries should make 75 percent effort. As I thought about this instruction, I realized that those of us from the United States are often highly motivated to succeed and drive ourselves beyond our natural capacities. My own cultural proclivities were leading me to make too much effort! I found that with less effort in meditation, I could relax into a quiet, aware state much more easily.

These observations and insights arose not after a week or several months but over the course of years of meditation practice. Remember, one of the requirements of scientific inquiry is replication of results. My experience of meditation was different from one day to the next, but a common thread emerged: the way I felt afterward. I began to experience a quiet satisfaction from my daily practice of quieting my mind.

After meditating for an hour in the morning, I would go to work—by now I was a professor at the University of Oregon—and experience throughout my day the benefits of the mental discipline I had given in the first hour. The word that comes to mind is "equanimity." After meditating, I was better able to watch what happened around me without jumping into reactions.

This was, after all, what I'd been doing in meditation. When the hum of the refrigerator came on while I was meditating, I just listened to the sound. I didn't embroider this sensory experience with any drama. I found that what created "noise" in my mind wasn't the sound of the appliance; it was my own narrative about the sound of the appliance.

So, I began applying that same principle to other stimuli in my life—the performance of my students, remarks from colleagues, disagreements with my husband. Even when a feeling would come up immediately, I found it easier to step back from the situation for a moment and to take it in from a neutral position before I assigned it a value. This didn't make for a dispute-free life, but it did calm down my day quite a bit.

And since much of the turbulence in my early meditations had stemmed from turbulence in my life, calming down my day also improved my meditation. It was a lovely self-enhancing cycle.

It may seem that I'm proselytizing here, beating a drum for meditation, but that is not my point. I'm not saying that meditation is the end-all and be-all, and I'm certainly not suggesting that it's a panacea for the ills of the world. What I am saying is that, through steady observation and deduction, I found the practice of meditation to be helpful in my life. I have also found my colleagues in neuroscience to be almost universally skeptical about such claims.

One factor that makes my personal foray into meditation seem insignificant to a neuroscientist is that it's difficult to measure the improvements in my life and impossible to know if they came specifically from meditation. In the time I am discussing, I moved from a city to the country, changed jobs, married, stopped eating meat, began playing oboe in an orchestra, and studied ballet. Did my new feelings of contentment and equanimity come from meditation? Or from some combination of these other factors? This is why a research sample of one subject is called "anecdotal" in science and is never considered conclusive.

There have, however, been thousands of studies on groups of meditators, conducted under carefully regulated conditions, with control groups and measurable outcomes, using statistical tools to analyze the findings. And what they have found, almost universally, is just what I found in my own life: meditation increases the subjects' sense of well-being, lowers their anxiety, and improves their attentional focus. Only with these scientific studies—some of which I have conducted myself—the results have been replicated by many other laboratories.[1]

These studies, as well—all of them, as a group—are largely ignored by neuroscientists. Let's look at some of them.

BRITTON: FOCUS AND HAPPINESS

Recently, I heard a brilliant presentation on the nature of happiness, a TED talk by the neuroscientist Willoughby Britton in which she told a gathering of Brown University students about a dialogue between neuroscientists and what she referred to as people in the "mental training practices." These are contemplative practices like meditation in which, as Britton put it, "you learn how to give your attention to what you're intending to give your attention to." Surprisingly, such focus turns out to be crucial to the experience of happiness.

"It would make sense," Britton said, "and we've sort of assumed, that if we get everything we want and we get rid of everything we don't want, we'll be happy. Makes sense; totally logical: totally wrong!" According to the data, she said, the United States is one of the wealthiest countries on the planet but not one of the happiest. And the wealthiest U.S. residents aren't necessarily happier than the poorest.

"What we've learned about happiness is that it seems to be inextricably tied to the faculty of attention. Or, more specifically, to our pervasive tendency, or habit, to *not* pay attention."[2]

Britton then spoke about a recent study that was done on this habit of ours. Harvard psychologist Matthew A. Killingsworth developed an iPhone app asking 2,250 volunteers at random times how happy they were, what they were currently doing, and whether they were thinking about their current activity or something else that was pleasant, neutral, or unpleasant.[3]

"What was most interesting," Britton said, "is that people were happier when they were paying attention to what they were doing—and they weren't paying attention very often. Fifty percent of the time they weren't paying attention. Fifty percent of the time, they were unhappy."[4]

That particularly struck me. In the mornings, when I take a shower, sometimes I relish the warmth of the water, the feel of the water on my skin, the fragrance of the lavender soap. And yet, as Britton observed, at least half of the time I'm in the shower, my mind isn't present for that experience. I'm going over my day; I'm thinking about a lecture I'm about to give; I'm rehashing a conversation I had with someone recently and coming up with a better response, defending myself more effectively than I did in the moment. What that means, of course, is that I wasn't completely present for the conversation either!

Notice that I don't spend all of my shower time thinking of other pleasant activities. This is another point Britton makes in her lecture. Our neural pathways are like subtle muscles, and just as our physical muscles become strong and pliant and adept through regular exercise, so our neural pathways become more efficient and accessible the more we use them. And what most of us are doing is exercising the pathways for negativity—for anger, for envy, for criticism, for dissatisfaction with ourselves and our world. We're *practicing* the means to unhappiness.

The good news here is that those pathways can be altered. The scientific term for this is "neuroplasticity," meaning the pathways are not permanent. We establish certain habits, certain ways of using our minds, and if we decide to do it, we can establish new habits. The man who wrote one of the first compendiums of spiritual experience, the nineteenth-century psychologist William James, describes habit as "the basic structure of mental life."[5] If happiness is about the mental habits we practice from moment to moment, and it's possible to change those habits, then it is possible for each one of us to be happy.

We might say, "No, that can't be the way it is. I can't be happy right now. I'll be happy when ____," and then we fill in the blank—*when my husband changes, when I have a new job, when I have a job at all.*

I held onto my fill-in-the-blanks for years even while I was meditating, even while I was developing the positive habits of mind that would, in time, change my mental landscape profoundly. Attention seems like such a small thing. It's so everyday, so minute-by-minute. It's with us all the time. How can something so intimate have that kind of power?

For me, it took studying meditation as a researcher before I understood the potential this practice had to change me. In my rational mind I had told myself that the focus of meditation was a way to become a better scientist, a more effective lecturer, a more attentive and powerful person. It was only later I saw that by improving my ability to attend— that is, to be present in the moment—I was also becoming happier.

Interestingly, in the Shaivite tradition I have studied, which was a spiritual foundation for my sister's teacher, some of the names of God are translated as "attention," "consciousness," "awareness." This tradition posits that attention itself is God.

LAZAR: CHANGES TO THE BRAIN

One question about meditation that is of interest to neuroscientists is whether the practice has an effect on the structure of the brain itself. The answer is yes. This subject was explored by neuroscientist Sara Lazar, from the Harvard Medical School, who first looked into it for personal reasons. Lazar, who took a hatha yoga class on medical advice in order to stretch her muscles after an injury, was initially put off by claims the teacher made that the practice of yoga would increase her compassion and open her heart.

The very idea was an affront to Lazar's scientific training. But then, she reported in a talk to Harvard students, she found after three weeks that she was calmer, better able to handle difficult situations, and, indeed, more compassionate and openhearted. She wondered, how could this be? Was it a placebo response—the teacher had said it would happen and so it did?

To find out, Lazar initiated a research study on the effects of meditation. She recruited people in the Boston area. "These were not monks or meditation teachers," she said. "They were just average Joes who, on average, practiced meditation 30 or 40 minutes a day."[6]

Using an MRI (magnetic resonance imaging) scanner, Lazar measured the sections of the prefrontal cortex associated with working memory and executive decision making. She found that in the control group, the people who didn't meditate, those sections of the brain became thinner in the later decades of life. In meditators this cortical thinning did not occur. In other words, meditators are better able to retain memory and decision-making functions as they get older. We think of being thick-headed as a bad thing, but Lazar explains that this thickness is related to more connections between neurons, which means that meditators have a greater ability to process, retain, and integrate information. And because of their cortical thickness, aging meditators can have the same mental agility they had in their twenties.[7]

Lazar found that the study was not greeted with enthusiasm. She reported, "The critics—and there were a lot of critics—said, 'Meditators are weird. Maybe they were like that before they started practicing. And a lot of them are vegetarians, so maybe it has something to do with their diet. . . .' To be fair," Lazar added, "that could be true."[8]

So, she did a training study, taking people who had not previously meditated and randomly assigning them to a group to learn meditation or to a wait-listed group—waiting to learn meditation at some point in the future. The brains of all of the subjects were measured before the study began, the meditators were taught how to meditate and instructed to practice thirty to forty minutes a day, and then eight weeks later everyone was measured again. The findings were, I think, dramatic.

The wait-list participants did not change. The meditators did change: they experienced less stress in their lives and underwent physical shifts in three specific areas of the brain: the hippocampus (which controls memory and learning) became larger, the temporal parietal junction (which controls perspective-taking and compassion) became larger, and the amygdala (which controls the flight-or-fight response) became smaller. In short, that means that after only eight weeks, the meditators had changed not only in their personal assessments and behaviors but also in the structure of their brains. They were better able to learn and remember and less likely to become stressed or to panic.

"Nothing had changed in their environment," Lazar pointed out. "They still had their stressful jobs, the difficult people in their lives were still being difficult, the economy still sucked, but yet their amygdala got smaller and they were reporting less stress."[9]

This study, as well, had its critics. This is not surprising to me because "meditation" itself is a loaded term for many neuroscientists. In fact, in the first meditation research that I know about, a Transcendental Meditator, Robert Keith Wallace, had done his dissertation on the effects of the practice at UCLA and was invited by Harvard physiologist Herbert Benson to join him in a study on the effects of meditation. By the end of that study, in 1971, Benson had renamed meditation "the relaxation response" and replaced the mantra given to the subjects with the word "one."[10] I'm sure Benson wanted to make the study more accessible, but I think what he did in changing his terminology was to dilute the research. He didn't allow for an investigation of the very practice that had inspired him to do the research in the first place.

ATTENTIONAL PROCESSING

My own first foray into meditation research happened precisely because of the low esteem in which the scientific community holds this topic. I mentioned being approached by the psychology professor who didn't want to offer his credentials and time in support of meditation research. The graduate student wanted to measure the effect of meditation on attentional processing—the ability to attend to one stimulation over another. For her study she chose the Stroop test, which has words like "blue," "red," and "yellow" printed in colors other than those named. The subject is asked to name the color of the word rather than the color it names. In Western culture, we're so word-oriented that our tendency is to name what we see in print rather than what we see as a color, and for this test subjects were asked to suppress that tendency. The meditators were measured against a control group of random subjects. I was interested in the study and delighted to step in—especially since the results showed that the amount of time the subjects spent meditating every day was correlated with high performance on the Stroop test and stronger functioning in their attentional networks, the anterior cingulate and prefrontal cortex.[11]

The next study I worked with, also initiated by a graduate student, involved a greater attentional challenge and additional groups. This student wanted to compare adults who practice tai chi, those who perform aerobic exercise, and those who are sedentary. Many other studies had looked at the positive effects of aerobic exercise on the brain and had shown that it can improve the function of the attention networks.[12] This student's hypothesis was that tai chi, which is a form of moving meditation, would have even greater positive effect. I told her that this sounded good but that she had to include sitting meditation—which I suspected would improve the subjects' attention even more than tai chi.

As it turned out, I was both right and wrong: it was good that we included meditation, but meditation and tai chi had virtually equal impacts on how subjects performed. I should mention that we could not find any sedentary meditators in Eugene, so all our meditators also exercised.

We asked the subjects to play a computer game in which they needed to press keys quickly and respond to ever-changing rules. The task required intense focus. There had been a lot of public interest in earlier tests showing the benefits of aerobic exercise on attention, but our study demonstrated that the aerobic exercise group didn't do much better than the sedentary group, while tai chi and meditation practitioners performed significantly better.[13]

Besides their performance, we also measured their brain response during the task, what is known in neuroscience as an ERP (event-related potential). The subjects' heads were covered with an EEG system, to measure the activity that arose in the regions of the brain associated with attention. When a subject saw the signals, they were to respond as quickly as possible. The height of the EEG wave that was registered showed the amount of attention the subject had given to the stimulus. The waves for meditators and tai chi practitioners were almost double those of the sedentary control group, and the aerobic exercisers were about halfway in between.[14]

TRANSCENDENT AWARENESS

I enjoyed turning my professional skills to a research subject that echoed a personal interest. For one thing, the research validated my meditation practice. At the end of the day, however—and this is a big "however"—none of the research I've participated in has addressed my own keenest interest in meditation: the experience of meditation. Nor has any other study done by anyone else that I am aware of. And there have been thousands—thousands!—of meditation studies. To my mind none has addressed the nature of the meditation experience. I'm not talking about brain activity during or after the experience. That has been investigated. I'm talking about looking at the energetic experience itself, about what the meditator *experienced!* For this, the researcher needs to *consult* the meditator, to describe the meditator's own account of the experience. This means first-person accounts.

Of course, there have been a number of studies in which meditators were interviewed and have described their experiences as a part of the research, but their accounts have been incidental to what was actually being measured: the differences in brain activity associated with "transcendental experience." This sort of experience is defined as an awareness of pure consciousness. Rather than describing the subject's perception of such an experience or the changes this state might inspire in the subject's life afterward, we are given the label the subject put on the experience and shown the simultaneous brain activity that oc-curred.[15] I find this type of research unsatisfying. Having had any num-ber of transcendental experiences myself, I find it inappropriate to con-sider them to be merely functions of the brain, as if such an experience could be defined by the activity level of certain neurons. As an example of what I mean, here is an experience drawn from a diary entry a few years ago when my husband and I went to a neuroscience retreat:

> I woke up as usual to shower, do hatha yoga, and meditate. . . . [Later that morning,] as the talks began I noticed that I could feel the same energy pulsing inside me as I often do in meditation. First I began feeling it as a loving, softly euphoric energy in my heart—inviting me to turn inside. It then moved up to the space between my eyebrows, pulsating there as well. And then it shifted to the top of my head—vibrating, tingling—and there was a quiet euphoria when I felt it again in my heart. I was listening to the talks . . . able to understand, but all my attention wasn't engaged with the words. The energy kept coming into my awareness again and again all morning long. . . . As we drove home, the energy was there—between the eyes, in the heart, at the crown of the head. It was so sweet, so satisfying, this

inward awareness as I watched the forest and the pastureland going by us on the drive.

How do you test for such an experience? How do you measure it? Yet how could you possibly discount it? There are many valid questions to explore regarding the effects of meditation, but from my knowledge of the subject I would like to suggest that objectivity is not the only approach.

Some of the criticism of meditation research comes because the researchers are almost always meditators as well. It's suggested that we don't have proper scientific objectivity. I once had a colleague call me an "enthusiast," and he didn't mean it as a compliment. My way of seeing this is that I *am* a meditation enthusiast—and I use this term in its most positive sense. The word "enthusiasm" comes from the Greek *enthusiasmos*. The syllable *en* means "in" or "within," and *theos*, the other root syllable, refers to the Divine. As an enthusiast, I know that there is a great deal more to meditation than the description of its effect on brainwaves.

I do not want to denigrate the neurological testing of meditation done by my colleagues, my graduate students, or myself. Such work brings meditation into the mainstream. It treats meditation as a legitimate topic of interest. It might even encourage some who would never have otherwise considered such a pursuit to embark on the practice of meditation. What this research also does, however, is attempt to reduce a spiritual endeavor to the realm of the material, the merely physical.

At a conference in Arizona on the subject of consciousness, I heard a fellow neuroscientist admit that he'd been exploring psychotropic drugs because he was sure this would show him a way to simulate meditation. "I thought we could find a shortcut," he said. "I thought all we would have to do is find a way to produce those brain chemicals and we'd have the experience."

As a meditator, I know his supposition to be absurd. There is a level accessed in meditation that is beyond the neuron. This level has many names; one we could use is infinite awareness. Whatever we call it, this transcendent level of awareness is what most scientists do not acknowledge exists. If we are to explore it, I am absolutely certain the only way we can is with subjective experience—we have to include the first-person perspective.

The Nobel laureate physicist Erwin Schroedinger discusses this quandary with great eloquence:

> The scientific picture of the real world around me is very deficient. It gives a lot of factual information . . . [but] it cannot tell us a word about red and blue, bitter and sweet, physical pain and physical delight; it knows nothing of beautiful and ugly, good or bad, God and eternity. So, in brief, we do not belong to this material world that science constructs for us . . . the scientific worldview contains of itself . . . not a word about our own ultimate scope or destination.[16]

This is precisely my concern. Science may be able tell me which neurons in my brain are activated in a meditative state, but this is not enough. I find that most neurophysiologists, biologists, even medical scientists who were trained as I was are interested in examining science from only the third-person perspective. From this remote vantage point, the physical world is seen as a machine with dynamic parts that move in certain ways to perform certain functions. When colleagues review my grant proposals, the question that's always raised is "What neural mechanisms do you hypothesize might explain the phenomenon you observe in the lab?" They consider it essential that I explore any question from this mechanistic perspective.

DRAWING MATHEMATICAL PICTURES

There are some areas of mathematics and subatomic physics that have, of necessity, rejected the classical mechanistic worldview. Delving into the nature of increasingly smaller particles, these researchers have found that the rules governing classical science no longer apply. Electrons are now viewed as a probability cloud rather than moving particles and can be either particles or waves, depending on how we observe them. Quantum physicists now consider that electrons do not move around the atom's nucleus in the way planets move around the sun but that they exist around the nucleus as standing waves. This means they are never located at a single point in space.[17] Sir James Jeans, who was a physicist, astronomer, and mathematician and made fundamental contributions to our understanding of the nature of nebulae and the evolution of stars in the early twentieth century, speaks of our exploration of reality in these terms:

> The essential fact is simply that all the pictures which science now draws of nature, and which alone seem capable of according with observational fact, are mathematical pictures. Most scientists would agree that they are nothing more than pictures—fictions, if you like, if by *fiction* you mean that science is not yet in contact with ultimate reality. [18]

By "mathematical pictures," Jeans refers to the way subatomic physicists must track the objects of their study by plotting positions, which are perceived along a course that exists only in the mind of the scientist. The scientist can infer how a particular particle is going to relate to other particles, and he can describe what he expects those particles to do. This description takes the form of mathematical formulas, mathematical pictures. Even if the particles seem to express the reality of these mathematical formulas, what we are seeing is never a full reality—never, as Jeans says, "ultimate reality." It is only a series of clues. The pictures we draw are of a closed system, like a machine that we have devised in our own imagination.

Jeans goes on to say:

> To my mind the laws which nature obeys are less suggestive of those which a machine obeys in its motion than of those which a musician obeys in writing a fugue, or a poet in composing a sonnet. The motions of electrons and atoms do not resemble those of the parts of a locomotive so much as those of the dancers in a cotillion. [19]

Here, I think Jeans is reminding us that there is an aspect of these subatomic particles that is not mechanistic. I appreciate his relating these particles to artists. I like to think that each of us is an artist, a distinct being, and not simply the mechanistic product of the movement of our own subatomic particles. I'm certain there is more to us than mechanics. If there weren't, we'd be no better than robots.

In relation to awareness, one way of expressing this dichotomy in science is "bottom-up versus top-down." I think of this as the fundamental theme of this book.

"Bottom-up" is the perspective of Newtonian science—there is nothing governing conscious awareness beyond the physical, and whatever inspires, drives, repels, or prompts an individual can be found, explained, and quantified within that person's physical body. In other words, the activation of neurons is the sole determinant of human consciousness.

"Top-down" is the perspective of mystics (a category that does include some quantum physicists)—there can be input into conscious awareness from a source beyond the body. This input could be from the mind itself or from another person's mind, or it could happen at a time when the body is not functioning. In other words, "top-down" implies that the mind has an existence apart from the brain.

From the third-person perspective, I have no concept of how we might measure a force that engages consciousness from beyond the physical body. There is, however, ample evidence of such a force from the first-person perspective. There are accounts from every culture and religion, from every epoch of human history, and from people of all races and both genders to suggest that human consciousness is connected to a higher reality. We just have to be willing to consider them.

3

AN UNACCOUNTABLE ENERGY

The most challenging aspect of meditation for me to explain as a neuroscientist is the way my interest in it was sparked—and "sparked" is, I think, the perfect word for this. In chapter 1 I describe my initiation by the swami, the moment when he touched my forehead and I experienced what felt like a current of electricity enter my body and move to the center of my chest. As I mentioned, I could feel the exact point in my body where this energy stopped. I've always called it my heart, even though it was not the physical heart, which, as we all know, is an organ made mainly of muscle fibers and encased in the left rib cage.

What I experienced was directly in the center. It was as if I had a cluster of cutaneous receptors at the center of my chest, toward the front, and they were tingling. If there are receptors at that precise physical spot, I don't know about them. So, from a neurological standpoint, the sensation makes no sense to me.

This isn't something I felt just that one time, either. When I meditate, I often experience the same tingling in that spot and also at the bridge of my nose and at a point deeper, in the center of my head. There are receptors at the bridge of my nose, but when I'm meditating no one is touching them. So, why are they tingling?!

As for the tingling in the center of my head, that's where the brain sits, and there are no sensory receptors in the brain. Once a brain surgeon has anesthetized the skin and layers over the brain, he can put a drill into the brain itself, and the subject won't feel a thing. There are neurons in the brain that communicate and integrate information to and from other parts of the body. I don't know if putting these neurons into an energetic field—of the sort one could hypothesize was created by the initiation I described—might not affect them in such a way that I could experience tingling. When parts of the brain are stimulated with an electric probe, however, the subject feels that sensation not in the brain itself but in the fingertips, the forearm, the left foot, the stomach—in the specific place associated with the sensory receptors going to those particular neurons.

So, as a neuroscientist, I have no physical explanation for all of this sweet tingling. What I do know is that I experienced it.

CHI, KI, SHEKINAH, N/UM, KUNDALINI

Fortunately, I am not the only person who has ever undergone such an awakening—and, yes, I will call it an "awakening." Much has been written about this subtle—and by this I mean nonphysical—energy. In the swami's tradition, which is the various religions and philosophies of India, the energy is known as *kundalini*. In China, this same energy is called *chi;* in Japan it's *ki;* the Hebrew tradition speaks of the *shekinah;* and the Christians refer to the Holy Spirit. This energy is spoken of by different names all over the world.

African tribesmen, the !Kung, are known to dance for long periods to activate or "heat up" the energy they call *n/um* so that a transcendent experience, the *!Kia,* can be awakened. One tribesman reported,

> In your backbone you feel a pointed something, and it works its way up. Then the base of your spine is tingling, tingling, tingling, tingling, tingling, tingling, tingling . . . and then it makes your thoughts nothing in your head.[1]

When a member of the !Kung tribe is in this state, he is said to have power to cure the sick and to see across great distances. In fact, tribesmen seek the experience not for themselves but so they can help others, by being empowered to battle the forces that, they believe, cause sickness.[2]

The Russian-born Irina Tweedie traveled to India after the death of her husband, a British naval officer, in 1954, searching for something but not sure what it was. She found a Sufi master and underwent a profound awakening. Her diary, published under the title *The Chasm of Fire,* was a source of great interest for me in my own spiritual search. Here is how Tweedie describes *kundalini*:

> Burning currents of fire inside; cold shivers running outside, along the spine, wave after wave, over legs, arms, abdomen, making all the hair rise. It is as if the whole frame were full of electricity. . . . Then it happened. It was as if something snapped inside my head, and the whole of me was streaming out ceaselessly, without diminishing, on and on. There was no "me"—just flowing. Just being. A feeling of unending expansion, just streaming forth.[3]

One of the most widely read accounts of *kundalini* awakening is from an Indian bureaucrat and social reformer, Gopi Krishna, who one morning in 1937, after seventeen years of daily meditation, had this experience:

> I was meditating with my face towards the window on the east through which the first gray streaks of the slowly brightening dawn fell into the room. Long practice had accustomed me to sit in the same posture for hours at a time without the least discomfort, and I sat breathing slowly and rhythmically, my attention drawn towards the crown of my head, contemplating an imaginary lotus in full bloom, radiating light. . . . During one such spell of intense concentration I suddenly felt a strange sensation below the base of the spine, at the place touching the seat. . . . The sensation was so extraordinary and so pleasing that my attention was forcibly drawn towards it.[4]

Krishna writes that the sensation disappeared when he lost his concentration. This happened twice again before he was able to keep his focus on the lotus. At that point

> the sensation again extended upwards, growing in intensity, and I felt myself wavering; but with a great effort I kept my attention centered round the lotus. Suddenly, with a roar like that of a waterfall, I felt a stream of liquid light entering my brain through the spinal cord. Entirely unprepared for such a development, I was completely taken by surprise, but regaining self-control instantaneously, I remained sitting in the same posture, keeping my mind on the point of concen-

tration. The illumination grew brighter and brighter, the roaring loader. I experienced a rocking sensation and then felt myself slipping out of my body, entirely enveloped in a halo of light. . . .

I was now all consciousness, without any outline . . . without any feeling or sensation coming from the senses, immersed in a sea of light simultaneously conscious and aware of every point, spread out, as it were in all directions without any barrier or material obstruction. I was no longer myself, or to be more accurate, no longer as I knew myself to be, a small point of awareness confined in a body, but instead was a vast circle of consciousness in which the body was but a point, bathed in light and in a state of exaltation and happiness impossible to describe.[5]

Gopi Krishna wrote of his experience in an autobiography, *Kundalini: The Evolutionary Energy in Man*,[6] in which he documents the awakening—beginning with this state of exaltation and leading into an extended period of physical exhaustion, anxiety, and depression all the way to the edge of a nervous breakdown. What tormented Krishna was that he didn't understand what was happening to him. Continuing his meditation practice and his introspection, Krishna was able to stabilize the active *kundalini*, and he spent the rest of his life, until 1984, writing and teaching about what he learned from his extraordinary awakening.

BEING IN A WIDER LIFE

The person I consider the pioneer of *kundalini* research never mentions the word in his writings, never posits the existence of a subtle energy. What he does, however, is directly explore scores of people's accounts of spiritual experience, including spiritual awakening and its aftermath in their lives, and in this endeavor William James broke new ground with his book *The Varieties of Religious Experience: A Study in Human Nature*, which was first published in 1902. Besides being a philosopher and educator, James was a physician and a psychologist. I first became acquainted with James's voluminous writings in high school, at which point I was awed by his clarity and insights regarding human psychology and the brain. I didn't read his book on religious experience until 2000, while on sabbatical from my teaching position and in preparation for entering a master's program in Asian studies.

Again, I was enormously impressed by his approach. Not only did James bring his excellent training in psychology to bear on religious experiences, he was strongly critical of the stance on this subject taken by his medical colleagues. He called them "medical materialists" and said that these errant professionals often equate spiritual awakenings with crises of puberty and adolescence, hysterical personalities, sexual confusion, "organic disposition," or medical conditions such as epilepsy or schizophrenia.[7]

I mention this because I have found similar biases among my own colleagues and because I, like James, see that spiritual experiences are neither pathological nor evidence of a low level of psychological development, but something else again. James reports that one of the hallmarks of what he calls "religious awakening" is "a changed attitude toward life which is fairly constant and permanent."[8] He delineated the effects of such an awakening in this way:

> A feeling of being in a wider life than that of this world's selfish little interests; and a conviction, not merely intellectual, but as it were sensible, of the existence of an Ideal Power . . . a sense of the friendly continuity of the ideal power with our own life and a willing self-surrender to its control . . . an immense elation and freedom, as the outlines of the confining selfhood melt down . . . and a shifting of the emotional centre towards loving and harmonious affections. . . .
> The world might look shining and transfigured.[9]

James also observed that these changes in the inner perception of life have practical consequences, including characteristics such as increased patience and fortitude, blissful equanimity, purity, and greater charity and tenderness toward fellow creatures.[10]

Since my own spiritual awakening some forty years ago, I have often pondered how to understand the experience, how best to describe it, how to convey it to those who haven't had it themselves. In science we are trained to think metaphorically, and for me spiritual awakening is best exemplified by an image: an unlit candle being ignited by a spark from a lit candle. This popular metaphor has power for me because so many points on this image are parallel to my own experience. First, the awakening came to me through the agency of another being, a person I now believe to have been himself fully awakened—fully lit, so to speak. The experience of receiving the awakening was something like a spark moving from the swami into me. And that transmitted energy, which I sensed as a tingle, then ignited the same sensation in me. Something in me was kindled.

What was that "something"? I experienced it as love—a deep, pervasive, unconditional love. I could feel I was connected to this love; I knew I was a part of it because I could feel this all-encompassing love within myself. I knew, intuitively, that this was the heart and core of the entire universe, what some people might call God. Until that moment I had been an atheist. When asked my religious affiliation, I would say, "None." I was one of the people known as a "none." I had experienced nothing in regard to a higher power, and so to my mind nothing could possibly exist. Once this love was ignited within me, though, I knew that the universe I live in is not confined to material dimensions. How could it be? I experience a powerful energetic force, a profound sense of love. I could never deny this experience of the Divine; it is utterly real to me.

In India *kundalini* awakening is called initiation or, in Sanskrit, *diksha*, which means, etymologically, "to cut." There is profound significance to this term, for yogic texts speak about this initiation as the means for an individual to sever, to cut, the three impurities that are said to bind each human being. The first impurity, known as *anava mala*, is also considered the foremost: our sense of separation from God. It is this impurity that is cut with the awakening itself—as I had experienced.

The second mala, *mayiya mala*, involves our sense of separation from each other and from other forms in the universe, something I recognized experiencing as well. In the week after my awakening, I became aware that I was feeling a warm connection to the people I ran into at school, both my colleagues and students. Then one day something extraordinary happened in an otherwise insignificant interaction with a total stranger. I was at the grocery store, buying food for my evening meal, when I became aware that I also felt a bond with the clerk who was ringing up my purchases. She handed me my change and, counting it quickly, I saw that she'd given me too much.

In the past when something like this happened, I would treat it as "found money," as a gift from the universe. In this moment, I had a different response. I felt as if I were in this transaction with a friend, and because I was aware of the connection I felt with this woman, I knew I did not want to shortchange her. It was as if she and I were in a dance together, and my part in the dance was to let her know there had been a mistake so that we could correct it. The only way I could behave with integrity in that moment was to play my part—and so that's what I did. I will never forget the feeling of that exchange. I had never met that young woman before, might never see her again, but we were connected, as two living beings, and my acknowledgment of our connection was a source of great joy for me. *Mayiya mala* was, for me in that moment, gone.

Even though this was just a few days into my spiritual awakening, I was already experiencing the power of *kundalini* to create personal transformation. "Transformation" is one of those words that has lost its meaning through overuse, but in this moment I can't think of a better term for this. To be transformed is to change not so much how we behave but our reasons for behaving as we do. As I've just indicated, in my twenties I would take what didn't belong to me as if it were something I'd been offered. In fact, this tendency was present when I was a child, as perhaps it is present in many children. At five, the same year I was cutting up gophers, I was entranced by a set of tiny teacups I saw in the kindergarten playroom and decided to take them home with me. My mother, investigating, learned my story—I didn't think I'd done anything wrong—and let me know the rules regarding personal property. In later years, my habit of keeping "gifts" of extra change in financial transactions was a little different. I knew it wasn't right, but in a largely unconscious exchange with someone I felt no connection with, it didn't feel *wrong* either. Besides, no one else would ever know. There was no reason why I shouldn't.

With *kundalini* awakened, I could now feel the reason behind *thou shalt not steal*. We could say, *thou shalt not take what belongs to another because to do so would be to injure that person—and you are intimately connected with that person, through the heart.* Now, no one needed to tell me this; I could feel it.

So, even though I don't have an explanation that satisfies me to explain what happens in *kundalini* awakening, I find this energy's presence in my life to be irrefutable.

DRAWING A MAP

There are thousands of books on *kundalini* in the tradition that I'm most familiar with, and over the years I have drawn some of my knowledge of *kundalini* from these sources. In many of these books, and now on many websites, you can find maps of the subtle centers known as chakras.

I am certain I never noticed any of these maps before I took the meditation workshop, where I experienced a sensory awareness of two of the chakras—the *ajna chakra*, or third eye, just above the bridge of the nose, and the *anahata chakra*, the heart center, at the front and center of the rib cage. These are, as many of the texts will explain and I will insist, *not* locations in the physical body but points in a subtle energy system that, I believe the term is, "interpenetrates" the body. What does this term mean? I cannot say for sure. In one of these yogic texts, the *Shat-chakra Nirupana*, the following description appears:

> Outside of Meru, the spinal bone, are situated on its left and right respectively the nerves of the Moon and the Sun and inside it is the nerve Sushumna of three aspects—lunar, solar, and fiery. [11]

According to this translation of the text, the spinal column is the location of the channel through which the *kundalini* energy travels, and in the sympathetic and parasympathetic nervous systems around the spinal column are subchannels for this energy. I won't go so far as to say that this is wrong, as some of my meditating colleagues have done in my presence, but I will say that it doesn't match my own view of the process. This particular author, Swami Vishnu Tirtha, translated the Sanskrit word *nadi* as "nerve." The literal meaning, I believe, is "flow" or "pulse." And, while it may be true that one biological reference for *nadi* could be "nerve," the term is more typically defined as a channel for energy rather than an anatomical structure.

I want to point out that all of us, neuroscientists and yogis alike, are operating under the same constraints that Sir James Jeans describes for his colleagues, the quantum physicists. We are creating pictures of phenomena for which we have only sketchy evidence. From a few pinpoints of information, we fill in the intervening lines in an attempt to create a total image, a map. And our evidence is subtle, while the maps we draw are material. We may be right—who knows!

Even so, what I will not do is discount my own experiences of this energy because some of its proponents describe it in ways I can't agree with. Let me give you an analogy from science: in describing the movement of electrons, some physicists say that electrons move out from the nucleus in varying spheres of excitability while other physicists say they should be viewed as clouds of probability because we never actually know where the electrons are; we're just saying that they're probably here. I might disagree with one or both of these viewpoints, but in any event I wouldn't throw out the concept of subatomic particles altogether. In fact, I can't even say for certain that one view is right and the other wrong. We don't yet know.

Besides, our propensity as human beings to create pictures out of a few points of information is not a negative attribute. This is what we as a species, and especially those of us who call ourselves scientists, are called upon to do: to construct our best guess at reality and then to test our hypotheses.

So, coming back to the yogic texts, we might find it remarkable that there is so much parallel between the various depictions of *kundalini* and its path through the human system. I certainly do. I also find it remarkable that these maps indicate points I have experienced. Fellow neuroscientists would say that, now that I've seen the maps, I have taken in a mental picture that could be forming my continued experiences of this subtle terrain. To this I would reply that I still haven't experienced all of the chakras shown. I've had experiences of only three chakras in meditation and a fourth at certain points in my work; there are seven chakras in all. If I were suggestible, it seems to me I would have gone the gamut. Why wouldn't I have had experiences of all of them?

MEDICAL CLASSIFICATIONS

I must admit, however, that I'm suggestible enough to be pleased when I see a sympathetic account of *kundalini* awakening from the Western scientific tradition. It's like finding an ally. The first of these that I discovered was a book from a San Francisco psychiatrist, Lee Sannella, who in 1976, the year my *kundalini* was awakened, published *The Kun-*

dalini Experience: Psychosis or Transcendence? In Sannella's view, it is clearly the latter. The book begins with a vivid image:

> Tissues are torn, blood vessels severed, blood spilled, much fluid is lost; the heart races and the blood pressure soars. There is moaning, crying, and screaming. A severe injury? No, only a relatively normal human birth. The description sounds pathological because the symptoms were not understood in relation to the outcome: a new human being.
>
> In a darkened room a man sits alone. His body is swept by muscular spasms. Indescribable sensations and sharp pains run from his feet up his legs and over his back and neck. His skull feels as [if] it will burst. Inside his head he hears roaring sounds and high-pitched whistling. Then suddenly a sunburst floods his inner being. His hands burn. He feels his body tearing within. Then he laughs and is overcome with bliss.
>
> A psychotic episode? No, this is a psycho-physiological transformation, a rebirth process as natural as physical birth. It seems pathological only because the symptoms are not understood in relation to the outcome: an enlightened human being. [12]

Sannella raises the question of psychosis, I think, in part because psychiatry is his field and in part because of the timing of his book. In the mid-1970s many physicians and psychiatrists considered *kundalini* experiences of the sort he described to be psychotic episodes.

Though there hasn't been much direct writing on *kundalini* awakening from scientific circles, there has been interest in meditation and in *kundalini* meditation, and these topics are most often viewed now not as an impetus to mental illness but as a possible therapy. One recent review article from Norway concludes that meditation-based therapies are associated with robust and substantial reductions of psychological problems in patients with anxiety disorders and depression. [13]

There have, however, also been a few recent studies noting concern by the medical community with what is called "meditation-induced psychosis," [14] including psychotic symptoms like hallucinations as well as mood disturbances. In a case study from the Netherlands, the authors note that one such meditation-induced psychotic episode had many contributing factors, including the individual's being under stress and going to extremes in his physical, emotional, and meditation-related activities. This twenty-four-year-old man had just lost 7 kg (15.4

pounds) in training for a marathon and had at the same time been under stress at work and in a relationship. With all of this going on, he undertook an unguided and intense meditation session, which ended with a psychotic episode: hallucinations, pananxiety, and feelings that he had caused the end of the world. His psychosis was short-lived.

The authors of the case report note that over the past decades, there have been several similar case reports citing brief psychotic episodes like this one. In summarizing the results of the published case studies, the authors note that half of the patients described had had a psychiatric history of previous psychotic symptoms. In these reports the patients were also said to be in states of physical exhaustion (typically caused by fasting and sleep deprivation) and to be participating in lengthy sessions of unguided and intense meditation. The authors described this type of regimen as "malpractice of meditation."[15]

"People with a previous history of psychosis have been recognized as more vulnerable to have a psychotic breakdown during intensive meditation," a second group writes in an article on meditation and psychosis that delineates other, similar case studies. The authors conclude that in such cases it is, arguably, not meditation alone that is the cause of the psychosis, citing especially factors such as sleep deprivation and fasting. They also note that there are data to suggest that meditation in moderation can be helpful in treating a number of psychopathological conditions and that, when carried out under proper guidance and in moderation, such meditation can lead to greater psychological well-being.[16]

Another article states that two patients in Denmark who had been diagnosed earlier as schizophrenic were found instead to be going through a spiritual crisis, related to *kundalini* awakening. The physician G. V. Hansen states that this experience is perhaps not a disease but should be medically classified as neither normal nor psychotic. He predicts that when allowed to progress to completion, this process would result in deep psychological balance, strength, and maturity.[17] Sannella's point precisely.

RECEIVING GUIDANCE

In summary, there is a point concerning the potential benefits and dangers of *kundalini* awakening that I'd like to broach not as a researcher but as an enthusiast: it helps to have a guide. This is something the swami said again and again in his talks, and my colleagues have borne it out in their research findings. Those case reports indicate that problems related to *kundalini* awakening tend to occur when an individual is undergoing intensive self-directed meditations—the "malpractice of meditation"—and is also under great personal stress. Inner work is subtle and can be confusing; our own inner drives to succeed can lead us astray. In my own experience, the swami was helpful in much more than just awakening the *kundalini* but also, and just as significantly, in letting me know what I needed to do to both nourish the energy and remain balanced as the energy did its work in me. I received clear instructions on how to combine appropriate periods of meditation, chanting, and study in a regular discipline that included wholesome food, physical exercise, adequate sleep, and rewarding work—in short, on how to live a balanced life.

The meditation teacher is understood in most traditions to be a pure channel for a phenomenon I brought up in chapter 1: top-down communication. It is considered especially valuable to have such a guide when undertaking inner exploration because with so subtle an endeavor as this, the voyager inevitably encounters many—many!—bottom-up suggestions. These suggestions can come from our past habits, our misconceptions about the goal or our own capacities, our well-meaning (but mistaken) friends, and the possibly well-meaning (but equally mistaken) teachers who present themselves as guides on a journey they themselves have yet to complete.

With all of this information coming at you, it's quite helpful to have a teacher you can trust to help you discern which suggestions are truly from the top.

4

CONSCIOUSNESS,
VIEWED AS BOTTOM-UP

The brain is a phenomenally complex organ. Your brain contains an almost unfathomable number of cells: ten to the eleventh power—ten multiplied by itself eleven times. One hundred billion! And each of these hundred billion cells—though some say it's eighty-seven billion—includes hundreds of different types of neurons. Plotting the relationship between this complex apparatus and consciousness, the awareness we call "the mind" is no simple matter. Neuropsychiatrist Eric Kandel, who won the Nobel Prize for his research into the physiological basis of memory storage in neurons, calls it the ultimate challenge:

> The last frontier of the biological sciences—their ultimate challenge—is to understand the biological basis of consciousness and the mental processes by which we perceive, act, learn and remember. [1]

For the layman who wants to explore this understanding, a first step would be to take an overview of how the brain functions. Let me simplify this and break it down for you:

Inputs: First, there is all of the information that comes into the brain through our sensory receptors and sensory nerves—the eyes, the ears, the skin, the muscles, and so on.
Outputs: Then, all of the reactions and actions that result from that information influx leave the brain through the motor pathways,

from the neurons that register feelings all the way down to the final motor neurons that activate our physical muscles.

The cognitive functions: These are the processes by which we perceive and understand the inputs. The cognitive functions are controlled by the **cerebral cortex**, the rippled and furrowed gray matter that most of us picture when we think of the brain. This gray matter covers our cerebral hemispheres, the left and right halves of our brain. Our cerebral cortex has four lobes, and each of these has a specialized function to help us move through our lives.

1. The **frontal lobe** involves, among other things, the planning and the control of all of our movements.
2. The **parietal lobe** interprets our physical sensations, forms our body image, and relates the body to the world around us.
3. The **occipital lobe** interprets the images we see.
4. The **temporal lobe** interprets the sounds we hear. Along with some deeper structures like the **hippocampus** and **amygdala**, the temporal lobe is also involved with learning, memory, and emotion.[2]

The brain is further organized in modules or regions, each of which controls specific functions. One of the most amazing examples of this modular organization is the fact that our sense of "I"—the feeling "I am a conscious, coherent being"—emerges from the connections between circuits in the left and right hemispheres, each with its own function to play in our awareness. Separating the brain's two hemispheres results in an individual's having feelings (which are perceived in the right hemisphere) but not being able to express them (because the power of speech rests in the left hemisphere). That same person might see a dog (the right hemisphere) but not be able to identify what it is (the left hemisphere).

The neurophysiologist Roger Sperry and his colleague Michael Gazzaniga discovered this hemispheric division through their work with epileptic patients who had undergone an operation to split their brains as a last-resort treatment.[3] They found that with no connection between the two halves of the brain, a person has two sets of experiences, each with no awareness of the other. One of their split-brain patients would violently shake his wife with one hand and defend her with his right.[4] When another patient, Paul S., was asked what work he wanted to pursue, his right brain said "an automobile racer" while his left side answered "a draftsman." In each case, the oppositional behaviors were independent because there was no connection between the two sides of the brain.[5]

If we don't yet understand the mental activities of the brain, Kandel says, it's because we are dealing with biology's deepest riddle: the neural representation of consciousness and self-awareness. It is Kandel's view that what we commonly call "the mind" is a set of operations carried out by the brain.[6] On this question, I disagree.

It's my premise that the scientific perspective has been colored by the approach neuroscientists took to this enormous subject, the functions of the brain, in the very beginning. Historically, we began our investigations with the motor neurons. Why? This was the easiest and fastest route to take. The motor neurons are huge; a motor neuron can be impaled with an electrode. Its functions are simple, its activity easily recorded. This is what I was doing so many years ago with the *Navanax*. The sensory neurons, which are almost as large, were also an early focus for neuroscientists. So, in studying the brain, we started at the periphery of the human nervous system and worked our way inward.

In the central parts of the brain, the cognitive cells are infinitesimal, typically one-twentieth the size of a motor neuron. These small cells work together in various ways as they process, evaluate, and integrate sensory data. Vast numbers of them contribute to any one cognitive function. These tiny, intricate cognitive cells in the central brain have received less scientific attention.

And then we come to the brain's most complex function: its connection to awareness, to the mind. Here, there is little research and many questions. What is it that allows all of these diverse and distinct sensory perceptions to emerge for us as one, single awareness? How does the brain contribute to this process of sensory integration? Does it happen wholly within the brain? Or is there a separate consciousness that exists apart from the brain? that interacts with the world through the brain, is itself affected by the brain, but has the potential to be the brain's master?[7] As you may have guessed, I lean toward this latter viewpoint.

I want to underscore that both points of view are, right now, nothing more than that. They're perspectives, models, theories. I don't think science is even close to understanding the relationship between the brain and consciousness beyond the most elementary functioning. Scientists investigating this arena are trying to find the neural correlates for various states of consciousness—being asleep or in a coma as opposed to being awake and aware—and they're asking what happens to a person's consciousness when the particular neurons whose activity is associated with those states are damaged or removed.

We will look at some of this research, but first I'd like to make the point that it covers only the most primitive questions regarding human awareness. There is nothing to address the exaltation of hearing a Beethoven symphony or Pachelbel's Canon, the inspiration of perceiving an idea, the quiet joy of watching the sun rise. These issues, fascinating to me, do not interest most neuroscientists.

HOW THE BRAIN CONTROLS AWARENESS

In the 1940s Reynold Brown enjoyed great success as an artist and illustrator. Extremely prolific, he worked for such magazines as *The Saturday Evening Post, Popular Science*, and *Boys' Life*, and, beginning in the mid 1950s, he created posters for dozens of Hollywood films: *Creature from the Black Lagoon* and *Attack of the 50 Ft. Woman, Cat on a Hot Tin Roof* and *Ben-Hur*. Then in 1976, at the age of fifty-nine, Brown suffered a stroke on the right side of his cerebral cortex, including the right parietal lobe, leaving him with a paralyzed left side and a type of "blindness" to objects on the left side of his world. The medical term for this condition is a "left-sided hemi-neglect syndrome." This handicap had significant consequences for Brown's artwork, as we see in the accompanying illustration (figure 4.1). On top is one of Brown's portraits from the period prior to his stroke.

After his stroke, because of the extensive damage to his brain, his doctors predicted that Brown would be unable to return to his painting. But he was able to begin the arduous task of retraining himself with the help of his wife, also an artist. As can be seen in his early post-stroke paintings (figure 4.1, middle and bottom), Brown tended to leave the lower left portion of his canvas blank. This happened because he could not perceive the lower left part of his visual field. He was unaware of it. He began every painting, and indeed every session, working on the

Figure 4.1. Paintings created by Reynold Brown, a California artist, prior to a stroke (top) and after a stroke (middle and bottom), which affected the right side of his cerebral cortex. Source: Reprinted with permission from the Estate of Reynold Brown. © Estate of Reynold Brown / Artists Rights Society (ARA), New York.

right side of the canvas. This caused his artwork to be heavily weighted to the right-hand side, with only minor details of objects painted on the left.[8]

Not only did Brown not perceive objects in his lower left visual field, his mind could not direct him to bring that area into his awareness. He wouldn't move his eyes, which would have shifted the functional part of his visual field into this space. Thus, in the morning when he ate breakfast, Brown didn't see the lower left part of his plate and, of course, left the food there untouched. Only when his wife rotated the plate would he see the food and eat it.

This case study, and many others like it, give neuroscientists detailed evidence to support the view that when neurons in specific parts of a person's brain are destroyed—which can happen easily by the formation of a blood clot and the oxygen deprivation associated with a stroke—that individual will, as an inevitable result, lose awareness of at least some aspects of the environment. And when motor areas of the brain are destroyed, as Brown's were, this individual loses the ability to move the arm on the opposite side of the body.

This is what happens when neurons are damaged: functions are lost. The connection between neurons and function can also be demonstrated with healthy neurons. Two neuroscientists from the National Institutes of Health, Jeffrey Moran and Robert Desimone, ran experiments with trained monkeys to show that when the animals moved their awareness from one object to another, the neurons engaged in the task also changed. This shift, which happened even though the monkeys' eyes didn't move, could be tracked by measuring the activity levels of the neurons in question. The neurons attending to the new focus increased their activity significantly, while the neurons associated with other parts of the visual field became less active.[9]

One thing that's apparent from this research is that the brain takes in vast amounts of information, and a healthy brain then selects certain parts of that information to attend to. A brain with damaged neurons receives the same information but has fewer choices. After Brown had his stroke, all of the information regarding his left visual field was still coming into his brain; he could not, however, see it because he didn't have the neural support from higher areas of this brain to give it his attention.

So, in reference to our initial point, at least some of our awareness of the environment around us is demonstrably tied to neural functioning. Now, we'll look at the way one part of the brain "binds," or translates, the information that comes through a particular sense into a cogent whole. Without this function, we would perceive nothing more than a sweep of color and form, something like a kaleidoscope, without meaning.

HOW THE BRAIN CONTROLS UNITY AWARENESS

I once assigned the best-selling book *The Man Who Mistook His Wife for a Hat* as the textbook in an introductory science course for students not majoring in science. This survey course was designed to fulfill general science requirements for students who cared very little for science. Unlike previous survey courses, this one seemed to engage students. I think that was because the author of this book, the neurologist Dr. Oliver Sacks, is highly entertaining and compassionate as well as being a careful observer of his patients' challenges with their brains. In this, his first book, Sacks writes of a Dr. P., a renowned music professor who, as he became older, began to act in unsettling ways.

Sometimes when a student arrived for his lesson, Dr. P. wouldn't recognize him. Only when the student spoke would Dr. P. realize who the student was. He recognized only the student's voice. Sometimes, too, Dr. P. acted a bit like the nearsighted Mr. Magoo. One time when he was out walking, Dr. P. patted the top of a fire hydrant and was surprised when there was no response—he'd thought it was a child. At first the professor and his friends laughed at these occurrences, as if they were jokes, but over a number of years this behavior continued and worsened even though his musical abilities continued to be impressive. [10]

Dr. P. talked about his difficulties with a physician who, recognizing that the symptoms pointed to problems in the brain, referred him to the neurologist. When the patient arrived for his first visit, this is what Dr. Sacks observed:

> He faced me as he spoke, was oriented towards me, and yet there was something the matter—it was difficult to formulate. He faced

me with his ears, I came to think, but not his eyes. These, instead of looking, gazing, at me, "taking me in," in the normal way, made sudden strange fixations—on my nose, on my right ear, down to my chin, up to my right eye—as if noting (even studying) these individual features, but not seeing my whole face, its changing expressions, "me," as a whole.[11]

During the examination, Dr. Sacks held up a magazine and asked his patient to describe some of the pictures. The physician reports,

His responses were curious. His eyes would dart from one thing to another, picking up tiny features, individual features, as they had done with my face. A striking brightness, a color, a shape would arrest his attention and elicit comment, but in no case did he get the scene-as-a-whole. He failed to see the whole, seeing only details, which he spotted like blips on a radar screen. He never entered into relation with the picture as a whole.[12]

Later, Dr. Sacks pulled out his Platonic solids, a set of geometric objects, from his neurological exam kit. When shown these one at a time, Dr. P. instantly identified them: a cube, a dodecahedron, and so on. When the patient was asked to identify family members in photographs, however, Dr. Sacks observed that the patient's acuity disappeared.

He approached the faces—even those near and dear—as if they were abstract puzzles or tests. He did not relate to them, he did not behold. No face was familiar to him, seen as a "thou," being just identified as a set of features, an "it." Thus, there was a formal, but no trace of personal, gnosis. And with this went his indifference, or blindness, to expression. A face, to us, is a person looking out—we see, as it were, the person through his persona, his face. But for Dr. P. there was no persona in this sense—no outward persona, and no person within.[13]

Later, Dr. P.'s wife told the physician that her husband had once been a gifted painter. She took Dr. Sacks to the room where these paintings were hung in chronological order. He could see that Dr. P.'s first paintings were realistic and detailed, while his later paintings were more abstract. The most recent paintings were no more than chaotically arranged lines with blotches of color. Dr. Sacks could see that, rather than expressing an artistic intent, Dr. P.'s paintings were documentation of the advancing neurological illness that was now obvious: a profound visual agnosia in which the ability to integrate visual information into a schema had been destroyed.

Dr. P. was diagnosed with a massive tumor in the parts of his brain involved in integrating visual sensory information and binding it into a whole scene. It is this "binding" capacity that allows us to recognize the sum of the parts as a person or a fire hydrant or a hat. Like other patients with this problem, Dr. P. could easily identify individual sensory stimuli but had lost the visual processing circuitry that binds these separate features into a recognizable whole. [14]

Dr. P. is another example of someone with a damaged set of neurons—in his case, neurons in the circuitry required to process visual information into an integrated and recognizable whole. I don't think science yet knows precisely which neurons fill this binding function, but we do recognize that a connection exists between our neural function and our awareness. In other words, it's clear that the inability of these particular neurons to function meant that Dr. P. could not perceive and interpret the world in a systematic way.

We also know that the same neurons that bind sensory information into a single, perceptual whole also serve to help us screen out irrelevant information. Sensory input that doesn't fit in the "picture" being constructed often doesn't even enter our conscious awareness. And it isn't just visual information that's bound together by this processing, either. If we're to associate a woman's voice with her face and the touch of her hand, our brains must bind together the appropriate tactile and auditory, as well as visual, information. We recognize our world through the agency of these binding neurons.

In fact, neural activity in specific areas of the brain appears to be required for waking consciousness itself.

HOW THE BRAIN CONTROLS WAKING AWARENESS

In 1984 at age nineteen, Terry Wallis was involved in an accident in which a truck he and two friends were riding in went over the rail of a bridge in Stone County, Arkansas; careened off a twenty-five-foot bluff; and landed upside down in a dry creek bed. One of the young men died, and Wallis suffered a profound and persistent head injury. For two weeks he was in a coma, which means he was completely unconscious, and from there he moved to the waking unconscious state that is called vegetative. After another few months, he entered a state with a bit more awareness—he would respond to his environment with grunts and nods—but he still could not communicate through words or even gestures. Wallis remained in this minimally conscious state for almost twenty years. Then in 2003, to the amazement of his caregivers, Wallis began to speak.

His mother came to visit him one day in the nursing home where he stayed. Afterward, as she typically did, the nurse asked Wallis who had been to see him that day.

He said, "Mom."

For someone who hadn't spoken for two decades, this was a profound shift. Over the next few days, Harris spoke more and, while his speech was garbled, he began to become more fluent in his communication. His family could recognize the return of the consciousness they identified as the young man they had known. Brain scans done on Wallis supported the researchers' hypothesis that neurons in his brain that had remained intact were able to form new connections avoiding the damaged parts of the brain.[15]

This parallels a set of findings we once obtained in my laboratory. I was working with one of my students in a study in which we trained stroke patients who had lost much of their ability to use one side of the body in balance and walking. We found that with a certain minimal amount of neural circuitry in place and forced use of the abandoned lower limb, the patients could regain much of the ability they had lost.[16] Researchers have discovered that neurons in the opposite, undamaged hemisphere often take over the function originally controlled by the damaged neurons.[17]

Wallis still, of course, had difficulty forming words and remained quadriplegic—paralyzed from the neck down. Though he had moved up from a minimally conscious state, the damage to his brain was profound and continued to affect him. He had, for instance, no awareness of the passage of time since his accident. Though he was by now thirty-nine, when his clinicians asked his age, he guessed that he was under twenty, the age he had been at the time of his injury. When asked the current date, he guessed that the year was 1984, the year he had been injured. Further, he was unaware that he had any physical or cognitive problems, and when a doctor asked him to explain the reasons for his physical challenges, he gave logical but incorrect reasons for his various physical problems.[18] This is a response often seen in stroke patients who have attention impairments. When asked why they are not using an affected limb, these people will reply that there's no reason for it; they'd just rather not.

What is most interesting to me is that Terry Wallis had no memories of the almost twenty-year period between the accident and his returning to an improved consciousness. This could be interpreted to indicate that neural activity in the specific areas damaged in Wallis's accident is a requirement for awareness. This is one reason most neuroscientists take the perspective that it is impossible for individuals to be aware of their surroundings or to participate in normal thought processes if primary neural activity is not present.

BUT IS THE BRAIN THE ONLY CONTROL OF AWARENESS?

One of the family legends my mother repeated to me again and again was that the first word I ever said was "no." Only it was "NO!" And Mom said that when my "no" didn't prevail, I would pout. "A rooster could have perched on your lower lip," she'd tell me. She called me Tuffie.

So, from the very beginning I was willful. I wanted things to be my way. The ability to set and defend parameters in our lives is an expression of what most people think of as free will. Free will is the ability to make unconstrained choices. As a neuroscience student, I was shocked to learn that many, if not most, of the eminent leaders in neuroscience maintain that human beings do not have free will; they say that we are constrained, controlled entirely, by our genetics and our neural circuitry.

The first time I read this, I put the book down and thought, *NO!* It just wasn't my experience. The way I put it then was, *I am NOT a robot.*

Most neuroscientists would say that my response originated not in the conscious part of the brain, the cerebral cortex, but in the unconscious or involuntary parts—in the amygdala or the hippocampus.

There is, of course, some evidence to suggest this, but I take solace in the knowledge that the person whose research provides this evidence—the distinguished neurophysiologist Benjamin Libet—agrees, at least in part, with me.

Libet, a professor at UC San Francisco, was a pioneer in the area of human consciousness and free will. He had noticed that epilepsy patients going into brain surgery had a half-second delay between the activation of a sensory stimulus and their awareness of that stimulus. What this meant was that the stimulus was acting on the brain before the person was himself aware of it. Libet wondered if this lag time meant that we perform actions in response to a stimulus before we are truly aware of that stimulus. In terms of response, a half a second is a long time. Runners who start a race at a whistle are reacting in less than half that time. If it took us half a second to respond, we wouldn't be able to play ball or dance or even drive very safely.[19]

So, Libet hypothesized that most of what we do in life is initiated automatically from involuntary neural functions. In the terminology we used earlier, this is classic bottom-up reasoning. In one experiment Libet asked his subjects to flick their wrists whenever they felt the urge or wish to do so. They could make these acts capriciously, he said, without any restrictions.

This type of action had already been shown to be correlated with a "readiness potential" in surface EEG recordings from the brain. This is neural activity that typically begins about half a second before our muscles are activated to move, in this case to flick the wrist. Libet wanted to find out at precisely what point we become conscious of our intention to perform an action. The results of his test surprised him: his subjects became conscious of the impending movement about a quarter of a second after the readiness potential had occurred.[20] His finding clearly suggests that the idea to perform what we call "voluntary" acts is initiated involuntarily—unconsciously—and that we then appropriate the desire to perform the action. We say we're performing an act of conscious will. Libet writes,

> The initiation of the freely voluntary act appears to begin in the brain unconsciously, well before the person consciously knows he wants to act![21]

The reason I say Libet was surprised is that telltale exclamation mark: scientists never use dramatic punctuation in writing up their findings. Libet must have felt pressed by his results, and, in fact, he goes on to caution against their universal application. He notes that after unconsciously initiating an action, we can still consciously decide whether to stop that action or to allow it to continue, since conscious awareness occurs about a fifth of a second before the act is begun. This is plenty of time to decide to either promote or block the final progression of the nervous system activity that began the motor action. So, in Libet's own view, his findings do not rule out the possibility of human free will:

> The role of conscious free will would be, then, not to initiate a voluntary act, but rather to control whether the act takes place. We may view the unconscious initiatives for voluntary actions as "bubbling up" in the brain. The conscious-will then selects which of these initiatives may go forward to an action or which ones to veto and abort, with no act appearing. [22]

Haven't you experienced this? I do, all the time. When I drive home from campus at the end of the morning, there is a point in my commute when I'm just about to get to my favorite bakery and I have the feeling *I'm hungry, I'm hungry, I'm hungry.* Then, on cue, I will get mental images of the bakery showcase: baguettes, Marionberry scones, and my favorite, the chocolate croissants. There have been times in the past when I've pulled into the bakery, but on most days I choose to follow another impulse, one that takes me home to a healthy salad.

This is the process that occurs in any situation in which we need to make a choice. We could hypothesize that the brain spontaneously offers to our consciousness many different next steps, possibilities, or solutions to a quandary, and that the conscious will screens out all but one. Most neuroscientists would say that my ultimate action, eating the salad, was also a result of neural conditioning and activity and my thought that I'd exercised free will a delusion. For Libet—and obviously for me—the question remains open.

Libet concludes his study with the observation that this profound question regarding free will has not yet been answered.

There remains a deeper question about free will that the foregoing considerations have not addressed. What we have achieved experimentally is some knowledge of how free will may operate.[23]

Here, Libet is referring to the way an individual chooses between the various possibilities presented for action by the unconscious forces of the brain.

But we have not answered the question of whether our consciously willed acts are fully determined by natural laws that govern the activities of nerve cells in the brain, or whether acts and the conscious decisions to perform them can proceed to some degree independently of natural determinism.[24]

"Natural determinism" is the doctrine that all of our actions—choosing a career, choosing a spouse, choosing whether or not to hike or eat ice cream or read a book—are determined by causes external to the power of will. Determinism holds that all our thought processes are reducible to the fundamental forces of physics—that they are, in other words, mechanical in nature. If the determinist view is accurate, then our sense of having free will is illusory. Neuroscientists would call this illusion an "epiphenomenon," an outcome of the brain's activities that has no effect on our actions. Libet disagrees.

Determinism has, on the whole, worked well for the physical, observable world. That has led many scientists and philosophers to regard any deviation from determinism as absurd and witless, and unworthy of consideration. But there has been no evidence, or even a proposed experimental test design, that definitively or convincingly demonstrates the validity of natural law determinism as the mediator or instrument of free will.[25]

Libet is saying that both perspectives—free will *and* determinism—are no more than ideas, unproven theories. I find this observation amazing because most of the scientists I know assume that determinism is fact, supported by abundant evidence.

The argument about an unexplained gap between physical and subjective phenomena, Libet points out, has been going on for quite some time. He cites the eighteenth-century philosopher Gottfried von Leibniz, who pointed out that when we look into the brain with a full knowledge of its physical makeup and nerve cell activities, we find nothing that describes subjective experience.[26] Libet says that when his own experiments on the physiology of conscious experience began in the 1950s, they were predicated on the need for a double-pronged focus: the externally observable brain processes and—at the same time, as an independent category—any accompanying subjective experiences. As he points out, only by giving full credence to subjective experience can we begin to understand the relationship between brain processing and consciousness.

> The phenomenal fact is that most of us feel that we do have free will, at least for some of our actions and within certain limits that may be imposed by our brain's status and by our environment. The intuitive feelings about the phenomenon of free will form a fundamental basis for views of our human nature, and great care should be taken not to believe allegedly scientific conclusions about them, which actually depend upon hidden ad hoc assumptions. A theory that simply interprets the phenomenon of free will as illusory and denies the validity of this phenomenal fact is less attractive than a theory that accepts or accommodates the phenomenal fact.
>
> In an issue so fundamentally important to our view of who we are, a claim for illusory nature should be based on fairly direct evidence. Such evidence is not available; nor do determinists propose even a potential experimental design to test the theory.[27]

For me Libet's point about our intuitive acceptance of free will is crucial. The notion of determinists that physical processes decide my every choice is not the way I see my life and, if they were to think about it, not the way my colleagues in the neurosciences see theirs either. It certainly isn't the way I've observed them to behave. I watch these scientists in faculty meetings attempting to influence the decisions of others; I see them in class attempting to inspire their students to greater focus; I observe them becoming outraged at what they consider heinous actions on the part of criminals, politicians, and university administrators. If my colleagues were truly determinists, it seems to me they would feel that each human being is simply living out his neural destiny. What, then, would be the point of endeavor or outrage?

This, then, is the paradox of bottom-up reasoning.

So, if we have no scientific evidence to prove the authenticity of either determinism or free will, where do we go from here? I find myself intrigued by what philosophers and scientists who support the concept of top-down processing have to say.

5

THE TOP-DOWN PERSPECTIVE

In chapter 4 we had only a glimpse of the bottom-up perspective—the view that, as humans, all our thoughts and actions are authored by activity in our neurons. There are innumerable scientific studies in support of this understanding, which I myself shared until I experienced an event that didn't fit that model, an event that involved phenomena beyond anything that normally occurs in the human nervous system.

I describe this event in chapter 1 as an infusion of energy that not only affected but also transformed the functioning of my nervous system. I understood it at the time to be an awakening—an awakening of an energy known in India as *kundalini*. As I have said, when this event occurred, I was sitting quietly in a darkened room, and another individual, the swami, touched me on the bridge of my nose and the top of my head. This much could be viewed as a sensory experience. The result, however, had nothing to do with my five physical senses. I have been touched by many other people in my life, and I know what the sensation of touch feels like on my skin. With this experience there was more. It seemed that a current of energy entered through a point between my eyebrows and moved deep inside my body and that a corresponding energy began radiating from the center of my chest cavity.

I want to stress that this was a felt sensation. I would say it was a physical sensation, but, as a neuroscientist, I know that a touch on the bridge of my nose would not excite sensory receptors in the core of my body to account for the sensations I experienced there. In chapter 6, I discuss the yogic view of this event. Here I want to explore another line of research I've followed over the years: what I call "top-down process-ing." This top-down perspective on consciousness has received some attention in scientific journals. What do my colleagues have to say about the prospect of receiving conscious input from a source other than one's own five senses?

From the perspective of neuroscience, any input to the brain that comes from something other than the usual sensory inputs would be considered "top-down." The yogic view differentiates between various levels of input. For instance, the effect of our own thoughts or of an-other's thoughts on our mind are seen by a yogi to be collegial influ-ences. We could call them "side-to-side." In the yogic sense, "top-down" would come from a higher level of consciousness than the mind: what a yogi might call supreme consciousness—although the yogi would probably capitalize the term. This we discuss in the next chapter.

First, let's look at the Western view of top-down: the influence we experience from others' ideas (emergent interactionism) and from our own thoughts (mind to brain). These provide us with some evidence regarding the top-down process that counters the bottom-up claims that our conscious awareness comes solely from activity within our own neurons.

SPERRY: EMERGENT INTERACTIONISM

One of the earliest proponents of top-down—and critics of the absolute determinism of some neuroscientists—was the Nobel laureate Roger Sperry, who taught at Cal-Tech, Harvard, and the University of Chica-go. Initially, Sperry gained recognition by demonstrating how the brain can be modified. Then, as we explored in the last chapter, he went on to examine changes in states of consciousness in split-brain patients, show-ing that the two halves of the brain sometimes behave as two separate individuals. This is why, seeing someone fall on an icy street, we might laugh at the same time we're feeling compassion for his or her pain and urgency about the need to offer help. It was for this work in 1981 that Sperry was awarded the Nobel Prize. His research on the strangely divided mental state that occurs when humans undergo surgery for epilepsy, cutting the brain pathways (the corpus collosum) between the two brain hemispheres, helped bring to the forefront research questions about the possibility of a top-down relationship between mind and brain. This work also led him to a new theory of consciousness as a causal force in brain activity. He calls this top-down theory "emergent interactionism."[1]

The term may sound dense, but the meaning is crystal clear. Sperry says that once we go beyond the simpler neural functions (smell, digestion, locomotion) and rise to more complex levels of existence (expressing love, explaining cause, applying ethics), there are, by necessity, additional laws that emerge to govern the component interactions. The perspective is, thus, "emergent interactionism." Sperry says neurons alone cannot determine the relationship between brain function and human behavior; the principles involved in human physiology and behavior are both subtle and complex. He says the idea that all causality can be reduced to neural functioning—the view of his reductionist colleagues—is, simply speaking, overly simplistic.

We haven't spoken much yet about the difference between the brain (the physical apparatus with its circuitry and connections) and the mind (the thoughts that play along those connections). According to the common neuroscientific view, the mind is the creation of the brain. In other words, material processes in the cerebral cortex—somehow!—generate thoughts and feelings. One of the supporters of this materialistic view, Tufts University cognitive scientist Daniel C. Dennett, claims that our brains are nothing more than

> a cobbled-together collection of specialist brain circuits, which . . . conspire together to produce a . . . more or less well-designed virtual machine. . . . By yoking these independently evolved specialist organs together in common cause, and thereby giving their union vastly enhanced powers, this virtual machine, this software of the brain, performs a sort of internal political miracle: It creates a virtual captain of the crew.[2]

The "virtual captain" is what we usually think of as the self—our sense of individuality, humanity, personhood. It's the one who watches us move from one life circumstance to another; the one who has been looking out of our eyes from childhood onward; the one who sees our dreams, who witnesses the movement of our moods, who plays all of our various life roles. To Dennett this virtual captain is an illusion, produced by the workings of our brain circuitry. This, then, is the view of most neuroscientists.

One reason Sperry gives for rejecting this materialist view is his observation that our thoughts and the patterns of our thoughts, rather than coming out of our brain, can change the form of the brain and, in this way, change our behavior. Let me repeat this: thoughts and patterns of thoughts can change the form of the brain.

This is, I think, the way most people view themselves. As I say in the previous chapter, it's the way I live, the way most of my colleagues live. We've discussed the plasticity of the brain, how the brain itself can alter when we alter our behavior. While I can't prove that I've changed the form of my own brain by changing the way I act, I have many times experienced changing habits and, thereby, changing my experience of my environment. Neurologically speaking, a habit is a pathway from a sensory stimulus coming in to a motor response that has been used so often that it is now automatic. No conscious thought is needed between stimulus and response.

One of my less helpful habits, I have long known, is a propensity to be critical, of myself and of others! Remember how in chapter 2 Willoughby Britton demonstrated to a class that criticism is most people's strongest mental circuit. She went on to say that this habit of criticizing comes up most often with our spouses. That was the case with me. I had always thought of my critical nature as a neutral aspect of my perfectionist personality, and then one day about twenty years ago when my husband and I were on a quiet walk together, he said, "When you criticize me, it really hurts." In that moment he wasn't attacking me or defending himself; he was communicating from his heart, and so I took in what he was saying. A few years later I came across a commentary on a classical yogic text, Patanjali's *Yoga Sutras*, that gave my husband's observation even greater meaning for me. The commentator writes about obstacles to knowing our true nature:

> The word "obstacle" is worth considering. . . . When Patanjali speaks of an "obstacle" he refers . . . to the negative effect which follows a [harmful] act—the whirling dust cloud of ignorance which then arises and obscures the light of the Atman [the Self] within us.[3]

To me this says that every action I perform that is harmful to myself or others has an invariable and inescapable consequence: it creates an obstacle to enlightenment that is, according to its magnitude, either great or small. And this obstacle is its own automatic, self-contained punishment: alienation from the Self. Anything harmful I do moves me into the "dust-cloud of ignorance" and further away from "the sun of Self." Reading this, I was transfixed. What I'd been thinking of as an issue with my husband was actually an issue with myself.

The next day when I noticed that my husband had forgotten to do something I considered to be important, I had a new perspective on the situation. The fact that he'd forgotten was his problem; the fact that it bothered me was mine! Instead of correcting him, I kept quiet. More opportunities for me to keep quiet continued to come up—and as I pulled back from bickering, I found that my mind was becoming more concentrated during meditation. My meditations were more peaceful, more intoxicating, and a certain quiet joy began spilling over into the rest of my day.

Weeks later my husband said, "What's happened? You've been so nice lately!" So, I told him about my revelation.

That was twelve years ago, and I must admit I'm still working on the same issue—but at new levels. I have observed that I still have a moment of irritation when my husband doesn't take an action that, in my perfect world, I would prefer for him to take. My irritation, however, dissolves almost immediately into the thought, *That's the way I used to be*. In place of the irritation comes a feeling of peace. It's a vastly different experience from my habits of the past.

From the determinists' perspective, my dropping this habit of—let's call it "nagging"—came about because my neural circuits were responding to painful stimuli. These painful stimuli were my husband's comment on the nagging's effect on him and, years later, the discovery of a philosophical comment on the nagging's consequences for me. These painful stimuli weakened the neural connection between the original sensory stimulus (my husband's various less-than-impeccable behaviors) and my patterned response. This is the Pavlovian or Skinnerian view (the salivating dog and the shocked rat, respectively): bottom-up.

My viewpoint of what happened in this alteration of my mind/brain apparatus is that I was influenced by two ideas. The first came from my husband: his observation that my nagging had a negative effect on him that I hadn't before considered. The second, years later, came from a philosopher, by then dead, who pointed out that a behavior that affects anyone negatively has additional consequences as well for the one engaging in that behavior—and those consequences were for me in relation to what is my most closely held life goal. I have to admit that both of these notions had been expressed to me before. For reasons I cannot fully understand, I didn't truly hear them before—I didn't take them in. I suppose I wasn't ready to. I think this is a phenomenon that Sperry may be referring to when he speaks of emergent interactions. With the involvement of the mind—and ideas definitely involve the mind—new laws regarding interaction emerge, and we must take these new laws into consideration.

Here is Sperry's own description of determinism:

> A traditional working hypothesis in neuroscience holds that a complete account of brain function is possible, in principle, in strictly neurophysiological terms without invoking conscious or mental agents; the neural correlates of subjective experience are conceived to exert causal influence but not mental qualities per se.[4]

He restates what we've discussed: that the traditional approach to brain function is strictly physical, strictly neural. By the "neural correlates of subjective experience," Sperry means the action-potentials in the circuits of the brain—the neurons that determinists say are the sole cause of our behaviors and our experience of our behaviors. This is not Sperry's view of it.

> This long established materialist-behaviorist principle has been challenged in recent years by the introduction of a modified concept of the mind-brain relation in which consciousness is conceived to be emergent and causal.[5]

I think Sperry defines "consciousness" in the traditional way: as our self-reflective awareness. He is, then, saying that this self-reflective awareness emerges (appears at a certain point in an individual's development) and thereafter is a driving force (is "causal") in relation to our behavior and experience.

> Psychophysical interaction is explained in terms of the emergence in nesting brain hierarchies of high order, functionally derived, mental

properties that interact by laws and principles different from, and not reducible to, those of neurophysiology.[6]

What emerges, Sperry says, to explain psycho-physical interactions, are "nesting brain hierarchies of high order"—our "functionally derived, mental properties" (the capacities to determine, to reason, to create, and so on)—which are subtle, complex, high-level systems that function under laws and principles entirely different from those governing our physical system. And here comes Sperry's main point:

> Reciprocal upward and downward, interlevel determination of the mental and neural action is accounted for on these terms without violating the principles of scientific explanation and without reducing the qualities of inner experience to those of physiology. Interaction of mind and brain becomes not only conceivable and scientifically tenable, but more plausible in some respects than were the older parallelist and identity views of the materialist position.[7]

So, in Sperry's theory, the fundamental forces of physics are seen as building blocks to create bigger, more competent entities. Once a new, more complex system (like the human mind) is created, the properties of this new system supersede the properties of the lower level subunits. Though these forces at the atomic, molecular, and cellular levels (the neurons) continue to operate, their significance is eclipsed by the power that emerges from the new, more complex whole.

The causal properties of our thought patterns, for instance, are highly significant. This is one of the complex systems Sperry mentions specifically in his analysis. As our various thought patterns evolve, he says, they begin to replace neurons as the dominant feature of our reality. Our world, then, may be partially controlled by the laws of our neurons, but it is also controlled by a complex group of powers—such as thought patterns—that have emerged from the neurons. Sperry points out that the randomness of movement often observed in subatomic particles, atoms, and molecules is seen only rarely in human behavior, since this tendency has been superseded in humans by these non-random higher-level forces that keep moving evolution to more competent forms.[8]

In Sperry's view, the flow of nerve impulses isn't affected solely by other nerve impulses but is also regulated by mental controls. This is the most significant difference between Sperry's emergent interactionism and the traditional reductionism: Sperry considers that while physical and chemical events impact, and even cause, some mental events, the mental events can also have a casual effect on the physical and chemical. In other words, we can change our brain with our thoughts.

Sperry says that our mental states or activities—our moods or thoughts—can change the "cerebral set," priming some brain circuits and inhibiting others. This change creates a shift in our focus or feeling or thought in that moment.[9] By "cerebral set" I think Sperry means the interactions between our various competing desires and predilections. That the influence of new ideas created a change in my cerebral set resonates for me as a description of the inner process that took place when I was inspired to stop criticizing my husband. It's the same sort of change that might happen for a smoker who reads an article on the carcinogenic effects of tobacco. Many times, such articles have no effect whatsoever, but once in a while, a reader will instantly decide to stop smoking and never again pick up a cigarette. The same thing can be said of an inspiration to change your diet or your exercise routine or to take up meditation. This moment of inspiration, which I know many people experience, has no adequate explanation in the reductionist view—which, in my opinion, reduces people to chemical or electrical response mechanisms.

According to Sperry, at the top of the command system of the brain are our ideas and ideals. The most influential concept in the examples I've given so far is the importance of good health. Sperry says that such an idea has as much potential to initiate change as a nerve impulse does. Ideas can interact with other ideas and with other mental forces, like emotions, within the brain of a single individual and across the brains of two or more individuals. In addition these ideas can interact with the external environment to produce evolutionary advances—changes in many people and at rapid rates. In other words, information itself can be seen as a key factor influencing mental activity and, in that way, brain activity. It's top-down.

Depending on the ideas and ideals two individuals hold in their minds, those individuals may behave differently in response to exactly the same environmental inputs. When, for instance, a person holds the long-term ideal of health and longevity above that of the immediate sensory enjoyment of a cigarette, they will respond to the sight and smell of a lit cigarette differently from someone who does not hold that same ideal. If the first person transfers those ideals to the mind of another, as new information, the ideals themselves can then transform the behavior of the second individual. The actions of any individual—and any group of individuals—are determined substantially by what this individual or group holds in highest esteem.[10]

"Free will," a concept cherished in the United States, has no place in traditional neuroscience, and, here again, Sperry's view is considerably different from that of most of his colleagues. As I mention in the final chapter, most neuroscientists see free will as an illusion and say that the mechanisms underlying brain and behavior are determined purely by the sensory inputs received by neurons and the interactions between neurons. Sperry proposes that choice happens at the level of conscious thought and that it involves the interplay of ideas, reasoning processes, and emotions. He is saying that an individual does determine, with his own mind, how he will act from among the many alternative possibilities. This does not, however, mean that the individual's decision-making apparatus is unaffected by his inherited makeup, lifetime memories, beliefs, ideals, feelings, physiological impulses, and unconscious desires. All of these exert a causal influence on any mental decision, creating an inevitable—but self-determined and highly personal!—outcome.[11] In other words, Sperry says that the influences on our behavior are both top-down and bottom-up. This is my own view of it.

Coming back to the example of people who decide to stop smoking, Sperry says that a number of factors determine whether or not individuals will be able to carry out this decision—the level of their physical addiction to nicotine (related partly to genetic makeup), the duration of their smoking habit, the strength of their ideals regarding the importance of good health, and the strength of their unconscious desire to smoke. All of these factors—some of them at the level of conscious thought and some at the level of unconscious neural events—come into play in their attempt to make a positive change in their behavior.

In summary, Sperry's emergent interactionism doesn't deny the atomistic, molecular, and animalistic in human nature. Rather, he is saying that human behavior cannot be reduced to these influences. His view is that new forms of causal control emerge at the level of conscious mental processing and that these higher forces can supersede controls at the molecular and physiological levels. So, the flow of our nerve impulses is not regulated *only* by other nerve impulses but is *also* regulated by mental controls, which encompass complex information—including ideas and ideals—received by the mind of the individual in question.

ECCLES: DUALISM

Another Nobel Prize–winning neuroscientist, Sir John Eccles, takes criticism of biological determinism a step further. In his book *How the Self Controls Its Brain,* Eccles discusses his alternative theory of brain-mind interactions, which he calls "dualist-interactionism."[12] This term comes from Eccles's hypothesis that there is a nonmaterial mind, or self, that exists apart from the brain (dualism) and that interacts with the brain (interactionism). This is substantially different from Sperry's view, which posits different levels of complexity in one apparatus. Eccles turns to the probability element of quantum theory—remember the cloud of electron particle positions in chapter 3?—as a way to account for parts of human experience that cannot be explained under the rigidly material precepts of Newtonian physics.

Eccles, working with the German physicist Friedrich Beck, considered the interaction between an individual and his or her own brain. The resulting theory brings together quantum mechanics and the brain—or, specifically the physiological mechanisms of the synapses between nerve cells in the brain. Eccles won his Nobel Prize in 1964 for his work on the junctions between neurons, the synapses, and it is these synaptic structures that play a crucial role in his theory. Eccles points out that the membrane channels forming neural synapses are so small—a nanometer in size, ten to the minus nine power of meters—that we can no longer approach them with classical physics. We have moved into the quantum world. And this, you will recall, is a world of probabilities. It is, further, a world in which there must be a subject—one who observes an action. At the quantum level, the presence and effect of the subject is critical to the outcome of any experimental observation.[13]

We did not make this crucial point in our necessarily truncated discussion of quantum theory in chapter 2, so we'll introduce it now. The behavior of particles is not only a probability, but that behavior has been shown to change according to the expectation of a viewer. A tree may, indeed, fall in the forest if no one is there to see or hear it, but we have no idea if quantum particles move when there is no one present to observe them. In the quantum equation, the subject and the subject's choices are more than just a matter of material logic; their effects on the physical system have been introduced, mathematically, at the most basic level as a part of the logical structure.[14]

Therefore, Eccles posited a subject, an experiencer, which he called "the self." We might also call this entity "the mind." And beyond conceptualizing a subject, Eccles hypothesized a way for this subject to interact with his own brain. Eccles, writing in 1992, was one of the first to consider that quantum processes might affect mind–brain interactions, and it took later scientists to refine and expand his theories and make them more accessible.

Henry Stapp, a physicist at the Lawrence Berkeley National Laboratories at UC Berkeley, addressed this issue in 2005 to point out that one of the crucial components of Eccles's theory is the detailed study he made of the mechanisms underlying synaptic transmission. Stapp took the theory further, to include the movement of calcium through the synaptic membrane and into the neurons. It is the calcium ion that activates the neurons. In the view of classic physicists, the number of calcium ions, the direction in which they move, and the velocity at which their movement occurs are all determined by mechanistic forces—sensory inputs, neural programming, and so on. In Stapp's view, calcium ion movement is viewed as a probability.

Let's look at this in detail. First there is a sensory event—you sniff a fragrance you like, you taste chocolate, or perhaps run your car into a telephone pole. The particular event causes action potentials (which we won't go into) leading into the brain and right up to the neuron in question. Once the neuron has been activated, an electrical charge moves along the neuron's membrane from the receiving end to its terminal, which has synapses to other neurons. Between these neurons is fluid full of calcium ions. The activation of the neuron opens up the tiny channels Eccles describes, and the calcium ions now move into these channels and enter our neuron. Once inside the neuron, the calcium finds and attaches itself to a tiny ball (the synaptic vesicle), which is filled with transmitter molecules—acetylcholine, dopamine, or serotonin, and so on. The impetus of the calcium ion moves the synaptic vesicle to the neuron's membrane and the transmitter molecules are then released into the gap between the neurons. This process activates the next neuron or neurons.

This is a process that is memorized by all beginning neuroscience students. Now you know why the field is not overpopulated. I, on the other hand, was *so* excited to find out how this one tiny function in my brain actually worked!

One factor is most important for us here: what ultimately determines the effect of this sensory event is the amount of calcium that enters the initial neurons—and that is determined, Stapp explains, by the degrees of attention and intention the subject gives to the sensory event.

You've probably experienced this yourself. Say you're at a football game and you care enormously about the outcome of this contest while a person you're with cares not at all. The various dramatic turns of this game will have a vastly different impact on the two of you. Most of the events in our lives, of course, do not elicit either our attention or intention, and for these the descriptions of classical physics are completely adequate. It's as if the brain were a potential—a cloud of possibilities, representing different alternative possible plans of action—waiting for the subject to make an intention.

Once an intention is made, and carried through—which means it's made again and again—then sensory events cause calcium to enter the synaptic vesicles and radiate into further neurons at a tidal clip in neurons throughout your brain. Your life changes. You intended that it would, and it does. Your transformation affects others. As Stapp puts this:

> [T]he choice made by an observer about what sort of knowledge to seek can profoundly affect the knowledge that can ever be received either by that observer himself or by any other observer with whom he can communicate. Thus, the choice made by the observer about how he or she will act at the macroscopic level has, at the practical level, a profound effect on the physical system being acted upon.[15]

CHALMERS: THE HARD PROBLEM

The Australian philosopher David Chalmers takes yet another step, identifying what he calls "the hard problem of consciousness," which he distinguishes from easy problems—such as the ability to understand how we categorize and react to stimuli, how we control our attentional focus and our behaviors, and so on. The hard problem, Chalmers says, is the problem of experience.

> When we think and perceive, there is a whir of information-processing, but there is also a subjective aspect. As Nagel has put it, there is *something it is like* to be a conscious organism. This subjective aspect is *experience*. When we see, for example, we experience visual sensations: the felt quality of redness, the experience of dark and light, the quality of depth in a visual field. [16]

This question of experience relates to the methodology issue I mentioned in chapter 2. Scientists invariably use the objective perspective (third-person: he, she, it) because that's the easiest from which to track data. When we attempt to measure subjective experience (first-person: I) we have a problem—as Chalmers points out, a hard problem. How can we correlate one first-person experience to another? And how do we connect any first-person experience to our third-person data? Chalmers goes on to raise another question:

> What makes the hard problem hard and almost unique is that it goes beyond problems about the performance of functions. To see this, note that even when we have explained the performance of all the cognitive and behavioral functions in the vicinity of experience— perceptual discrimination, categorization, internal access, verbal report—there may still remain a further unanswered question: *Why is the performance of these functions accompanied by experience?* [17]

A number of neurobiologists feel they have answered this question; Chalmers does not agree.

First, the British Nobel laureate Francis Crick and Cal Tech's Chris Koch have put forward the "neurobiological theory of consciousness," which hypothesizes that the basis of experience is neural oscillations in the cerebral cortex. [18] These oscillations seem to be connected to awareness in a number of modalities—sight and smell, for instance—and they also suggest a mechanism through which binding can take place. Binding, as you will recall, is the process by which the brain brings disparate pieces of information together into a cogent whole. Chalmers describes their theory in this way:

Following others (e.g., Eckhorn et al., 1988), Crick and Koch hypothesize that binding may be achieved by the synchronized oscillations of neuronal groups representing the relevant contents. When two pieces of information are to be bound together, the relevant neural groups will oscillate with the same frequency and phase.[19]

Looking back to our case studies from the previous chapter, Mr. P. was unable to put together the image of a person's face; he could not unite his separate perceptions of eyes, nose, mouth, and length of hair into a distinct and coherent picture of an individual. Crick and Koch would say this was because these specific neural circuits of Mr. P.'s cortex were not oscillating in synchrony. Chalmers says that, even though this theory could prove to be correct, it does not answer his initial question.

> Such a theory would be valuable, but it would tell us nothing about why the relevant contents are experienced. Crick and Koch suggest that these oscillations are the neural *correlates* of experience.[20]

. . . and not the experience itself.

Another neurological answer is the "global workspace theory of consciousness" put forward by Bernard Baars from the Neurosciences Institute in La Jolla, California. This theory is that the contents of awareness are contained in a global workspace, which can be understood to operate as a kind of theater. In this workspace, a spotlight of selective attention shines its bright light on the stage, revealing what we are giving our attention to from the wide spectrum of possibilities. In other words, the various sense perceptions, memories, emotions, and so on are all like actors on a stage, each with their own lines and gestures. Chalmers says,

> One might suppose that according to this theory, the contents of experience are precisely the contents of the workspace. But even if this is so, nothing internal to the theory *explains* why the information within the global workspace is experienced. The best the theory can do is to say that the information is experienced because it is *globally accessible*. But now the question arises in a different form: *why should global accessibility give rise to conscious experience?* As always, this bridging question is unanswered.[21]

Chalmers does more than just discount theories—he puts forward some of his own. The one I find most elegant is offered in his book *The Conscious Mind,* in which he posits a fundamental law for the theory of consciousness.[22] Chalmers's basic principle is the notion of information. He theorizes that everything in the universe, even the most basic particle, is made up of information—what he calls an "information state" in an "information space." He further theorizes that all information contains two basic aspects: physical and experiential.

> This has the status of a basic principle that might underlie and explain the emergence of experience from the physical. Experience arises by virtue of its status as one aspect of information, when the other aspect is found embodied in physical processing.[23]

And so we have another unproven view of the mind and our world—yet isn't it wonderful to have a plausible explanation that couples scientific data with what we all experience! Our consciousness and the entity of our complex physical organism can be seen as one coherent whole. Of course this theory is, as Chalmers goes on to say, highly speculative and also counter-intuitive. Does all information have an experiential aspect? Does the falling tree experience its "tree-ness," or its movement, or its demise? Chalmers suggests that might be the case, but not in the way we, as humans, might think:

> Where there is simple information processing, there is simple experience, and where there is complex information processing, there is complex experience. A mouse has a simpler information-processing structure than a human, and has correspondingly simpler experience; perhaps a thermostat, a maximally simple information processing structure, might have maximally simple experience?[24]

I particularly like that Chalmers takes the experiential aspect of information all the way down to an individual electron. Though he doesn't go into them, he raises fundamental questions of philosophy. He's saying that you cannot differentiate matter from consciousness—from experience. In Chalmers's view, there is no inert matter; all matter contains within it some sense of being, primitive and crude though that might be.

It's a question we look at next from the yogic perspective.

6

OR IS CONSCIOUSNESS
ON A CONTINUUM?

The quantum physicist David Bohm takes the stance, with Niels Bohr and others, that our greatest obstacle to understanding how consciousness works is the very means we use to describe it: language, especially the Western languages. Because of the subject-verb-object structure of Western languages, we are led to perceive our world in fragments and as a series of relationships between separate and unchanging entities. Scientists are particularly myopic in this regard, according to Bohm, because besides being led by language, those of us who explore the whys of the material world are also "theory-laden." We look through the lens of whatever scientific theories predominate in our own time: Copernican, Newtonian, Einsteinian, and so on.[1]

When I encountered this premise, quite recently, I could feel the truth of it. For the whole of my scientific career, I'd been looking at the world of science through the lens of Isaac Newton. As I've said, as a neuroscientist I most often worked with young cerebral palsy victims learning to sit and reach, stroke victims regaining their balance, and frail (usually elderly) individuals relearning how to walk without falling. For such physical endeavors as reaching, balancing, and walking, the Newtonian model is an efficient and functional way to order the universe. These actions are largely automatic rather than thought-based; your neurons can take care of all this by themselves. Insects perform these actions easily. On the other hand, for meditation, for interpersonal interactions, for any form of transformation in thought patterns, I found this materialist perspective to be not so helpful because, in my experience, such endeavors involve the conscious mind. But I've mentioned this already.

What Bohm's analysis helped me understand is that the world of yoga has its own lens, its own theories, its own very specific way of seeing and describing reality—and this perspective imposes, I have found, its own form of limitation. When I've taught meditation, I've often spoken about the *kundalini* energy, the subtle energy I'd experienced in my own awakening. I'd describe the *chakras*, the seven energy centers arrayed along the spinal column "from the root of the spine to the crown of the head " and describe how the *kundalini* energy "interpenetrates" the spinal column and moves between the *chakras* through subtle channels, called *nadis*, of which there are said to be seventy-two thousand, seventy-two hundred thousand, or seventy-two million, depending upon which source book you consult.

After one of these talks, another neuroscientist who meditates walked up to me and said, "Marjorie, how can you *say* that!"

As I mention in chapter 3, the yogis do not claim that this system exists in the physical body. The *kundalini*, the *chakras*, and the *nadis* are all seen to be part of a subtle system that overlays the physical system. I have myself had experiences of aspects of this subtle system. I'm sure that most of the yogis who speak of it have had their own experiences—visual, auditory, or kinesthetic—but I'm also fairly certain that few yogis have experienced the entire terrain as it's most often depicted: the vivid colors associated with each *chakra*, the resident deities, the mantras, the specific number of "spokes" or *nadis* coming in and out of each *chakra*—and I doubt that anyone actually counted those seventy-two million *nadis*! Just as scientists do, yogis are drawing what we've called "mathematical pictures," connect-the-dots images constructed by filling in the gaps between experienced subtle events.

Coming back to the comment from that critical neuroscientist—who is also a friend and fellow yogi—I must say that on one level I agreed with him. In my talk on *kundalini* I'd been drawing from various texts I'd been directed to read. I'd reported what those texts had said. But what does it mean to say the energy "interpenetrates" the spine? How would that happen? Through what receptors would *kundalini* even enter the spinal column? This is one reason I couldn't even bring the subject up with my scientific colleagues at school.

And it was often just as difficult to raise scientific questions about *kundalini* at the meditation center. Once people have had experiences of this subtler-than-subatomic reality, they are no longer interested in what science has to say. They drop the scientific model and take on the yogic model in its place. When I would try to suggest to a yoga student that the yogic view is just that—a viewpoint—they were usually incredulous, irritated, and dismissive. "What do mean, it's just a way of seeing things. I've experienced it! And so has _____ and _____," and they'd name various authorities: great yogis, saints, and beings of attainment from many traditions.

The disparity between these perspectives is the crux of the disconnect I experienced between science and yoga, the two most significant parts of my life. At the university, I lived with one worldview; at the weekly meditation *satsang* and on my vacations when I visited an ashram, I was operating with another. I felt divided, torn, schizophrenic—and it chafed me. More than anything else, I wanted to bring the two halves of my existence into resonance.

One day listening to an ashram teacher speak on an abstruse point from the Shaivite text *Pratyabhijna-hrdayam*, I was amazed to hear her refer to the work of David Bohm. This teacher was describing the perspective that, rather than existing as a static aggregate of forms, the universe is created anew in each moment through a process known to students of the philosophy Kashmir Shaivism as *abhyasa,* which means "shining forth." The teacher said that while the general population may think subatomic particles orbit the atom's nucleus along a smooth path, in quantum physics it's now accepted that these particles disappear from one moment to the next. They're seen in one place around the nucleus and then in another . . . and then another. The elliptical trajectory that's been drawn for particles is a guess—a literal connecting of the dots—and a number of physicists, like Bohm, take the perspective that the particles are appearing and disappearing and reappearing from one nanosecond to the next.

It was my first glimmer of a connection between the scientific and yogic perspectives. Bohm had just published his seminal work *Wholeness and the Implicate Order*, and when I returned to Oregon, I ordered a copy.

BOHM: THE IMPLICATE ORDER

Bohm claims there are two ways of seeing the universe. The first is the mechanistic order in which the universe is thought to be made up of entities that exist independently in time and space and interact through forces that do not cause any change in the essential nature of these entities. This is the Newtonian perspective, following fundamental laws of classical physics, in which each atom, molecule, cell, or organism exists independently in time and space and acts according to classical physical laws of motion.

The second perspective, the view Bohm himself takes, is based on quantum and relativity theories, which cannot be accounted for by the mechanistic order. In quantum theory, movement is generally seen as discontinuous. This means, first, that an electron can move from one spot to another without going through any of the space between. This, the opposite of flow, is what we were just discussing in terms of the yogic notion of *abhyasa*. In addition, particles like electrons can show different properties depending on the environment they are in; in some places they're particles, in others waves. Finally, two particles can show "non-local relationships." This means they can be far apart but react as if they were connected to each other.[2]

These new features of quantum theory—"new" when compared, say, to Newton and the apple—require that the entire universe be considered as an unbroken whole, with each element in that whole demonstrating properties that depend on the overall environment. Bohm writes,

> The three key features of the quantum theory given . . . clearly show the inadequacy of mechanistic notions. Thus, if all actions are in the form of discrete quanta, the interactions between the different entities (e.g., electrons) constitute a single structure of indivisible links, so that the entire universe has to be thought of as an unbroken whole.[3]

The notion of an "unbroken whole" is clearly resonant with Kashmir Shaivism, which I describe in greater detail later in this chapter. Kashmir Shaivism is the Indian philosophy I have been most drawn to because it best describes to me the workings of my mind. It's also the philosophy the swami said most accurately describes his experience of the world, explaining as it does the varied states of consciousness at the highest levels of manifestation. For now, however, we haven't come close to finishing our exploration of Bohm.

Focusing on the undivided wholeness of the universe, he proposes a new perspective he calls "the implicate order." "Implicate" (pronounced to rhyme with "cricket") comes from the Latin *implicare*, which means "to enfold." According to this theory, enfolding takes place in the movements of the various universal fields, including electromagnetic fields, sound waves, and so forth.[4] Bohm uses three metaphors to explain his implicate order.

The first comes from a point in the 1960s, when the scientist began to more carefully examine the notion of order in the universe. Bohm was shown a mechanical device that gave rise to his notion of the enfoldment that occurs in the implicate order. The device was made of two concentric glass cylinders, placed one within the other, with the space between filled with a viscous fluid, glycerin. Bohm was shown that when a droplet of ink was placed in the fluid and the outer cylinder was rotated, the ink drop was drawn out into the shape of a thread that finally became so thin it disappeared. He saw that the ink particles had become "enfolded" into the glycerin.

What especially fascinated me is that when the cylinder was rotated in the opposite direction, the threads of ink reappeared and finally turned once again into the droplet. The droplet, from Bohm's perspective, had been "unfolded." The insight the scientist had from this demonstration was that when the ink is spread through the glycerin by turning the cylinders, that ink is not in a state of disorder but is, in fact, part of a hidden order.[5] Bohm says,

> When the dye was distributed in what appeared to be a random way, it nevertheless has *some kind* of order which is different, for example, from that rising from another droplet originally placed in a different position. But this order is *enfolded* or *implicated* in the "grey mass" that is visible in the fluid. Indeed one could thus "enfold" a whole picture. Different pictures would look indistinguishable and yet have different implicate orders, which differences would be revealed when they were explicated, as the stirring device was turned in a reverse direction.[6]

Another image Bohm presents to explain the implicate order is a piece of paper that was once folded and was at that time pierced through in certain spots. In the unfolded sheet we see a pattern of holes that appear to us to be separate and unrelated. However, if the paper is folded back into its initial position, all the holes come together into the single spot that was pierced through. Again the enfolded or implicate order is the basis of the explicit pattern that we perceive in the unfolded state.

One way I've understood Bohm's implicate order is by applying it to my own life in relation to the yogic principle known as "the law of karma." I speak more about karma in a later chapter, but right now I'm considering its most basic aspects: cause and effect. If I drop a crystal glass, that glass will fall, at some point hit the ground, and, in all probability, break. That's simple Newtonian physics. Here's another easy example: during the holidays, when there are lots of parties and dinners out, I tend to gain weight. More calorie input, greater fat production: physical cause and effect. There's nothing hidden there.

With smokers, however, the effects of their habit may take years to manifest in a way that can be physically measured. This is true even though statistics show that in more cases than not, smoking has unhealthy consequences that will, in all likelihood, appear: cancer, emphysema, strokes, arthritis, osteoporosis, and more new ones that come up with each new study. The same is true for those of us who live on a planet where we breathe air that has been polluted by carcinogenic toxins. The toxins have an effect on our body even when that effect is hidden.

Another example of an even more hidden effect is what happens when we indulge in anger or sarcasm or unkindness, and say to another person something that would have been better left unsaid. The other person may show no apparent reaction, but with our words we have created a new implicate order: we have implanted in another human being a negative seed—frustration, doubt, irritation—and my own experience has shown me that unpleasant consequences do, almost always, appear.

So, with many of our actions we create a reality for ourselves that is not immediately apparent but is, nonetheless, real. These can be positive as well as negative: study for a test, and you are more likely to pass; exercise, and you will develop strong muscles. Our lives turn just as

Bohm's cylinders do, and in time the traces we create will unfold into something that appears to us in an undeniable form; they will become explicate. And when, as it can so easily happen, a circumstance or problem appears in my life as if from nowhere, I remember Bohm's unfolded paper and think that I must have created this "hole" some time when I wasn't aware of doing it.

The point is that if you accept Bohm's view of the implicate order—and the yogic view of karma—you can't stop with just these few examples. If the perspective is correct, it affects everything: it means that everything we do has consequences. This law of karma is a perspective I consider undeniable; again and again my experience has given this concept reality. Much of my life is spent trying to gain greater awareness of what I actually am doing, right now, in this very moment.

Bohm, of course, does not refer to karma. He speaks of the implicate order, "in which everything is enfolded into everything," to draw attention to the relevance of distinguishing between what is hidden and what is apparent. He proposes that when scientists of the future formulate the laws of physics, they give primary relevance to the order they cannot perceive and secondary significance to such factors as physical properties, location in the three dimensions, and so on. His main point, it seems, is that what is hidden also exists and must be considered in any schema that attempts to describe the whole because, apparently, it has greater power than what can be easily seen.

Bohm's third, and preferred, metaphor to explain the implicate order is that of the hologram: a three-dimensional likeness of an object. Holograms are made by splitting a laser light into two beams. One beam is then reflected off an object onto a photographic plate, which causes it to create an interference pattern with the second beam. The interference pattern viewed on the photographic plate looks chaotic when viewed normally. However, as in the case of the ink drop diffused in the glycerin, the interference pattern contains a hidden order that can be seen when it is illuminated with laser light. It creates a hologram, a three-dimensional image that can be viewed from any perspective.

Another of the hologram's characteristics is that if the holographic film is cut into pieces, any portion of the holographic film will create a likeness of the entire original object. The only difference is that the likeness is less distinct in the smaller piece than in the original film.

This shows that both the shape and organization of the whole object are encoded in every part of the film.[7]

Bohm concludes that a hologram functions as it does because it is recording detail at all levels, down to the wavelength of light itself. That makes it an especially dense form of information storage.

Aside from the fact that the holographic particles create an image that is less distinct, they also reflect what I consider to be the most significant aspect of consciousness from the Kashmir Shaivite perspective: everything that exists in the universe, even if only as an idea, is seen by the Shaivite as a form of consciousness.

Bohm goes on to relate these ideas to the structure of the universe and to consciousness. First, he shows that what we ordinarily think of as empty space is possibly full of background energy. He notes that if we apply the rules of quantum physics to general relativity theory, we find that the gravitational field is made of wave particles. He writes,

> As we keep on adding excitations corresponding to shorter and shorter wavelengths to the gravitational field, we come to a certain length at which the measurement of space and time becomes totally undefinable.[8]

This is the "zero-point" energy of space. It is the lowest possible energy that a quantum mechanical system can have. The estimated size of this infinitesimal wavelength is 1/1,000,000,000,000,000,000,000,000,000,000,000 of 1 centimeter; scientists read this as 10^{-33} cm. It is the point when time and space become indefinable. Bohm's computation of the amount of energy contained in this "shortest possible wavelength" in one cubic centimeter of space shows it to be greater than the sum of the energy of all matter in the known universe. Thus, what many would consider to be "empty space" may contain an immense amount of background energy, Bohm says, with "matter as we know it [being] a small 'quantized' wavelike excitation on top of this background."[9] Taking this vast sea of energy into account would significantly change human understanding of the universe. Think of it: space not being empty; space being full—full of energy!

Coming back to the implicate order, it is this that Bohm describes as the ground of all existence and as "an immense background of energy." The implicate order is seen by Bohm as the undivided wholeness of the universe.[10]

As I look at the physical universe, I'm intrigued by the notion that within all that is so very explicit, quantum physics posits the existence of an implicate order. An unseen order. A subtle order. While Bohm's thesis doesn't echo philosophical terminology, his perspective is perfectly in keeping with that of Kashmir Shaivism—indeed, with that of all monistic Indian philosophies. The pan-Indian view is, simply, that pure consciousness is the substratum of everything. It is the classic statement of unity and a pure expression of the implicate order.

The philosophers, of course, do not leave it at this. As human beings, we have a propensity to organize and categorize and theorize about the nature of reality. Every philosophy on the planet, including materialism, has its own cosmology. What the Indian philosophers mean is that the one subtle order—pure consciousness—is thought to take the form of an infinite number of sub-orders. I have found this perspective to be quite helpful. Let me explain how.

Underlying all Indian philosophies is a perspective on creation that shows twenty-five to thirty-seven levels of subtlety, called *tattvas*, the number depending upon the particular point of view. *Tattva,* which is Sanskrit, can be translated as "that-ness" and means a category incapable of being reduced beyond its current level, its current that-ness. The *tattvas* are arrayed from the subtlest expressions of cosmic will to the densest forms of matter, and encompass all the powers of understanding, perception, and interaction as well as the physical means for putting those powers into action.

The pan-Indian view of the *tattvas* is that they are neither sequential nor separate; the *tattvas* exist continuously and are overlaid, one upon the other. Another way of saying this is that they are enfolded, one within the other, the subtlest level being the predominant and the most powerful of all.

When I was introduced to the *tattvas*, I thought of them as a map. The schema is often presented as the means by which pure consciousness—the immense background of energy—contracts to become the universe and each individual being and particle within it. As a student of yoga, I saw the *tattvas* as a route for getting back to pure consciousness. Not that I wasn't pure consciousness already, but my awareness . . . that was another thing entirely. I saw the *tattvas* as a route my mind could take to create my own reality.

And over the years, I have continued to experience it that way. About ten years ago, I became aware that one of the main ways I would lose my state was to become embroiled in a challenging project, particularly one with a deadline. In that situation I had no inner mechanism to pull me back from my wicked tendency to overwork. I'd feel incredible tension in my chest and would have difficulty sleeping at night, and still I would push on. Naturally, I wasn't very good company at such a time—for me or anyone else—and it was no path to enlightenment either. My ferocious, I've-got-to-get-this done focus mired my awareness at a low and quite material level of manifestation.

As I thought about how I could bring more light into my life, I had the idea that I might give myself a place to relax when I was home. I pictured a sunroom with lots of huge windows, a room wide open to the trees and flowers in our garden, wide open to the sun and sky. It was as if I were opening myself when I thought of that room. I got very specific about my creation: I pictured a black cast-iron fireplace in the corner, a beige and Sedona red travertine floor, chestertown buff walls . . .

In the Shaivite view, the *tattvas* begin with Shiva having an idea, a mental image of this universe he might create; he plays with the idea in his own consciousness before he finally brings it into manifestation. That is what we all do. It is precisely what I did, one step at a time, in bringing my own little world into form. It took time and negotiation and resources to make that sunroom manifest, but I did, and now I have this beautiful place to sit and be peaceful. I love to sit there, and when I do, I remember my reasons for bringing it into being. All of that is implicate in the sunroom.

Home renovation is, of course, not a spiritual practice, and it didn't eradicate my tendency toward overachievement. I'm still working on that. Five years after I put in the sunroom, I retired, and now, four years into retirement—which still involves an NIH grant, overseeing graduate students, teaching some classes, and writing a book—I'm now considering taking up a more relaxing kind of work.

What hasn't changed is that I continue to work with the same inner map and use the same creative process to find my way from the explicate to the implicate.

WOOLLACOTT: A QUEST

Something else that didn't change was my experience of a split between my work and my spiritual path. Bohm's theories were wonderful for me to contemplate, but my colleagues and I weren't actually working with them. In neuroscience, we don't explore the substratum of existence; we measure the functions of the brain. At one point it occurred to me that, rather than expecting science to bridge the gap, I could take a closer look at yoga—specifically at the texts I was quoting. Perhaps a common ground could be found in the original Sanskrit.

I had a sabbatical coming up, my third, and after twenty-one years of teaching at the University of Oregon, I felt that this time I could do what I most wanted. One of the courses I taught was on meditation, and I was working on a research project that involved tai chi. These were my stated reasons for asking to spend a year at the University of Rochester, an upstate New York school with an active Asian Studies Department. I would study Sanskrit and Eastern philosophy.

It was an absorbing endeavor. First, Sanskrit is the most difficult language I've ever tried to learn. I love studying language: I know a bit of Spanish and Italian, I'm fluent in French, and I'm getting fluent in German. Sanskrit is something else. Our class began with thirty enrolled, and half dropped out by the end of the semester. It was that hard. To begin with, Sanskrit has another alphabet entirely, and a script that's oriented syllabically. Sanskrit nouns have eight declensions with a single, dual, and plural form for each. I spent months with flash cards; I never even went for a walk when I wasn't trying to memorize vocabulary.

It was, however, worth it. By the end of the year, I was just scratching the surface in terms of learning the language, but I was able to read a word in Devanagari script and look it up to check the translation. I began to see that many texts I'd read had been translated by Indians not fluent in English or by Americans or Europeans unfamiliar with Indian culture. As I've mentioned, I found many times when *nadi* was translated as "nerve" rather than "conduit" or "channel." I also found rituals depicted as superstitious habits when the practitioners themselves might describe them as spiritual research. Reading about *samadhi* (an objectless absorption) in three sources, I found the term translated as 1) the cessation of all wisdom, 2) the suppression of all modifications, and 3) the restriction of all [the contents of the mind].[11] Studying San-skrit taught me to look much more carefully at "source" texts.

I took philosophy courses at the same time, and this opened another avenue of exploration for me: looking with a finer focus at practices I'd been doing, and teaching, for years. One lecture that stands out was from a class on the first book of Patanjali's *Yoga Sutras*, a classic yogic text. The professor said that the subject of this book was stopping thought, and his focus for this particular class was mantra. I'd been using a mantra in meditation for a quarter of a century by then and had been teaching mantra as a tool for stilling the mind for some two decades. I saw mantra as a kind of incantation, a series of syllables I would repeat to replace my other thoughts. I had a mental charge about many of the thoughts that circled through my mind but none at all on the mantra. So, for me the mantra was a neutral alternative thought. Mine was a Skinnerian view of mantra repetition.

In this class I learned that mantra repetition is also considered by some scholars and yoga practitioners as a way to flush out *samskaras*, which is a name for the memory traces—embedded karmas—that all of us are said to carry within our bodies. Initially, in meditation the intel-lect becomes silent, and we have an experience of our inner being. Then—as many meditators experience—the impulse to think arises again from our stored impressions, breaking our focus. The professor interpreted the first section of the *Yoga Sutras* as saying that when a meditator focuses on repeating a mantra, he is able to traverse these "material layers of domain" within his own mind. The "material layers" refer to our sensory experience in that moment, our memories, and also these deeply buried impressions that are subtler than memory. So, the scripture is saying that repeating a mantra actually takes the practitioner past the barriers to concentration that he carries in his own body, open-ing him to what this professor referred to as "the ocean of content-less consciousness" and allowing the meditator to "step into the inward cur-rent."

While your own focus is moving inward, the sound of the mantra bounces against your thoughts and pushes them out. Those thoughts may become more apparent with mantra repetition, especially at first. You think things are getting worse because in meditation you're notic-ing more thoughts than you usually do. But what's happening is that the mantra is bringing up these thoughts and impressions to be expelled—

they are, as one commentator said, "swallowed" by the mantra. At the same time, you, the meditator, are establishing new impressions: memories of the delight of moving deeper inside yourself.

This was, I think, the best college class I've ever taken. It was exciting to me to be given a way to be more observant about the effect mantra repetition was having on my mind—and to see how a scripture that was supposed to have been initially recorded in the first century BCE was offering me hints about how to deal with the movement of my thoughts concerning my classes, my colleagues, my cats, whether I'd be able to find a good French Brie at the market for tonight's dinner, and what I could say to my husband about his latest high-tech purchase.

In another course this same teacher started introducing *sutras* from another philosophical work, the *Pratyabhijna-hrdayam*, from Kashmir Shaivism.[12] This was where I tasted the difference between true scriptural study and academic learning. This class was offered not in a university but in the ashram, so here the professor was addressing study from the perspective of the medieval sage who authored this work—not for indifferent college sophomores, not for people who wanted to "fill in an elective" so they could graduate, not even for scholars who approach the work as an intellectual exercise. He was speaking to spiritual seekers.

The work was written by the Kashmiri sage Kshemaraja for students who had themselves received spiritual awakening and were attempting to understand subtle experiences they were now having. It can be assumed that, even in Kashmir in the tenth century, the general population worked within a materialistic view, and authentic guidance on the inner world of the spirit was not easily found.

This was several centuries before the advent of the printing press, and students in those days learned the texts they studied "by heart." The primary means of delivering teachings in this tradition was the *sutra*, which means "thread" and refers to the way that each teaching is tied to the one before, as if by a thread. Each *sutra* is the shortest possible statement of the teaching in question.

The professor directed us to a method of studying these *sutras* that I had never before considered: focusing on each of the words individually. He said,

Think that the light of this great being's attainment is congealed and crimped into every word. Each *sutra* contains the power of Kshemaraja's enlightenment. The gift he gives us is that if we allow the understanding contained in this text to enter into our awareness, to penetrate deep within us, these *sutras* will precipitate an experience of recognition of the Lord. [13]

It was a revolutionary thought. I had been teaching classes for more than two decades, and I'd never had occasion to instruct a class in that way. As I looked at the *sutra* under discussion, I found myself enthralled, word by word. *Sutra* 1 of the *Pratyabhijna-hrdayam* is a definition of supreme consciousness, *chiti*. The *sutra* is this:

Chiti svatantra vishva siddhi hetuhu [14]

Let's look at those words, one at a time:

chiti: consciousness, the power of ultimate consciousness, the Absolute

svatantra: freedom, independence, self-rule

vishva: everything, the totality, the completeness, the all

siddhi: attainment, perfection, power

hetuhu: cause, means

So, translated, this would be: Consciousness freedom totality power attainment cause.

Notice there is no verb. As the professor indicated, the best way of taking in this *sutra* is to look at the words individually and then ask, *What is the relationship between them?* In this case, it's as if there were an equal sign between each word. And, for me, because *chiti*, consciousness, is the first word, it is also the most telling. It is "consciousness" itself that is being defined.

In neuroscience, "consciousness" is awareness. In Kashmir Shaivism, "consciousness" is synonymous with freedom, with everything in the universe, with all power and attainment, and it is also the cause of all that. One way to translate this sutra is

Consciousness, out of its own freedom, is the source and power of everything.

"Everything" is a lot. It certainly includes each one of us; it also includes whatever it is we want to call God. Consciousness is seen as the energy and the origin of all that is—and, as some Shaiva commentators have said, all that isn't as well. Because consciousness includes every thought, every wish, every emotion, every sliver of feeling, and it is the force by which these manifest into form. How does it do this? Consciousness takes form as an act of pure self-determination.

Doesn't this sound a lot like Bohm? Another of the *sutras* on consciousness that reminds me of the implicate order is *sutra* 5 from the same text. It's a more complex idea, so there are more words involved:

Chitireva chetana padadavarudha cetya samkochini chittam[15]

Consciousness itself descends from the expanded state to become the mind, contracted by the objects of perception.

We can see that the sage views pure consciousness, the consciousness of the universe, as a united whole, with one exalted and essential nature. This pure consciousness has the capacity to contract into the separate awareness of an individual—defined here as "the mind"—taking the form of the individual's material reality. This "material reality" is whatever a person chooses to perceive and understand about that perception.

As a student of yoga, I resonate with this *sutra* in particular because it deals with the importance of choices I had long seen as crucial to my own path: *What do I take into my mind? How do I relate to those things? Where do I put my attention?* This *sutra* is saying that the mind actually takes the form of its perceptions and thoughts. The next *sutra* says that the person whose nature is the contracted mind experiences *maya,* illusion.

Returning to a perspective we explored in earlier chapters, this is a clear demonstration of top-down for a yogi. "Top" in this case is pure undifferentiated consciousness, and "down" is the human mind, set, as it were, within the context of the brain, which is even further "down." The *sutra* itself—indeed, the entire text—is seen as a "top-down" communication, coming as it does from an enlightened master, one who is established in a state of ecstasy and, thus, not driven by his thoughts or his impulses, for the sake of his students, who are seeking enlightenment themselves.

Sutra 5 is a perfect dovetail to Bohm's worldview. He criticizes those who take the perspective of the Newtonian model, saying that they perceive the world only as separate fragments, divided by time and space. In reality, Bohm says, the universe is a continuous and ever-moving whole.

I've mentioned only two yogic texts so far, and an uninitiated reader might get the impression there are just a few. There are, in fact, thousands. Another text seminal to Kashmir Shaivism, the philosophy I've most carefully studied, is the *Shiva Sutras*, which is credited to the sage Vasugupta.[16] This is a classically top-down collection of teachings, as it is said to have been not just heard but also revealed. The first *sutra* gives us another way of looking at a topic so vital to our exploration: consciousness. It says

> *Chaitanyam atma* [17]

Once again, there is no verb, and so I feel the best way to look into this sutra is, once again, to just consider the words:

chaitanyam: consciousness
atma: the soul, the innermost self

Chaitanyam is another word for consciousness, and *atma* is who we are, each one of us, at the deepest and purest level. So, either way you look at it: consciousness is what we are; we are consciousness.

This is, once again, an echo of Bohm's implicate order, and the second *sutra* from this text reiterates a point from the physicist I made earlier. *Shiva Sutra* 1.2 says

> *Jnanam bandhaha* [18]

jnanam: knowledge
bandhaha: bond, fetter, chain, binding

In the yogic sense, bondage is due to one thing: our knowledge, our *limited* knowledge. Because you know you are Suzy or Bill, you don't know you are God, pure consciousness. This is, I think, what Bohm was referring to when he said that our greatest obstacle to understanding consciousness is our language—our divisive and fragmented means of thought and expression. This is especially true, he said, for scientists, who have developed a worldview that inspires us to focus on the particulars and on certain ways of understanding those particulars.

LIFE INTERVENES

Since I was on the East Coast for this sabbatical, when I heard from my father that he needed to pay a final visit to his brother on Cape Cod, I said Dad and I could meet at the Boston airport and I'd drive him there. My uncle Marion was a major figure in my own life, something of a role model in my early years as a scientist, and I wanted to pay my final respects to him as well. Marion was a self-contained man who took his greatest pleasures from doing detective work in the scientific terrain he had chosen for exploration: the microwave in all its varied applications.

Once I'd accepted science as an avocation, at some point in my teens, Uncle Marion and I formed a bond. At family gatherings, while everyone else sat around discussing food and faith and family gossip, Marion and I would create a quiet interlude so the two of us could talk about what we most loved: scientific exploration. We had fewer of these talks after I took up meditation. I always felt that he was disappointed in me because of what he saw as my disaffection from science.

Now, in his early eighties, Marion had little time left; the melanoma he'd kept in check for about seven years was finally taking over. When Dad and I arrived, Marion was sitting in his living room in his summerhouse on Cape Cod. He looked tanned from the sailing he'd been doing, but, as happens with cancer, his skin cells were beginning to fill with water, and it was obvious to me that he would soon die. Beside him on the table I saw a book that surprised me: *Still Here: Embracing Aging, Changing, and Dying* by the activist-philosopher Ram Dass. The title was on point, and perhaps that's why Marion's daughter gave it to him. The author, I knew from my own reading, is someone my materialist uncle of the past would never have let into his mind.

I don't remember how it came up—probably I asked him about the book—but I'll never forget the gist of my uncle's reply: he said he'd come to a point in his life when he was having new experiences and so a new perspective was called for. He patted the book and said, "This makes a lot of sense." Though my uncle was certainly not embracing yoga, I think he was a bit more open to broader perspectives, including that of an aging yogi called Ram Dass.

For me, hearing my super-scientific uncle say this was as satisfying as a personal accolade: his step toward more openness made me think it *might* be possible to bridge the gap between yoga and science. I hadn't done it yet, of course, but going to Rochester had been a good first step. I was determined to keep looking for the right way to do it.

At the end of my sabbatical, I realized that I could get a master's degree in Asian studies at the good old U of O, at the same time I handled my teaching responsibilities in science. The philosophy and Sanskrit courses were there, my courses from Rochester were considered as appropriate prerequisites, I got an advisor, a committee, and chose what seemed to me to be the perfect topic for my thesis: *Unbounded Potentialities of Resonance: Perspectives on the Interface between Mind and Brain from the Neuroscience and Kashmir Shaivite Traditions.* The thesis is the basis for this very book.

7

AWARENESS WITHOUT A BRAIN

Can consciousness exist without activity in the brain? This question marks one of the major divisions between the yogic and the materialist perspectives. For materialists, and this means most scientists, consciousness arises from the physical brain; the yogic view is that the brain arises out of consciousness.

For now, let's consider the notion that consciousness, though linked to the brain, might also exist without it. So far we've discussed theories of two scientists in support of this thesis. We've looked at David Chalmers's proposal that consciousness exists along a continuum and that all matter—from the simplest forms within subatomic particles to the most complex forms within the human system—contains a level of consciousness. We've also discussed David Bohm's implicate order, which he says exists in its wholeness in every particle of the universe. The implicate order itself is consciousness.

For me, some of the most compelling evidence supporting the idea that consciousness can exist without the brain comes from the scientific literature on near-death experiences (NDEs). These are accounts of experiences people report from a time when the body—including, naturally, the brain—was judged by medical professionals to be nonfunctioning, to be dead. With advances in medical science, increasing numbers of patients in such a state are able to be revived—the body "brought back to life"—and a notable percentage of those who are, say later that they were conscious at the time their brain was not functioning. These are what are termed "near-death experiences," and they range from stories about what was happening in the operating room at the time of the patient's procedure to meetings with dead loved ones and visits to other realms.

This area, of course, has its detractors in the sciences. Many of my colleagues see the NDE research as "anecdotal" (by which they mean these are subjective stories, true only for this individual in this situation), "unreferenced" (which means the researchers' findings haven't been adequately reviewed by their colleagues to establish accuracy), and "explainable" through current theories of what happens in the dying brain.

I speak in chapter 4 about the need for the subjective exploration of topics—for example, awareness—that cannot be understood fully in objective terms. Such exploration, by its very nature, would be subjective and anecdotal. As for "unreferenced," I consider that to be a spurious criticism. Though there are, certainly, numerous accounts of NDEs in the popular press and in books that haven't been held up to even the most cursory forms of deduction and logic, there are also many—countless!—referenced reports and investigations offered by reputable academic psychologists and medical researchers. These professionals have published a variety of meticulously examined, peer-reviewed articles and books on NDE. There is, in fact, a scholarly journal devoted solely to this subject, the *Journal of Near-Death Studies,* which has published peer-reviewed research in this area quarterly since 1988. In addition, a number of NDE researchers, noted below, have carefully examined each claim by neuroscientists that NDEs are completely explainable through the subjects' neurophysiological mechanisms or psychological/cultural biases, and have carefully countered these claims that NDEs are not veridical.

Saying this, I must admit that it is impossible to perform randomized, controlled, blinded studies with a large number of people on near-death experiences. Not everyone who comes close to death will have a conscious experience of being in this state. I have, however, found some research studies done in this area and some reports of people who have undergone near-death experiences to be both carefully analyzed and compelling. In this chapter, I introduce several of these.

First, I describe the findings of researchers from a variety of academic disciplines: psychologist Kenneth Ring, sociologist Allan Kellehear, cardiologist Pim van Lommel, critical care physician Sam Parnia, and psychiatrist Bruce Greyson. I summarize and examine the many theories put forth by reductionist scientists to dismiss NDEs as being psychological, culturally induced, pathophysiological, or the product of a dying brain. Then we look at two personal accounts: first, from what was probably the most celebrated near-death experience, singer Pamela Reynolds, and another, more recent, from physician Bettina Peyton.

NDE RESEARCH: A SPECTRUM

The classic book in this area is *Life after Life*, written in 1975 by the psychologist Raymond Moody, who coined the term "near-death experience." From a study of 150 people who had almost died, Moody reported their experiences of being out-of-body, traveling through a tunnel, rising into the heavens, seeing people not physically present (often dead relatives), meeting a spiritual being (often identified as God), and reviewing the whole of their life. Many of Moody's subjects reported that they were reluctant to return to life. *Life after Life* is, in fact, largely anecdotal, but it's my observation that this is often the case in a new area of research—groundbreaking research is often more observational; careful studies come later.

For the near-death experience, the more meticulous research happened in the late 1980s, when the phenomenon caught the attention of Kenneth Ring, a professor of psychology at the University of Connecticut. Reading *Life after Life*, he felt Moody's findings would be strengthened by a scientifically structured study. Ring was the founding editor of the scholarly *Journal of Near-Death Studies* mentioned earlier, and in a 1993 issue Ring published the now-well-known account of the near-death experience of a woman in Seattle. This woman, a migrant worker named Maria, had a severe heart attack while visiting friends and was rushed to the coronary care unit of Harborview Hospital. A few days later, she had cardiac arrest and what Ring calls "an unusual out-of-body experience." His information comes from a report made by Maria's critical care social worker, Kimberly Clark. Ring writes,

> At one point in this experience, she [Maria] found herself outside the hospital and spotted a single tennis shoe sitting on the ledge of the north side of the third floor of the building. Maria not only was able to indicate the whereabouts of this oddly situated object but was able

to provide precise details concerning its appearance, such as that its little toe was worn and one of its laces was stuck underneath its heel.

Upon hearing Maria's story, Clark, with some considerable degree of skepticism and metaphysical misgiving, went to the location described to see whether any such shoe could be found. Indeed it was, just where and precisely as Maria had described it, except that from the window through which Clark was able to see it, the details of its appearance that Maria had specified could not be discerned. Clark concluded:

> The only way she could have had such a perspective was if she had been floating right outside and at very close range to the tennis shoe. I retrieved the shoe and brought it back to Maria; it was very concrete evidence for me. [1]

Ring includes two additional NDE case studies in this particular article and, in conclusion, cites three observations that he could have made from Maria's story alone:

1. Patients who claim to have out-of-body experiences while near death sometimes describe unusual objects that they could not have known about by normal means.
2. These objects can later be shown to have existed in the form and location indicated by the patients' testimony.
3. Hearing this testimony has a strong emotional and cognitive effect on the caregivers involved, either strengthening their preexisting belief in the authenticity of NDEs or occasioning a kind of on-the-spot conversion. [2]

As to the question of whether any particular near-death experience is either imaginary or actual, real, verifiable, or veridical, Ring does not attempt an answer. He says that he understands his observations do not prove the authenticity of NDEs. He feels, however, that such cases add to the increasing evidence that veridical and conventionally inexplicable perceptions do occur during near-death experiences.

Since Ring's report in 1993, many other studies examining the characteristics of the NDE have been carried out. Another academic who has pored over NDE research and writings is Allan Kellehear, a sociology professor and researcher in the Faculty of Health Professions at Dalhousie University in Nova Scotia, Canada. What struck Kellehear in his twenty-year survey was the scientific biases he observed among the researchers. He notes that, far from being "value neutral," all scientific explanations for the NDE are clearly partisan, as shown in the language, rhetoric, and metaphors employed by the scientists describing them.[3] He identifies the principal scientific evaluations of NDE, and what most interested me was the one that fell in my own area, neurophysiology, where researchers see NDEs as a form of hallucination. Of neurophysiologists, Kellehear notes,

> Much of their work uses descriptors designed to give the NDE an abnormal medical appearance. The NDE is described as part of temporal lobe "dysfunction"; as a neurotransmitter "imbalance"; and as an example of "abnormal brain functioning"; the model they put forward is a pathophysiological one.[4]

For example, he quotes one neurophysiologist as saying:

> The life review in the NDE can be understood as an abnormal retrieval of episodic memory contents by the dysfunctional limbic areas.[5]

As Kellehear points out, the pathophysiological model employed here is the model used for abnormal brain function—for insanity, epilepsy, oxygen deprivation, and so on. People in these conditions do report seeing and hearing things they couldn't physically see or hear—and yet there is no stated reason for assuming the NDEs arise from the same brain dysfunction. In fact, as we'll show later, there are reasons *not* to assume this. But for now, without the benefit of research that had not by this point been done, these scientists were placing a model from their own understanding over the phenomena they were attempting to evaluate. They were saying that if a person has an experience when they are approaching death, this experience must have come from the brain right before it stopped. These scientists then equate the subject's experience with what happens in a subject who is living with an abnormal brain. That is why the scientists see near-death experiences as hallucination. It's bias, pure and simple. They don't even consider the possibility that the experience is not coming from the brain.

All of these initial explanations concerning the mechanisms underlying NDEs are, of course, put forward as theories, theories for which there is no supporting evidence until carefully designed scientific studies can be performed. How would one go about gathering evidence? There are, basically, two kinds of studies that can be done: retrospective (where you look back over a number of incidents that have already happened) and prospective (where you pick a starting point and look at every incident that occurs after that time).

Prospective studies, the gold standard of research, are longitudinal studies with data collected over a period of months or years. They are designed to determine the probability of an event's occurring in a particular group of people—for instance, the likelihood of NDEs occurring among cardiac arrest patients. The data are collected immediately after each event occurs, and so both patient and physician are more likely to have a more accurate recall of the particulars—certainly a more accurate recall than in retrospective studies, in which research may be done even years after the fact.

With NDEs, naturally, much of the research up to this point is retrospective—looking at the people who have had NDEs in the past. Prospective research in this area is more difficult to do and, everyone would agree, more useful in its outcome. Fortunately, several academics have attempted this.

At least two prospective studies of NDEs have demonstrated no difference between patients who had an NDE and those who did not in regard to their brain electroencephalogram (EEG) activity,[6] their blood chemistry, or their brain-seizure activity.[7] The findings indicate that changes in these phenomena were not the cause of the NDE.

One of these prospective studies, from the Dutch cardiologist Pim van Lommel, happened because, after reading a book on near-death experience, the doctor started asking his patients who survived cardiac arrest if they'd had such experiences themselves. "To my surprise," he writes, "twelve out of the fifty patients (24%) reported an NDE, often with extremely poignant details."[8] The data were collected over a two-year period, following which van Lommel initiated a prospective study, which was published in 2001 in *The Lancet*, a highly respected medical journal.

Van Lommel and his colleagues from the division of cardiology in Hospital Rijnstate, in Arnhem, the Netherlands, aimed to determine the probability of NDEs in cardiac arrest survivors and, when NDEs occurred, to describe the characteristics of these experiences. The researchers interviewed 344 patients who had survived cardiac arrest from 10 hospitals in the Netherlands, and found that 41 patients—12 percent—reported a near-death experience. Interviews were done immediately after the NDE and again two and eight years later to determine what changes may have occurred in their lives as a result of the experience. Of those patients who had experienced an NDE, about 24 percent indicated they had been able to watch and recall events happening around them during their cardiac arrest.

In a review of the study, a report regarding one of these NDE events was summarized in this way:

> During this study it was reported that in one case, a nurse had reported having removed a patient's dentures and placed them in a drawer in a special trolley. Throughout the one and a half hours of his resuscitation, the patient had remained in a coma. One week later he had returned to the same ward where the nurse worked and, after seeing her, said, "Oh, that nurse knows where my dentures are." He went on to describe how she took his dentures out of his mouth and put them into the crash trolley. He added, "It had all these bottles on it, and there was this sliding drawer underneath, and that's where you put my teeth."
>
> The nurse is quoted as saying: "I was especially amazed because I remembered this happening while the man was in a deep coma and in the process of CPR. When asked further, it appeared that the man had seen himself lying in bed and that he had perceived from above how the nurses and doctors had been busy with CPR. He had also been able to describe correctly and in detail the small room in which he had been resuscitated as well as the appearance of those present. . . . At the time . . . he had been very much afraid that we would have to stop CPR and that he would die. And it is true that we had been very negative about his prognosis due to his very poor medical condition when admitted."[9]

In this study van Lommel addresses several of the scientific theories proposed by skeptical neuroscientists to explain away NDEs. Some skeptics say NDEs arise in abnormal physiological states caused by cerebral hypoxia, which is low oxygen in the brain. Some say these experiences are from excessive neurotransmitter release—like the endorphins and serotonin that come from eating chocolate and in a runner's high. And some liken them to ketamine-induced experiences that result when the NMDA receptor is blocked. (Ketamines are synthetic drugs used in anesthesia and, to my knowledge, have never been located in a natural form in the brain—so the only way these could have an effect is as a result of this specific type of anesthesia.) In response van Lommel writes:

> These [ketamine-]induced experiences can consist of unconsciousness, out-of-body experiences, and perception of light or flashes of recollection from the past. These recollections, however, consist of fragmented and random memories unlike the panoramic life-review that can occur in NDE. Further, transformational processes with changing life-insight and disappearance of fear of death are rarely reported after induced experiences.[10]

We look at the transformation that comes from NDEs in the next chapter.

The theories from skeptics that NDEs are due to cerebral hypoxia or neurotransmitter release are, in fact, connected. "Cerebral hypoxia" means that the neurons no longer have enough oxygen to function and they, therefore, begin to act abnormally and release extra neurotransmitters. Both of these conditions have been associated with hallucinations. A lowering of neural activity is not, however, a factor in the medical condition most often linked with near-death experiences. According to another researcher, critical care physician Sam Parnia, most studies on cerebral function in patients during cardiac arrest show there is *no* electrical activity in the brain.

> This has raised a number of questions regarding the mechanism of causation of cognitive processes and memory during cardiac arrest. It has also raised questions regarding the relationship of the mind and the brain. This is because, using current theories of neuroscience, this should not be possible.[11]

Isn't this interesting. The neuroscientist says you *have* to have an active brain to have an experience. In an NDE, you have no brain activity yet you *do* have an experience. It's quite a puzzle for neuroscientists—or would be if they accepted the NDE as reality. It doesn't fit, so it can't be right. You must have lied about your experience. Or you must have been hallucinating!

In a survey study of NDEs in 2001, Parnia and a team of researchers in London examined sixty-three cardiac arrest survivors over a one-year period, finding that 11 percent had NDEs. In the journal *Resuscitation*, Parnia and his team write:

> The data suggest that in this cardiac arrest model, the NDE arises during unconsciousness. This is a surprising conclusion, because when the brain is so dysfunctional that the patient is deeply comatose, the cerebral structures which underpin subjective experience and memory must be severely impaired. Complex experiences such as are reported in the NDE should not arise or be retained in memory. Such patients would be expected to have no subjective experience (as was the case in 88.8% of patients in this study) or at best a confusional state if some brain function is retained. Even if the unconscious brain is flooded by neurotransmitters, this should not produce clear, lucid, remembered experiences, as those cerebral modules which generate conscious experience and underpin memory are impaired by cerebral anoxia. The fact that in a cardiac arrest loss of cortical function precedes the rapid loss of brainstem activity lends further support to this view.[12]

There is yet one more alternative explanation for a person's having a near-death experience in cardiac arrest that is often put forward by skeptical neuroscientists: that the experience occurred not when the brain had stopped but in the liminal period before or after, when it was impaired but still partially functioning. This is what has been shown to happen when people faint. Parnia answers this "partial-function" theory in his article summation, saying that fainting involves a gradual slowing of the cerebral rhythms.

> In the case of cardiac arrest the process is accelerated, with the EEG showing changes within a few seconds. The transition from consciousness to unconsciousness is thus rapid, appearing immediate to the subjects. Experiences which occur during the recovery of consciousness are confusional, which these were not.[13]

LUCID AWARENESS AND LOGICAL THOUGHT

The longest and most inclusive NDE study to date was published in 2003 by Bruce Greyson, a professor of psychiatry and neurobehavioral sciences at the University of Virginia. He performed a thirty-month prospective study regarding NDEs in 1,595 cardiac patients—a huge sampling! NDEs were reported by 10 percent of patients with cardiac arrest. NDEs were found to be ten times higher in cardiac arrest patients than in any other cardiac patients—an answer to those skeptics who say that an NDE is not necessarily associated with a person's proximity to death. So, the fear of having a heart condition isn't enough to inspire an NDE; it takes being on the brink of death as you are when your heart stops working. Echoing Parnia, Greyson summarizes NDEs during cardiac arrest with this observation:

> The paradoxical occurrence of heightened, lucid awareness and logical thought processes during a period of impaired cerebral perfusion raises particularly perplexing questions for our current understanding of consciousness and its relation to brain function. As prior researchers have concluded, a clear sensorium and complex perceptual processes during a period of apparent clinical death challenge the concept that consciousness is localized exclusively in the brain.[14]

Let me paraphrase this: the surprising incidence of both "lucid awareness" and "logical thought" at a time when the brain does not have sufficient oxygen to function raises "perplexing questions" in regard to the current scientific view of the relation between consciousness and the functioning of the brain. In short, it challenges "the concept that consciousness" is located "exclusively in the brain."

And this groundbreaking research has been replicated by a four-year prospective study of cardiac arrest patients published in 2014 by Parnia, Greyson, and others. The more recent study explores the extent to which patients demonstrated retaining awareness during cardiac arrest, a period when brain activity is not present. Of the 140 surveyed, 2 percent "described awareness with explicit recall of 'seeing' and 'hearing' actual events related to their resuscitation."[15] One survivor said,

> I can remember vividly an automated voice saying, "shock the patient, shock the patient," and with that, up in (the) corner of the

room there was a (woman) beckoning me. . . . I felt that she knew me, I felt that I could trust her, and I felt she was there for a reason and I didn't know what that was . . . and the next second, I was up there, looking down at me, the nurse, and another man who had a bald head. . . . I couldn't see his face but I could see the back of his body. He was quite a chunky fella. . . . He had blue scrubs on, and he had a blue hat, but I could tell he didn't have any hair, because of where the hat was. . . .

I know who (the man with the blue hat was) . . . I (didn't) know his full name, but . . . the next day . . . I saw this man [come to visit me] and I knew [he was] who I had seen the day before."[16]

Parnia, Greyson, and their co-authors write that they verified in the patient's medical records his descriptions of the people, sounds, and activities from his resuscitation, including the use of the defibrillator. They add that the patient's account indicates that he maintained awareness for a number of minutes during cardiac arrest, a state in which it is unlikely that there was any brain activity, even deep brain activity. As Greyson had surmised in the initial study, authors of this follow-up write that they do not see how these data could possibly support a model of consciousness that "assumes a causative relationship between cortical activity and conscious awareness."[17]

Psychologists Edward and Emily Kelly from the University of Virginia take the point a step further, saying,

The most important objection to the adequacy of all existing psycho-physiological theories, however, is that mental clarity, vivid sensory imagery, a clear memory of the experience, and a sense that the experience seemed "more real than real" are the norm of NDEs, even when they occur under conditions of drastically altered cerebral physiology.[18]

Other issues addressed in various studies include the tendency of subjects to report experiences using images from their culture or previous beliefs and the possibility that an NDE is the product of the subject's imagination, abnormal personality traits, hallucinations (caused by lowered oxygen levels in the brain), or neurochemical response to stress.[19]

Basically, an attempt to describe *any* experience will prompt us to draw from our cultural background. That doesn't make our experience invalid. As for the NDEs being created by cultural expectation, the people who have NDEs come from diverse backgrounds, and their experiences often differ dramatically depending on those backgrounds. (Like meditators, those who have NDEs lean on their cultural conditioning to find descriptions that come close to expressing what they experienced: it's the universal function of a metaphor. Metaphor seems to be the only way a person who has experienced consciousness without the anchor of the physical body can communicate such an occurrence.)

There is also no correlation regarding personality traits or blood oxygen levels and the likelihood an individual will have an NDE. And for those who do have NDEs, the experience itself is distinctly different from the experience of someone who has an abnormal neurochemical release or abnormal activity in the limbic system or temporal lobes of the brain. Certainly, there are parallels. There are parallels between our brain activity when we're dreaming and when we're wide awake—yet we would never try to say that these are the same state.

Now we take a more detailed look at the near-death experiences of two people, one a musician, whose story is told by her cardiologist, and the other a physician, who was a skeptic until she'd had her own astonishing and extremely lucid experience.

REYNOLDS: "YOU CAN CHECK OUT ANY TIME YOU WANT . . ."

At thirty-five, Pam Reynolds was a suburban mom and, following her classical music training, she was a fixture at the Atlanta recording studio of her husband, William "Butch" Lowery. Reynolds sang; she did arrangements; she played backup piano, guitar, and keyboard. She was on tour with her husband, promoting a new album, when she found she had inexplicably forgotten how to talk. "I've got a big mouth," she told a journalist later. "I never forget how to talk, and I forgot how to talk."[20]

An Atlanta neurologist found Reynolds had a basilar artery aneurism, a ballooning of the blood vessel, in the middle of her brainstem. This was clearly the cause of her speech difficulties and had probably contributed to the headaches Reynolds had been experiencing for the previous ten years. The aneurism was already leaking blood into the brain, and the wall was thinning further. It could have broken at any time, which would have been fatal, as the blood would kill the brain tissue around it. The neurologist explained all of this, and told Reynolds the aneurism was placed so that its safe removal was impossible using standard neurosurgical techniques. [21]

This was 1991. Reynolds's mother had heard about a neurosurgeon in Phoenix, Robert Spetzler, who had developed a new surgical procedure to deal with risky aneurisms like this one. She called him and, when he heard the details of her daughter's case, the surgeon agreed to do the procedure on her for free. Reynolds flew to Phoenix, and two days later, at 7:20 am, she was wheeled into the operating room at the Barrow Neurological Institute.

Reynolds was given a sedative intravenously to put her to sleep. Her arms and legs were tied to the operating table and her eyes were lubricated, to keep them from drying out during surgery, and taped shut. An endotracheal tube was put down her windpipe, and she was given a barbiturate to, in the words of her surgeon, "stop her deepest brain functions." The surgeon knew these functions did cease because throughout the four-hour procedure Reynolds's brainstem was monitored by a device affixed to her ears and set to emit clicks of 90 to 100 decibels—roughly the sound of a jet engine firing up.

"As the brain goes deeper and deeper into sleep," Spetzler explained, "it becomes less and less of a signal, and in her case, they [the vital signs on the monitors] go completely flat." [22]

In the next four hours, Dr. Spetzler, assisted by a team of twenty doctors and nurses, performed the surgical procedure, a hypothermic cardiac arrest. Basically, this procedure involves stopping the patient's vital signs (the lungs, the heart), chilling the body to 60 degrees Fahrenheit, and draining the blood from the affected body part, in this case, the head.

"So not only is she given medication to put her into the deepest coma," the neurosurgeon explained, "but then you add on this hypothermia, which puts her into an even deeper coma. Her brain is as asleep, as comatose, as unresponsive, as it can possibly be." [23]

Asked if Reynolds could see or hear anything during this time, Spetzler said, "Absolutely not." [24]

Yet she did.

Reynolds's experience was reported in detail in 1998 by Atlanta cardiologist Michael Sabom in his book *Light and Death*, in which he gives accounts of the near-death experiences of fifty individuals encountered by himself and his colleagues. Sabom, originally skeptical about the authenticity of NDEs, was inspired to do this research by the detailed accounts he received from his patients. He began his research, called The Atlanta Study, in 1994. He did extensive interviews with both Reynolds and her surgeon, making it possible to pinpoint the specific times in her procedure when Reynolds had certain experiences. Her near-death experience began, Sabom writes, just at the point when the surgeon, using a pneumatically powered cutting tool, began to cut into Reynolds's skull. This is how she described it to Sabom:

> The next thing I recall was the sound: It was a natural D. As I listened to the sound, I felt it was pulling me out of the top of my head. The further out of my body I got, the more clear the tone became. I had the impression it was like a road, a frequency that you go on. . . . I remember seeing several things in the operating room when I was looking down. It was the most aware that I think that I have ever been in my entire life. . . . I was metaphorically sitting on Dr. Spetzler's shoulder. It was not like normal vision. It was brighter and more focused and clearer than normal vision. . . . There was so much in the operating room that I didn't recognize, and so many people.
>
> I thought the way they had my head shaved was very peculiar. I expected them to take all of the hair, but they did not. . . .
>
> The saw thing that I hated the sound of looked like an electric toothbrush and it had a dent in it, a groove at the top where the saw appeared to go into the handle, but it didn't. . . . And the saw had interchangeable blades, too, but these blades were in what looked like a socket wrench case. . . . I heard the saw crank up. I didn't see them use it on my head, but I think I heard it being used on something. It was humming at a relatively high pitch and then all of a sudden it went *brrrrrrr!* Like that.[25]

Pam Reynolds also remembered hearing a female voice say that her veins and arteries were small. In fact, while Spetzler operated on Pam's head, a female surgeon located the femoral artery and vein in Reynolds's right groin, and these did turn out to be too small. The left artery was used.[26]

As Spetzler made his way through the brain, underneath the temporal lobe, he found the basilar artery aneurism. The medical records note that the aneurism was "extremely large and extended up into the brain" and that the head surgeon decided the hypothermic cardiac arrest would be needed to perform the operation.[27]

At 10:50 am, Sabom writes, tubes were inserted into Reynolds's exposed femoral arteries and veins and connected to the cardiopulmonary bypass machine. Warm blood from her body flowed through hoses into the bypass machine, where it would be chilled before being returned to her body.

At 11 am Reynolds's core body temperature had fallen 25 degrees, and her heart registered irregular, disorganized fibrillation patterns on the monitor screen. Five minutes later, the remaining electrical spasms of the dying heart were extinguished with massive intravenous doses of potassium chloride. Cardiac arrest was complete.

Once her heart had stopped, Reynolds's brain waves flattened into electrocerebral silence. Brainstem function weakened, and clicks from the ear device produced increasingly lower spikes on the monitoring electrogram.

Twenty minutes later, the core body temperature had fallen another 13 degrees to a deathly 60 degrees Fahrenheit. The clicks from the ear device no longer elicited a response. It was a total brain shutdown—time for the daring surgical maneuver to begin. In this period, Reynolds's near-death experience progressed:

> There was a sensation like being pulled, but not against your will. I was going on my own accord because I wanted to go. . . . The feeling was like going up in an elevator real fast. . . . It was like a tunnel, but it wasn't a tunnel.
>
> At some point very early in the tunnel vortex I became aware of my grandmother calling me. But I didn't hear her call me with my ears. . . . It was clearer hearing than with my ears. I trust that sense more than I trust my own ears. The feeling was that she wanted me to come to her, so I continued with no fear down the shaft. It's a dark shaft that I went through, and at the very end there was this very little tiny pinpoint of light that kept getting bigger and bigger and bigger.
>
> The light was incredibly bright, like sitting in the middle of a light bulb. It was so bright that I put my hands in front of my face fully expecting to see them and I could not. But I knew they were there. Not from a sense of touch. Again, it's terribly hard to explain, but I knew they were there. . . .

I noticed that as I began to discern different figures in the light—and they were all covered with light, they were light, and had light permeating all around them—they began to form shapes I could recognize and understand. I could see that one of them was my grandmother. . . . They were specifically taking care of me, looking after me.

They would not permit me to go further. . . . It was communicated to me—that's the best way I know how to say it, because they didn't speak like I'm speaking—that if I went all the way into the light, something would happen to me physically. They would be unable to put this *me* back into the body *me*, like I had gone too far and they couldn't reconnect. . . . .

I wanted to go into the light, but I also wanted to come back. I had children to be reared.[28]

Once the blood was drained from the body, the aneurism sac deflated, and Spetzler could clip and remove it. The cardiopulmonary bypass machine was turned back on then, and warmed blood flowed back into Pam's empty body. After the warming had begun, the ear device began to register blips on the electroencephalogram—signs of re-emerging life. Waves of electrical activity from the higher brain centers once again moved across the EEG screen.

At 12:00 noon, a serious problem arose. The initially silent heart monitor began to register the disorganized electrical activity of ventricular fibrillation. It was a lethal cardiac rhythm that, if uncorrected, would bring about death within minutes.

Moving quickly, Spetzler placed two defibrillator paddles on Reynolds's chest and shocked her heart with 50 joules of electricity. No response. The defibrillator was then charged with 100 joules and reapplied. After this second jolt, the familiar *beep-beep-beep* of normal sinus rhythm signaled success. At this point, Reynolds became aware of "returning" from her near-death experience:

My grandmother didn't take me back through the tunnel, or even send me back or ask me to go. She just looked up at me. . . . Everything was fine. I did want to go.

But then I got to the end of it and saw the thing, my body. I didn't want to get into it. . . . It looked terrible, like a train wreck. It looked like what it was: dead. I believe it was covered. It scared me and I didn't want to look at it.

It was communicated to me that it was like jumping into a swimming pool. No problem, just jump right into the swimming pool. I didn't want to, but I guess I was late or something because he [her uncle] pushed me. I felt a definite repelling and at the same time a pulling from the body. The body was pulling and the tunnel was pushing. . . . It was like diving into a pool of ice water. . . . It hurt![29]

At 12:32 pm Reynolds's body temperature was 89.6 degrees—low but life-sustaining—and the cardiopulmonary bypass machine was turned off, the various instruments were removed, and the surgical wounds were closed. Spetzler's younger assistants had responsibility for the closing surgical duties, which they did to the accompaniment of rock music—a detail that Reynolds noticed.

When I came back, they were playing "Hotel California," and the line was "You can check out anytime you like, but you can never leave." I mentioned [later] to Dr. Brown that this was incredibly insensitive, and he told me that I needed to sleep more.[30]

Spetzler's report from the surgery states that at 2:10 pm the "patient was taken to the recovery room still intubated but in stable condition."[31]

In reading the details of the two concurrent reports—one from the head surgeon and one from the patient—I felt like a detective, trying to fathom what had actually taken place during that time period. When Pam Reynolds's awareness rose above her body and watched—verifiably!—what was happening to it, was that awareness, though separated from her brain, still intact? When her brain waves had flat-lined and her heart had stopped beating, were these authentic experiences she remembered of going through a tunnel and seeing and talking with dead relatives? Clearly they would have been subtle experiences, but were they veridical? Or were they, as many of my colleagues say, hallucinations caused by abnormal brain activity? Or, as others believe, were these simply comforting dreams that arose in response to Reynolds's fear of the death her body was, in that moment, undergoing?

One way to answer these questions is to examine differences in brain activity between cardiac arrest patients who report NDEs and those who do not. The prospective studies that collect such data report that no difference in brain activity has been found between these two groups, which indicates to me the possibility of a continuation of aware-ness without brain activity, at least in some individuals.[32]

There are other possible explanations, of course, and many neurosci-entists would say—do say—that all of Reynolds's experiences could have happened under anesthesia, at the beginning and end of surgery, while she was still able to perceive sounds in the room. I must agree that this is a possibility. We don't know precisely when Reynolds's expe-riences occurred in relation to her cardiac arrest and the cessation of her brain function. We do, however, know from the surgeons' accounts that it would be unlikely, almost impossible, for Reynolds to have seen or heard the bone saw with her eyes and ears taped shut and with loudspeakers in her ears.

Asked how he could explain Reynolds's perceptions of the events of her surgery, Spetzler said, "From a scientific perspective, I have abso-lutely no explanation about how it could have happened."[33]

The journalist then asked whether the drugs or neurotransmitters could create hallucinations. The surgeon said,

> Those are suspect, but not in this setting. . . . You can have patients who become hypoxic—who have too little oxygen in the blood. In that situation, patients may experience hallucinations, where you see yourself transported up into maybe a corner of the ceiling and you're looking down on things. But in virtually every one of those settings, you have a warm body which is missing something—either not enough oxygen, or it's metabolically missing something—or it is fe-verish. So that you can imagine all sorts of neurons firing in an unorganized fashion and it would give you an explanation.
>
> Here you have the opposite. . . . Here you have the neuron in a depth of a sleepy state, of a suspended animation, that makes it very hard to think that it's from active neural transmission.[34]

When the journalist asked Spetzler about what Pam Reynolds's case says about awareness, and whether it can be separate from the brain, he replied:

> It comes down to the metaphysical. . . . It comes down to the soul. It comes down to whether you're religious and believe in these things. I think it is the ultimate arrogance for anyone, whether they're a scien-tist, or anyone else, to say that something can't be. I accept Pamela's

account, although I have no explanation of how it could have happened. [35]

At the time of Reynolds's death, from heart failure, in 2010, her out-of-body recollection was, according Kenneth Ring, "the single best instance we now have in the literature on near-death experiences to confound the skeptics." [36]

PEYTON: ACCEPTS DYING AND HEARS "YOU MUST LIVE!"

Dr. Bettina Peyton was an avowed materialist until she had a near-death experience during the birth of her second child. At the time, 1988, she had been practicing internal medicine for two years. Peyton had never encountered a near-death experience in her own patients and, having been an atheist from childhood, she had never given the phenomenon so much as a thought. It was only after her vital signs flatlined in the delivery room of the Tufts-New England Medical Center in Boston—the hospital in which she had been working—that Peyton learned about NDEs firsthand. Her experience challenged what she described as her "strident materialism" when, under general anesthesia and without a heartbeat, she saw and heard everything that happened around her in the delivery room.

Peyton's story begins when an ultrasound revealed that her second pregnancy was more complicated than her first had been. A year earlier she had given birth to healthy twin boys. This time, however, the placenta obstructed the birth canal and would be at risk of bleeding as the uterus enlarged. The condition was life threatening for both mother and child.

In her seventh month Peyton did, indeed, begin to bleed and was put on strict bed rest on the medical center's ob-gyn floor. Night after night, her husband, also a doctor, brought their one-year-old sons to their mother's bedside for a hug and a story.

The medical plan was to deliver surgically, by Cesarean section, as soon as the fetus was sufficiently mature. Peyton, writing of her experience for this book, indicates that she spent this time in "uneasy anticipation":

Although I had great confidence in my healthcare team and had avoided fretting over possible complications, I was well aware that this surgery would be a high-risk procedure. Because the placenta extended across the front of the uterus, my obstetrician would have to make the incision directly through it, cutting across what was essentially a spongy mass of venous lakes. A substantial amount of blood loss was to be expected.[37]

Each week a unit of Peyton's blood was collected and stored, and her anesthesiologist recommended a general anesthesia rather than the less extensive spinal block that was customarily used in such cases. In the spinal block, the patient feels no lower body pain but is fully conscious.

Finally, after a month, the weekly amniocentesis indicated that the fetus's lungs were mature enough for delivery. The next morning, Peyton learned from her obstetrician—a seasoned doctor, the one who had delivered her twins—that instead of the usual (and cosmetically preferable) low-transverse incision he had originally described to her, he had decided to make a large vertical incision. This would give him better access to the fetus. Peyton writes:

> His decision forced me to face the gravity of the situation. I accepted the news with a valiant smile, but tears sliding into my ears sabotaged my show of courage.[38]

Peyton distracted herself by joking with the surgeon as the nurse laid down the surgical drapes and the anesthesiologist injected the induction drug into her vein. "Think good thoughts," she remembers him saying. She imagined jogging beside her husband on a sunlit country road while, relaxed and comfortable, she felt a tube advancing down her trachea. Peyton lost consciousness until, as she writes, she heard a voice:

> "Her blood pressure is too low!"
>
> My anesthesiologist's alarmed voice had snapped me awake as if from a deep sleep. Suddenly, right in the middle of the operation, I was wide awake. As if with a flick of a switch, I had become super aware and attentive. It was a form of heightened awareness the likes of which I had never before experienced, as if the majority of my brain, dormant all my life, had suddenly switched on. It seemed like the first time ever that my brain was operating at full capacity. I was

amazed, wondering how my mind had managed to break through the drugs bathing my brain. Even more amazing is how calm I was—given the circumstances. I was simply and fully present, listening in the darkness behind my eyelids to the sounds in the room. I could feel the painless tugging sensations in my abdomen of the surgery in progress.

"How's it going?" The anesthesiologist was asking the surgeon how far along he was in the delivery. He exclaimed that my blood pressure was plummeting fast.

"The baby's gone," muttered the surgeon from the other side of the tented drapes. His voice sounded strained. It appeared the operation wasn't going well at all, and my baby hadn't survived. But there was no time to grapple with that grim news. From over my right shoulder there burst forth a loud expletive.

"*Shit!*" The anesthesiologist couldn't detect any blood pressure whatsoever.[39]

Peyton's attention shifted then from what she was hearing to what she could feel in her own body.

In the next instant, a strange stillness spread inside my chest, a hollow feeling. . . . Something was missing . . . my heartbeat. My heart had stopped.

At the same time, my vision opened, and I discovered that I could see into the room. How amazing! The eyelids on my physical eyes had been taped shut to protect the corneas, yet by some other mechanism I could see perfectly clearly. Several units of blood were hanging from an IV pole directly over me, one already was being transfused. The anesthesiologist, seated to my right, was hunched over my right arm, inspecting the IV line.[40]

Peyton realized that she was the only one in the room who had noticed that her heart had stopped. Then the silence was interrupted by a volley of strident beeps—the cardiac monitor registering the lack of a heartbeat—and Peyton watched the anesthesiologist slam his fist into a large red button in the middle of the wall. In medical jargon, he was calling a code, initiating a chain of signals that would culminate in the arrival of the hospital resuscitation team.

Peyton knew the drill: throughout the hospital the team members would drop whatever they were doing and rush to the delivery room, taking steps two at a time—even though most of these codes were exercises in futility. Usually, such patients were too old or too far gone to resuscitate.

> My mind assessed the situation: My baby is dead; I am in cardiac arrest. I knew, as I watched my ghostly white chest flopping under the anesthesiologist's arms, that this code would be futile too. I was dying; there was no question in my mind of the outcome.
>
> So here I was, having a firsthand experience of dying. It was not at all as I'd imagined it might be. I was not feeling in the least bit scared. Nor did I feel lonely or helpless. Instead, there was a calm acceptance of the fact that my life was ending. From a place of power, I accepted the fact that I was dying. I felt absolutely unafraid. It was all very natural, surprisingly serene, and free of suffering. And that's because I knew "I" was separate from the limp white corpse that was my body. My body was dying, and "I" was watching the whole calamity from some untouchable place inside.[41]

Whatever it was that Peyton identified as "I" was doing just fine.

Her attention shifted then from the room and the drama around her body. She had the sense that it was time for her—the identity that she perceived herself to be—to make an exit. And with this thought,

> . . . there the exit is, actually perceivable—a spaciousness opening up in the back of my mind. I see in my inner vision a vast darkness expanding behind me, at the backmost boundary of my mind. I can sense the edge, beyond which there is only empty space. Instinct draws me toward it, and I let my attention approach it as one approaches the brink of a cliff. I know I must entrust myself to that spaciousness. My awareness reaches the edge of the precipice and I lean backwards, arching over the chasm of darkness below. Very naturally, I let myself fall, gliding downward in a graceful backward arc into the unknown.
>
> Free-fall . . . engulfed in a thick darkness . . . awareness dissolving . . . no sensation . . . blankness . . . nothing.
>
> Bursting through a thick barrier. A great crashing sound reverberated all around.
>
> Expansion. Freedom.
>
> Echoes of the explosion receded into profound silence. Empty space surrounded. No stars . . . no planets . . . nothing.

> The darkness was vividly black . . . fascinating . . . mysterious . . .
> gleamed like black velvet. Laced within the darkness were particles
> of shimmering light. The blackness sparkled, shimmered. This scin-
> tillating light was intriguing, intensely beautiful, mesmerizing.[42]

Peyton was entranced by this sparkling black light, whose brilliance
intensified as she moved through it. She sensed a pervasive presence in
this light, an intelligence, a pulsating power. She was deeply happy,
enveloped in peace. All was perfect, until Peyton's experience was
interrupted by a statement, which she perceived not in words but as a
quiet thunder with the message

> *You must live!*
> I must live? Though the command was crystal clear, I don't
> understand. It seemed like a koan.
>   A light glimmered in the depths of the darkness. I peered down-
> ward and saw, at a great distance, what appeared to be a miniscule
> luminous crystal. Its colorful flickering contained, as if in a hologram,
> the entire experience of someone who once lived, someone very
> familiar . . . and gradually I recognized that this was the life of
> someone I once impersonated, flickering dimly like a dream that had
> ended. That person had died; there could be no return. The com-
> mand to live seemed impossible to fulfill. How could a mere memory
> be brought back to life?[43]

The voice descended once again, interrupted Peyton's confusion, and
filled her with a will to survive. She understood that her own effort to
survive was crucial.

> In an unbroken stream of communication, I am given precise in-
> structions on just how to come back to life. The instructions are
> simple and clear: I must fix my focus on the present moment, main-
> tain a positive attitude, and hold the firm conviction that I will in-
> deed survive. Any distraction or negativity will jeopardize my survi-
> val. . . .
>   Funneling down through the darkness, my consciousness opened
> abruptly into the confines of the hospital operating room. The drama
> of the cardiac arrest was unfolding. Still connected to the expanded
> state, I was its direct extension: Bettina's disembodied mind, made of
> that pure energy. Watching from a vantage point a few feet above the
> head of the operating table, I was an instrument of perception and

cognition, fully available as an open conduit through which the power of the transcendent realm flowed, in service of its command to resurrect the life of Bettina. I gazed down at my body lying on the operating table. It appeared quite dead. [44]

Peyton observed the members of the code team burst through the double swinging doors and see their colleague's lifeless body on the table. It occurred to her that she could be embarrassed by the way her body looked, but that, she immediately understood, would be a perilous distraction. Sensing her colleagues' collective impression that she was already gone and beyond resuscitation, Peyton began to hold the strong thought, *I'm going to live. You can do this. Now, let's get to work.*

The room was churning with personnel. In the center of the action my surgeon was totally focused. He had a very difficult task. Amidst the clamor and urgency, working in a lurching surgical field filled with blood, he was performing what he would later declare was his first three-minute hysterectomy. . . .

A catheter was being inserted into my right jugular vein and threaded toward my motionless heart. A sharper pain was tugging at my attention: the anesthesiologist was trying to insert a line in my right wrist, but the artery was collapsed and the needle is poking the bone underneath. The persistent stabbing in my right wrist was becoming a distraction. I suggested to the anesthesiologist that he try the larger, more proximal artery at the elbow. I sensed his negative response as concretely as if he had shaken his head in refusal; he was concerned about injuring the nerve that runs alongside the larger artery. I urged him again and again, more forcefully, but he continued to poke at the collapsed artery. Finally, drawing on all the power of the expanded state, my mind shouted, *Just go for it!* With a start, he straightened up and turned to my elbow, gaining access to the larger artery on his first try. . . .

My attention was then drawn to a white-haired gentleman in scrubs—a senior surgeon—entering the room. He radiated a compassionate wisdom that I perceived as an aura of soft golden light around him. Slowly and deliberately, he wove a path through the crowded room, coming to my right side. Directly opposite him, my obstetrician didn't look up from his work. Without a word, the elderly surgeon reached deep into my blood-filled abdomen. He located the aorta, the large artery that runs vertically along the midline of the body, and wrapped his fingers around it. My attention became fully

focused on his hand. So tangible was his touch and keen my perception that I felt the warmth of his skin and saw the fingerprint whorls
on his fingertips. It seemed he had forgone surgical gloves in the
interest of saving time. Then, clenching his fist, he clamped the aorta
shut.[45]

The moment the surgeon's hand entered Peyton's abdomen, her center
of awareness shifted to inside her body. She understood this as a move
from expanded consciousness back into her own awareness. The surgeon twisted the core of her body into a knot, holding what remained of
her blood in the aorta in service of her heart and brain. It was the worst
pain Peyton had yet experienced in the operation—and it was, she
understood at the time, the turning point: she would live.

Shortly after, one of the nurses leaned over and whispered into
Peyton's ear that her baby had lived; she had a healthy daughter. Later
Peyton learned that "the baby's gone" meant not that the baby had died
but that it had been removed from her abdominal cavity and carried to
her husband, who was waiting outside the operating arena.

When Peyton first opened her eyes, she was in the critical care unit,
lying in a bed encircled by her husband and a team of doctors and
nurses. She still had a tube in her trachea, so she couldn't talk, but she
put up her hand to keep people from speaking and motioned to be
given something to write with. Before anyone spoke, Peyton had written on a napkin words to this effect: "I know I have a baby girl. I know
my uterus is out. I know my heart stopped."

> So, they did know I knew what had happened. They immediately
> knew that I had been aware. That confounded them, but they were
> far more concerned with my physical state. I wasn't out of the woods
> at all at that point. There were more brushes with death in the next
> twenty-four hours.[46]

Over the next few days and weeks, Peyton had conversations with many
of the personnel who had been with her in the delivery room, and one
by one, they verified that all of the perceptions she'd had—under anesthesia and with her eyes taped shut—about what was said and what
was done and by whom were accurate.

> I spoke with the surgeon and the anesthesiologist, and they were
> both aghast at what I had to say. They could not explain anything I

was reporting to them. They were willing to go on a TV news program on near-death experiences and to say that this was inexplicable.
They confirmed that I had perceived things that didn't seem physio-
logically possible. [47]

Finding an explanation became a motivating factor in Peyton's life—as,
in fact, it is in the lives of many who have an experience of consciousness unmediated by the brain.

8

FOLLOWING A NEAR-DEATH EXPERIENCE

What is most interesting about near-death experiences is what the person who has the experience makes of it afterward. Pim van Lommel and his colleagues spent a great deal of time and energy tracking this phenomenon and found that the majority of those who had NDEs not only remembered these experiences in the years that followed but were transformed by them.

Specifically, in interviews with 344 patients from ten hospitals in the Netherlands at two- and eight-year intervals after the original experience, the researchers found in both follow-ups that patients who'd had an NDE reported a significant increase in their belief in an afterlife and a decrease in their fear of death after the experience. These changes were not echoed in the control group, patients who had not had an NDE. The researchers noted that for the NDE patients their attitudes regarding afterlife and death were even more apparent at the eight-year compared to the two-year follow-up. Also, after eight years, patients could still recall their NDE almost exactly.

The staying power of the NDE makes perfect sense to me: it echoes my experience of meditation. After two years, I was well embarked on the practice, and after eight years of daily meditation, I had a deeper understanding of what I was doing and had begun to reap some of its benefits in my life.

Van Lommel suggests that the NDE is difficult for many patients to accept and integrate, apparently due to negative conditioning toward such experiences within our culture. Again, this is a phenomenon I can easily relate to. It's difficult to find words to express these ineffable experiences, and when people do begin to speak about an NDE, their family, friends, and colleagues may disagree with them, ridicule them, or—to me, even worse—change the subject. Van Lommel says:

> Our findings show that this process of change after NDE tends to take several years to consolidate. Presumably, besides possible internal psychological processes, one reason for this has to do with society's negative response to NDE, which leads individuals to deny or suppress their experience for fear of rejection or ridicule. Thus, social conditioning causes NDE to be traumatic, although in itself it is not a psycho-traumatic experience. As a result, the effects of the experience can be delayed for years, and only gradually and with difficulty is an NDE accepted and integrated. Furthermore, the long-lasting transformational effects of an experience that lasts for only a few minutes of cardiac arrest is a surprising and unexpected finding.[1]

In an interview van Lommel identifies this cultural prejudice as an issue that is often introduced by scientists themselves. He says the understanding that consciousness is primary, that everything originates from consciousness—a perspective that van Lommel calls "fundamental in the universe"—was lost to human wisdom over the last two centuries because of Western science. He says, "It was Newton with his physics and Descartes with the difference between the body and the spirit, the consciousness." Since then, we could study only the physical aspects of humanity, not our consciousness. "Consciousness," Van Lommel says, "*pfffft!* Get out!"[2]

Van Lommel points out that 50–60 percent of Americans believe in some form of afterlife, and when you add the dimension of spirituality with afterlife, the percentage is even higher. Of the two hundred scientists in the American Academy of Science, only 7 percent identify themselves as spiritual. That means 93 percent are nonbelievers. "These 200 scientists have positions in scientific journals, and so on," Van Lommel says. "So, it's hard to get this kind of subject into mainstream science."[3]

I think he is absolutely right. In my early years of science, it never occurred to me to look at near-death experiences as examples of anything. NDEs are outside the scientific worldview. *Weltanschaung* is the

German word for worldview; to me it means that which can be even considered in one's reality system. In science you might be able to speak of meditation experiences because the person having them is still alive. But you can't speak of experiences that happen when the body is dead. I won't say that the "person" is dead in a near-death experience because the person is still very much aware and later—once the body has come back to life—the person reports what has happened to them. This indicates something that is anathema to scientists: the idea that, as van Lommel indicates, awareness itself might exist when the brain is not functioning. In other words, between the brain and consciousness, consciousness might be primary.

REDEFINING THE NATURE OF CONSCIOUSNESS

After her NDE, once Bettina Peyton awoke—once she returned to waking awareness—she was utterly convinced that consciousness is primary. In her words,

> When I woke up in the intensive care unit, I had vivid recall of what had happened. My perception was—as it still is—that I am not this body, this individual; and that consciousness is real and is the substratum of everything that exists. That is what I immediately gathered from this experience.
>
> I knew that "I" am separate from my body. Because in that experience, I saw a little flickering light that was Bettina. That was the whole individual. That might have been the equivalent of the life review that other people have in near-death experiences, but I just saw it as this little hologram.
>
> My identity has never gone back to *I am Bettina*.[4]

The notion that she could identify a foundational "I" that was not physical, not cultural, not a personality, was an entirely new perspective for this physician, who had been an atheist from the age of seven.

What I find particularly interesting is the process Peyton underwent to return to the experience of expanded consciousness she'd had in her NDE. She knew, intuitively, that there must be a way back, and she set out to find that means of return, whatever it might turn out to be. She heard about meditation, the practice of quieting the mind and going within, and felt that this might be a means of accomplishing what she sought. Even though she had three children in diapers and was working full time as a doctor, she managed to attend a meditation session each week for three months. The sessions were facilitated by a psychologist for her clients; Peyton was an observer, but she was also there to learn to meditate, which she felt she did accomplish.

> I was very frustrated. I did exactly what we were being told to do, and at the end of three months, I had found no satisfaction. So, I sat with this psychologist and said, "I really need a teacher. I would like someone to sit with me one-on-one every week." I had in mind some elderly man with a long, white beard. Some Zen master, but a man and old. I asked if she had a teacher, and she did. She started to speak about this teacher's age and availability. When I heard that her teacher was young and wouldn't be able to meet with me, I said, "Say no more. I'll look elsewhere."[5]

In time, Peyton heard about a local meditation center, but when she arrived for a public session there, the place seemed all wrong. The walls were lined with five-by-seven-foot photographs of various people she knew must be teachers in this tradition. She felt it was obviously a cult, but rather than leaving, Peyton found herself sitting down with the others. People were informally grouped, sitting mainly on the carpeted floor, all facing a chair in which no one sat. When the group chanted, Peyton found herself weeping, inexplicably. When a video came on of one of the teachers, a fairly young woman, Peyton found herself staring at this person's eyes.

> I didn't hear a word she was saying. I kept looking at her eyes, thinking, *She knows.* I didn't even know what I needed to know, but I knew that she knew. The look in her eyes told me.
>
> I went up to the emcee afterward and said, "This is a cult. This is all wrong. But I just have to meet the teacher and get it over with. I have a question, and if I could just meet with her, I can move on with life."
>
> He said, "If you're at all curious, check it out."[6]

This teacher was giving a meditation workshop in two weeks in an ashram just four hours' drive away, and Peyton arranged with great difficulty to get a weekend off from her family and her job so that she could attend. No one understood why she wanted to go to this ashram; Peyton herself didn't understand it. Throughout the entire drive she wept.

> I thought I was on the edge of a new life. The feeling was that something precipitous was about to happen. I didn't know what it was. But I thought it was psychosis. . . .
>
> I thought I must be about to become psychotic. This is what it felt like. It couldn't be explained: why was I so compelled to do this? It wasn't rational to be drawn to an ashram, which just seemed like a silly and unsafe place to go.
>
> So, I was crying all the way there. I didn't even know if I was going to take the workshop. I just wanted to meet this teacher. Being very assertive, my plan was to barge my way in and sit with her for an hour and then turn around and drive back home.[7]

Peyton arrived at the ashram and asked for the interview she was seeking. After talking with several layers of organizational hierarchy, she was told that she could see the teacher at the ashram chant the following morning.

The next morning, the chant was already under way when the teacher entered the room. Before she saw this teacher, Peyton said she had a very specific sensation:

> I felt a ripple of energy, like it was flowing through the crowd, like we were seaweed, and it was rippling through us.
>
> Then I turned and saw her. This being was so graceful and radiated so much authority that I knew this was the real thing. The word I heard inside was—*phoom!*—"majesty." I just knew this was it, this was a master.[8]

With her eyes Peyton followed the teacher as she walked to her seat, as she sat in her chair at the front of the room, as she picked up her chanting book and began to sing. Peyton's heart pounded with what she recognized as fear. She thought, *Why am I so afraid?* She noticed that everyone around her had looked back at their books and continued to chant, but Peyton found herself unable to move.

> I was just staring at her, fixedly. I didn't know why. I knew it wasn't appropriate; I knew it was rude. But I couldn't take my eyes off of

her, and my heart was continuing to hammer. It was raw terror, like I was on the edge of a cliff. I felt like something huge was about to happen.

Suddenly my entire body was extended, along the spine. I became like a tall pole, with my head way higher than everyone else's, staring at this teacher like some beacon. Then I heard this voice inside of me, shouting, *look at me!*[9]

At the same time, Peyton thought, *This is rude. How could I say such a thing?* Then it happened again: *LOOK AT ME!* Peyton found her body extending up even further, and again from inside, she heard a roar: *LOOK. AT. ME.*

That third time, the teacher lifted her eyes from the chanting book, and looked at the crowd. I was off to the side. She slowly began rotating her face in my direction. As that happened, my heart went from pounding to fluttering, to what I would call fibrillation—to something I don't know how I could physically sustain. As her face turned toward mine, my whole system seemed to be preparing for death.

This was nothing like the near-death experience, which was absolute calm; this was alarm, terror. I knew the exact moment our eyes met, even though she was thirty feet away, because the instant they did, there was a bridge of beautiful sparkling black light between us. I merged into her. Or she merged into me. We became one. I was in the same experience of oneness I'd been in, in my near-death experience: this formless consciousness, which is all that is.[10]

At this point, Peyton did feel as she had in her near-death experience, but with one significant difference: another living being was now in the experience with her.

It was the same exact experience, but with one difference: the teacher was present. The Guru was that consciousness. . . . I could see that she was one with that consciousness, and that she also was a shell of a personality through which this consciousness flowed, unimpeded. . . .

In this experience, the next thing that happened was my hearing expanded consciousness saying, through this teacher, *Welcome home. You have come home.*

> She was in that state, welcoming me back to that state. She knew
> I had been here before. She knew everything there was to know
> about me. . . . I knew I had found in her the path back. [11]

Welcome home! These were virtually the same words I myself heard in my first meditation. In considering what they meant, what *home* truly is for me, I saw that I had come back to an experience that felt more authentic and joyful than any state I had experienced before. All the other perspectives I had ever taken felt like they were not really me, not truly my own. Up to this point I had been wandering outside of my homeland and now, only now, I had found my way home. I was in my core.

I think this feeling of being "home" is why people who experience consciousness without the filter of the brain—an image I've borrowed from Edward Kelly and speak more about in the next chapter—remember the experience, seek to understand it, and find ways to give it expression in their lives.

Bettina Peyton, for instance, brought her near-death experience into her medical practice. She had long been interested in working with end-of-life care.

> In medical school, I walked into a Hospice, and the minute I stepped
> over the threshold, I said, "This is what I want to do!" In my medical
> training, I wrote Elisabeth Kubler-Ross and said, "I want to do what
> you do; how can I do that?" She wrote back saying, "You are going to
> have to create a career for yourself." And so I did that. [12]

Working in Hospice and with palliative medicine, Peyton helped to establish the medical field that eases the experience of death, a field that came into being in the 1990s and received formal recognition from the American Board of Medical Specialties in 2006.

> Before my own near-death experience, I thought, "At least I can hold
> people's hands and make them feel better." I wanted to comfort
> them. [13]

Following her near-death experience in 1988, Peyton had much more than comfort to offer patients facing death. When she felt it would be helpful, she spoke about her own experience, and she was naturally sensitive to indications that patients were having subtle experiences themselves.

> Many of the patients had experiences of expansion, had religious experiences, saw deceased family members—all of the things that are part of near-death experiences. I would support them through that.
>
> The other thing that made me effective as an end-of-life doctor was my lack of fear of death. When I would enter a room that lack of fear could be felt. [14]

I met Bettina Peyton at a meditation retreat, and when I told her about this book and described some of the near-death experiences I'd read about, she spoke a bit about her own NDE. This conversation was when it first occurred to me that the most compelling aspect of NDEs is their power to transform the people who have them. Her experience had certainly touched Peyton, and there was another physician, Eben Alexander, whose powerful account of his NDE had recently come to my attention. Alexander's popular book, *Proof of Heaven*, charts his near-death experience and its immediate aftermath in vivid detail. He had contracted bacterial meningitis in 2006, when, for a week, he lay in a coma in a hospital in Lynchburg, Virginia. In his book he gives a lucid account of the experiences, teachings, meetings, and exalted expansions that he was conscious of in this time.

Alexander's story is exciting, but what I want to focus on is what happened to him afterward.

POST-NDE ANALYSIS

First, because Alexander is a Harvard-trained neurosurgeon and his subject is taboo among scientists, his book drew a kind of chilling scrutiny from some members of this sector: personal slurs, sloppy refutation of fact, that kind of thing. [15] Members of his medical team were interviewed and later complained that they were misquoted, that they had never made the critical comments attributed to them. [16] In the face of this, Alexander himself never wavered from his original account; he answered critics; he analyzed the negative views he himself had held on the subject of NDEs, going back and forth between the arguments.

Some people, for instance, speculate that his experience could have been a psychedelic vision produced by the drugs he was being given or hallucinations caused by a malfunctioning cortex.[17] Alexander points out that such drugs work on receptors in the neocortex, and without a functioning neocortex, there were no active neurons with which these drugs could engage.[18] Likewise, there were no active neurons in the neocortex to create hallucinations.

Alexander adds that the deeper he delved into the current perspective of science on NDEs, the more he "came up spectacularly short." He observes that everything about his experience—the uncanny clarity of both the vision and the conceptual flow of his thoughts—suggested higher brain functions. But his higher brain hadn't been available; it wasn't around to do the work.

> The more I read the "scientific" explanations of what NDEs are, the more I was shocked by their transparent flimsiness. And yet I also knew with chagrin that they were exactly the ones that the old "me" would have pointed to vaguely if someone had asked me to "explain" what an NDE is.[19]

In the previous chapter, I discuss these "scientific" explanations of NDEs, and how the validity of these arguments is refuted by researchers who work in the field. As I mention in chapter 3, scientists have similarly attributed experiences of the *kundalini* energy to aberrant mental functioning and have likened the feelings of euphoria, experiences of visual images, and performance of spontaneous movements—all of which can arise during meditation—to epileptic seizures. These scientists are attempting to show neural correlates of the meditative experience, but in doing so, they define that experience by its most basic component—as if neural activity were its sole characteristic.

Like Alexander's view of his near-death experience, I understand my meditative states as being something altogether different from hallucinations or fantasies created by my mind. They appear to be states in which my mind is so still that I am able to access levels of reality that are more subtle than those of which I am normally aware. Alexander describes the essence of his near-death experience in this way:

> If I had to boil this entire message down to one sentence, it would run this way: *You are loved.*

Love is, without doubt, the basis of everything. Not some abstract, hard to fathom kind of love, but the day to day kind that everyone knows—the kind of love we feel when we look at our spouse and our children, or even our animals. In its purest and most powerful form, this love is not jealous or selfish, but unconditional. This is the reality of realities, the incomprehensibly glorious truth of truths that lives and breathes at the core of everything that exists or that ever will exist. . . .

Not much of a scientific insight? Well, I beg to differ. I'm back from that place, and nothing could convince me that this is not the single most important emotional truth in the universe, but also the single most important scientific truth as well. [20]

From my perspective, the most important truth that Alexander—and Peyton—discovered regarding near-death experience is the understanding that the experience can be replicated by meditation. Alexander points out that it isn't necessary to almost die in order to, as he puts it, "glimpse behind the veil." What is needed to access these truths is that we do the work: go deep into our own consciousness, through prayer or meditation. [21]

LINKING NDE AND MEDITATION

This unusual link, between NDE and meditation, is worth dwelling on. Because he's had both kinds of experiences, Alexander can draw a correlation between what he experienced when he was near death and his brain had shut down and what he experiences in meditation, when he voluntarily makes his mind still. Each of these states is capable of opening a door to what a yogi would call true perception: an individual's awareness of his unity with the infinite awareness that is the foundation of all that exists. Here's how Alexander explains the mechanics of this state:

To understand how the brain might actually block our access to knowledge of the higher worlds, we need to accept—at least hypothetically and for the moment—that the brain itself doesn't produce consciousness. That it is, instead, a kind of reducing valve or filter, shifting the larger, nonphysical consciousness that we possess in the nonphysical worlds down into a more limited capacity for the duration of our mortal lives. There is, from the earthly perspective, a very definite advantage to this. Just as our brains work hard every moment of our waking lives to filter out the barrage of sensory information coming at us from our physical surroundings, selecting the material we actually need in order to survive, so it is that forgetting our trans-earthly identities also allows us to be "here and now" far more effectively. . . . (That's not to say we shouldn't be conscious of the worlds beyond now—only that if we are extra-conscious of their grandeur and immensity, they can prevent action while still here on earth.)[22]

This is, quintessentially, the "top-down" perspective of consciousness we discuss in chapter 5. As I've said, I adopted this way of seeing consciousness after analyzing and contemplating my meditation experiences and those of people whose meditations have gone deeper than my own. I suggest that the meditation and near-death experiences reported by many are glimpses into a higher reality—and by this I mean a reality more subtle than the one to which our nervous system usually has access. At those moments in our lives when the mind has been quieted, we may indeed go "beyond" our nervous system's usual capacities. Then the consciousness within us, freed from perceiving the machinations of the mind, is able to perceive its own expanded form. This is, though simply put, the view of the Kashmir Shaiva texts I describe in chapter 6.

Let me clarify this. A few years ago, in preparation for a talk at a Northwest conference of the American Academy of Religions, I came up with a model to describe my view of the relationship between the limited consciousness of the brain, the mind, and the expansion of absolute Consciousness. My model was based on what I'd gleaned from the medieval Shaiva texts as well as from meditation experiences, both mine and those of others. The model is shown in figure 8.1. Since this is top-down, let's start at the top, where there is an icon representing absolute Consciousness. This is another name for Bohm's implicate order, the energy thought to be within everything in the universe. This absolute Consciousness contracts (the arrow pointing downward) to become the mind, which is the mass of thoughts, memories, habits, and so on that we carry within us. This limited consciousness further contracts (another arrow pointing down) to become the neural activity of the brain. The model is not solely top-down, however, because the arrows point upward as well, showing that the brain also has access to experiences of absolute Consciousness. This is what happens when we still the normal brain activity in meditation or the brain is shut down temporarily because of illness.

As to why only one in ten cardiac arrest patients has a near-death experience, I cannot answer. Indeed, why do many people sit for hours in the practice of meditation with no experience? Meditation is not a mechanical process, as I've indicated, and so I surmise that there are other factors at play in these events, factors of which we are unaware.

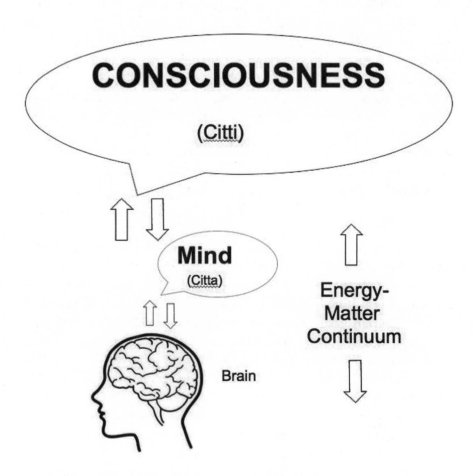

Figure 8.1.   Diagram of the continuum of consciousness extending from universal consciousness (citti) through the individual mind (citta) and the brain. Author's creation.

This does not, however, discount the thousands upon thousands of experiences that have been reported.

The next question that's often raised involves the nature of these reports of subtle experiences. Most people who have had near-death experiences don't mention flying over a terrain of the sort Eben Alexander describes in his NDE—and it's my hunch that, even though he likens meditation to his near-death experience, he's never had the same images arise again. The significant thread that holds together these subtle experiences was well described by Alexander: *You are loved.* There are other patterns to experiences, but as researchers have pointed out, many of these vary according to a person's culture.

From my observations of the reports of meditation and near-death experiences, even with overarching similarities, each is infused by its own unique flavor. One factor that accounts for the differences is the way they are, by necessity, filtered through each person's limited capacity to perceive and articulate subtle events.

Alexander experienced being greeted by a beautiful young woman flying on butterfly wings who turned out later to be a deceased older sister he had never before met. Another person experiences being greeted by angels; yet another sees a relative who appears to move through space effortlessly. One person may identify an all-powerful and loving presence as Jesus; Alexander identified such a presence with great love and the sound *om*, considered in the Indian traditions to be the primeval sound of creation. How is this different from what scientists do in creating models of the electron and the atom from a few mathematical points in equations that are themselves based on atomic theory? It's a human propensity to make sense of the universe we live in, and those who have subtle experiences attempt to convey them with familiar images and in words that, no matter what the language, are inadequate to the task.

Of his new view of the relationship between consciousness and the brain, Alexander goes on to say:

> We—the spiritual beings currently inhabiting our evolutionarily developed mortal brains and bodies, the product of the earth and the exigencies of the earth—make the real choices. True thought is not the brain's affair. But we have—in part by the brain itself—been so trained to associate our brains with what we think and who we are that we have lost the ability to realize that we are at all times much

more than the physical brains and bodies that do—or should do—our bidding.

True thought is pre-physical. This is the thinking behind the thinking responsible for all the genuinely consequential choices we make in the world. A thinking that is not dependent on linear deduction, but that moves fast as lightning, making connections on different levels, bringing them together. In the face of this free, inner intelligence, our ordinary thought is hopelessly slow and fumbling. It's this thinking that catches the football in the end zone, that comes up with the inspired scientific insight or writes the inspired song. The subliminal thinking that is always there, when we really need it, but that we have all too often lost the ability both to access and to believe in. . . .

To experience thinking outside the brain is to enter a world of instantaneous connections that make ordinary thinking (i.e., those aspects limited by the physical brain and the speed of light) seem like some hopelessly sleepy and plodding event.[23]

Clearly Alexander's model of the origins of consciousness and their relation to the brain was transformed by his own NDE. And as I think you may have surmised from the descriptions of the NDEs of other individuals by Sabom, Gray, and others, the researchers' and physicians' views of the nature of NDEs were also often transformed by carefully examining the details of the medical information and the experiences that their patients shared. Prospective studies of hundreds of patients who have undergone NDEs during cardiac arrest also offer additional information that makes the usual medical model explaining the neural origins of consciousness unlikely as it relates to these experiences.

So then, does one simply say, "These cases must have been anomalies!" Or "I don't know?" Or does one propose that *possibly* consciousness can exist without brain function?

UNFETTERED CONSCIOUSNESS

One of the resources Eben Alexander turned to in his attempts to understand his experience is the book *Irreducible Mind: Toward a Psychology for the 21st Century*. In this 800-page compilation, University of Virginia researchers Edward F. Kelly et al.[24] summarize the evidence from peer-reviewed research on NDEs to show a clear probability that consciousness is not necessarily tied to brain function. The authors say that there is evidence of conscious awareness when the brain is not functional in NDEs, adding this statement:

> NDEs seem instead to provide direct evidence for a type of mental functioning that varies "inversely, rather than directly, with the observable activity of the nervous system." Such evidence, we believe, fundamentally conflicts with the conventional doctrine that brain processes produce consciousness, and supports the alternative view that brain activity normally serves as a kind of filter, which somehow constrains the material that emerges into waking consciousness. [25]

Varying "inversely rather than directly" means that when the nervous system is quiet, this mental functioning is active; when the nervous system is active, this mental functioning doesn't happen. The evidence, then, suggests that an active mind actually inhibits certain kinds of expanded mental processes—precisely what meditation teachers have been saying for thousands of years!

One example of mental function that is often enhanced during the NDE is the "life review" that many people experience, in which they have a rapid review of their life memories, often covering their entire life. This occurs faster and more fully than it is ever observed in normal waking consciousness. The physiological theory that the NDE is caused by temporal lobe malfunction in a dying brain cannot explain this increased memory efficiency, as the memories evoked by temporal lobe stimulation or in temporal lobe epilepsy are typically single memories rather than summaries or compendiums. [26]

Another aspect of NDEs that supports the hypothesis that consciousness does not depend on brain function, and which is not explained by physiological models, is the experience of seeing the body from a point in space outside itself. Kelly et al. note that 48 percent of the persons whose NDEs they studied reported having this experience, and reported as well seeing and hearing events that verifiably took place nearby, such as the medical team's attempts to revive them. Skeptics have said that these are just "imaginative reconstruction attributable to a persisting ability to hear, even when unconscious, or to the memory of objects . . . glimpsed just before losing consciousness." [27] A counter argument is that, in fact, other patients normally have either a confused memory or no memory of events just before or after losing consciousness. In addition, researchers have found almost no evidence that patients retain hearing abilities when under general anesthesia.[28] This is, of course, even less likely when the senses have been blocked, for example, with the ears plugged or the eyes taped shut.

This particular hypothesis was tested in an experiment performed by the cardiologist Michael Sabom.[29] He interviewed cardiac patients who had NDEs during a cardiopulmonary resuscitation (CPR) and reported watching events from outside their body, comparing them to cardiac control subjects who had not had NDEs during their cardiac crises. Sabom said that 80 percent of the control patients made at least one error when describing the events, while none of the NDE patients made an error.[30]

Kelly et al. go on to propose a "transcendent" model of the NDE. By this they mean there may be characteristics or levels of reality not normally accessible to our senses and our consciousness that may be part of a transcendent level of reality. The authors propose that someone in a near-death experience accesses these more subtle levels of reality, in which consciousness functions outside of the body and without the support of the nervous system. They suggest this model because in their database most (81–82 percent) who have had an NDE believe that during the experience their consciousness separated from their physical body, and therefore they believe their individual conscious awareness may also survive a permanent separation from the brain when they die. Kelly et al. suggest that this model corresponds to those proposed by the well-respected psychologist of the late 1800s and early 1900s, William James, in addition to Frederic Meyers, and others that indicate consciousness

> has roots in a transcendental environment of some sort, accounting for its supernormal capabilities. It provides the overarching unity of the psyche . . . and it survives the shock of physical death.[31]

They also say that the characteristics of NDEs are often seen in mystical experiences related to meditation traditions, including out-of-body experiences, enhanced mental functioning, and heightened perception.[32] The comments of Kelly et al. support the experiences of both Bettina Peyton and Eben Alexander, in showing the many similarities between NDEs and experiences of deep meditation.

I talk more about this transcendent model of consciousness in chapter 11. Next, we look more closely at the possibility that conscious awareness might survive the death of the body.

9

CONSCIOUSNESS AFTER DEATH

There is yet another way of exploring the possibility that conscious awareness exists independently of brain function. In addition to near-death experiences, scientists have also looked at the possibility that some aspect of the personality may survive the body when it dies and may later enter a new body. This is the concept of "reincarnation"—that once the body dies, a part of a being, often called the spirit, continues to exist without the support of a nervous system or any other physical foundation; this spirit then takes birth, incarnates again, in another, new body.

Culturally speaking, reincarnation is a doctrine of most Eastern religions—Hinduism, Buddhism, Taoism, and so on—and also of many of the shamanic religions of tribal peoples. Though there are varied understandings of reincarnation, the unifying principle seems to be that the spirit continues its evolutionary growth or service from one lifetime to the next. In my years of meditation, I have never had an experience that suggests reincarnation, but I know a number of people who have. My own interest in the subject is the question we've been exploring: can consciousness exist without the support of a living brain?

A number of scientists have done research in this area, one of the best known being the late psychiatrist Dr. Ian Stevenson. Though this field of research may seem to border on, or to be outside of, the areas in which one could normally apply the scientific method, Stevenson had a strong foundational training in scientific methodology and applied this to his research with great care. His first degree was in biochemistry, and he then graduated from medical school, specializing in psychiatry and the development of personality in children. Stevenson was for many years the head of the Department of Psychiatry at the University of Virginia School of Medicine. As a new professor, he says, he was dissatisfied with the scope of current theories of personality and so began to broaden his research interests to include what he calls "psychical research and paranormal phenomena." He was specifically interested in the survival of the human personality after death.

Stevenson published his first article on cases suggestive of reincarnation (his term) in 1960, in the *Journal of the American Society for Psychical Research*. In this article he recommends accepting the possibility of reincarnation only if all other possible interpretations of a case can be excluded. The article won an award from the American Society for Psychical Research, an organization that the author himself describes as one of the most obscure in science.[1]

A few months after the article appeared, the head of the Parapsychology Foundation offered Stevenson funding to continue his research in India. Since reincarnation is a tenet of most of the religions practiced in India, it seemed the country would offer fertile ground for such an investigation. Stevenson accepted the offer, and so began the primary research of his more than forty-year career. By the time he died in 2007, Stevenson had accumulated more than 2,500 case studies, collected on six continents (all but Antarctica), including many countries in Asia (India, Thailand, Sri Lanka), the Middle East (Myanmar, Lebanon, Turkey), as well as Europe and the United States. Of this research and his relationship to it, Stevenson writes:

> Journalists have sometimes incorrectly (and unjustly) described me as trying to *prove* that reincarnation occurs. This allegation is wrong as a description both of my motive and of science. Outside of mathematics there is no proof in science; scientists make judgments about probabilities, and they rarely express themselves in statements of certainty. It is true that I search for stronger evidence than we now have for paranormal processes in the cases I study, and if that evidence points toward reincarnation I am not displeased. I have never hidden my interest in the results of my research. William James pointed out that "if you want an absolute duffer in an investigation, you must, after all, take the man who has no interest in its results . . . the most useful investigator . . . is always he whose eager interest in

one side of a question is balanced by an equally keen nervousness
lest he become deceived."[2]

In my reading of the peer-reviewed articles by Stevenson and others in
this area,[3] I have been favorably impressed by the care these researchers take to explore all the available evidence. They look not only at the
data supporting the possibility of reincarnation but also at any data
potentially invalidating their hypothesis.

   In this chapter I will review evidence from the writings of Stevenson
and other scientists in support of the concept of reincarnation—though
Stevenson himself never speaks that baldly. He refers not to evidence
"of reincarnation" or "in support of reincarnation" but to cases "suggestive of reincarnation." Even with his careful wording and his adherence
to scientific standards, Stevenson's research has been largely ignored by
other scientists. The American Medical Association, however, in a review of one of Stevenson's books, wrote,

> . . . [I]n regard to reincarnation he has painstakingly and unemotion-
> ally collected a detailed series of cases . . . in which the evidence is
> difficult to explain on any other grounds.[4]

"Difficult to explain on any other grounds"—this is, ultimately, the
hope Stevenson held to for this challenging area of research. He writes:

> Friendly critics of my investigations have pointed out that reincarna-
> tion is itself an irrefutable hypothesis. We can never show that it does
> not occur; nor are we ever likely to obtain conclusive evidence that it
> does occur. I can imagine the "perfect case," but have no expectation
> of finding it. All of the cases I have investigated so far have some
> flaws, many of them serious ones. Neither any single case nor all of
> the investigated cases together offer anything like a proof of reincar-
> nation. They provide instead a body of evidence suggestive of rein-
> carnation that appears to be accumulating in amount and quality. For
> the most part, science advances through the development of prob-
> abilities making one interpretation of a particular phenomenon more
> likely than another. I anticipate a gradual further accumulation of
> evidence that will make reincarnation seem to an increasing number
> of informed persons a more probable explanation than others for
> cases of the type that I have reported. This cannot happen, however,
> until larger numbers of scientists become aware of the evidence so

far obtained. This in turn may depend upon a greater appreciation by
other scientists of the explanatory value that the idea of reincarnation
may provide for a number of important unsolved questions of biology
and medicine.[5]

Unfortunately, the upsurge of scientific interest Stevenson hoped his
accumulation of evidence would inspire has yet to manifest. His research does, however, greatly interest me. In the following pages, I
examine some of the evidence suggestive of reincarnation—and suggestive, therefore, that an individual's consciousness can move, across time
and space, from one system of neurons to another.

EVIDENCE SUGGESTIVE OF REINCARNATION

In a chapter by Stevenson in the *Handbook of Parapsychology*, he defines the term "reincarnation," saying that it

> refers to the concept that human beings (and perhaps subhuman
> animals) consist of two separable components, a physical body and a
> psychical entity or soul. At the death of the physical body the soul
> persists and, after a variable interval, becomes associated with a new
> physical body.[6]

Stevenson identifies this as a short, working definition, and he notes
that various cultures around the world have specific and often differing
perspectives on the nature and particulars of reincarnation. The most
interesting question for him, as a scientist, was how to design his research to track the movement of this spirit, or soul, from one lifetime to
another.

Think about it. How could one do that?

In popular culture, there are what are called "past life readings" in
which, through hypnosis or the psychic powers of a spiritual intuitive,
an individual may learn of the passage of his soul through various identities of the past. Scientists generally avoid such avenues for gathering
information, however, and it's obvious why. How could you possibly
verify the talents of an intuitive? As for hypnosis, you would have to do
painstaking research to prove that the person under hypnosis had not

come into contact with the information he gave about a past life at any point in his current life.

Stevenson did consider hypnosis a possibility. He noted that while hypnosis can provide veridical information, there have been many cases where the subject unconsciously brought into his past-life "memories" information from something he'd read in his current lifetime. That said, however, Stevenson added that he knew of two cases in which hypnosis provided evidence of xenoglossy (being able to write or speak a language that one has not been exposed to before in life). In both of these cases, Stevenson said that the subjects demonstrated abilities during hypnotic regression that gave valuable information about the possibility of their previous lives.[7]

The mode of research that Stevenson turned to most often, and which most researchers in the area use to this day, is to interview the families of very young children who claim to remember previous lives.[8] Such cases come up when children, often only two or three years of age, begin to speak about events and people their parents know nothing about. These children have memories or dreams that, it seems, they cannot possibly know from their own very limited life experience. And, in fact, at such an early age, it is a fairly easy matter to verify whether this information has been given to the children—told to them by someone—or whether it is from a truly spontaneous memory.[9] Stevenson termed these "spontaneous cases of the reincarnation type."

The interview techniques that Stevenson developed for his research are similar to those practiced in the legal system in that they involve interviews of only firsthand witnesses. This means that researchers interview only those people who know the subject—this includes the child's parents, grandparents, older siblings, and other relatives. The child would also be interviewed, though not all children are willing to talk to the researchers. In the countries where there is a great deal of acceptance of reincarnation, Stevenson would always try to interview the child's family members before they had contacted anyone whom the child had mentioned knowing in a previous life. The researcher also studied relevant written documents, including any newspaper reports, birth records, and the like. Careful notes were taken and the number and description of items from the past life the child had said he or she remembered were documented.

After all of this was recorded in detail, Stevenson and his associates would search for the previous identity of the child and, if this had not yet happened, try to locate that family. Again, they carefully interviewed the members of this potentially "previous" family in isolation from the child's current family. When visiting the previous family, Stevenson also would independently verify the location of roads, houses, stores, and other landmarks that the child may have mentioned about this previous home environment. Then the researcher would compare the number of items remembered to the number corroborated through interviews with the previous family and the researcher's own on-the-ground observations. Finally, the researcher would make a note of any recurrent features that occurred in a large number of cases.[10]

In summarizing the general characteristics of these cases suggestive of reincarnation, Stevenson says:

> The child often begins talking about this previous life as soon as he gains any ability to speak, and sometimes before his capacity for verbal expression matches his need to communicate so that he mispronounces words that are later better understood or uses gestures to supplement what he cannot yet say clearly with words. . . . In most cases the volume and clarity of the child's statements increase until at the age of between 5 and 6 he usually starts to forget the memories; or, if he does not forget them, he begins to talk about them less.[11]

When the past lifetime can be traced, it is often noticed that the child has behaviors that are unusual in the context of the current family but normal in the previous life. In other words, phobias or special interests the child shows will often match what is said about the behavior of the deceased person. Also, these children will sometimes think of themselves as adults and act as if they are patronizing other children or expect to be able to behave in adult ways. The children often ask to be taken to the place where they say they previously lived and often shows concerns about their "family" there. In Asian countries, the child's current parents are often willing to search out the child's previous family and are able to find that family because the child gives sufficient and accurate information concerning the place where they live and their proper names.[12]

Another unusual factor in many of these cases, noted by Stevenson, are physical marks on the child's body:

> . . . [T]he subject has some birthmark or congenital deformity that corresponds in location and appearance to a wound (usually fatal) on the body of the related previous personality. The child may point to the birthmark as the place where "he" (in the previous life) was (for example) stabbed or shot.[13]

I find it particularly interesting that almost all of Stevenson's subjects describe past lives in which they were ordinary, undistinguished people. This refutes the idea that children, rather than describing their own experience, are describing a subconscious memory of a deceased but well-known person they had heard about from others.[14]

In other respects, the particular social stratum involved is not a significant factor, as cases suggestive of reincarnation have been found across all social and economic levels. Children from wealthy families may remember previous lives in poor families and vice versa.

Physical proximity, however, can be a factor. Although there are examples of a child's remembering a previous life in another country, typically the previous life is in the child's own culture and in a location within no more than 15 miles from where the current family resides.

Timing seems also to be significant as, from one culture to another, there are slight variations in the intervals between the death of the previous person and rebirth. These times range from, typically, nine months (in Turkish cases) to about forty-five months (in Indian cases), though some cases have much longer intervals between the previous hypothesized death and rebirth.[15]

Since the time between incarnations might vary from one culture to the next, one might well ask if reports of reincarnation are culturally influenced and, therefore, not truly valid. In fact, the distribution of cases suggestive of reincarnation differs across countries. As one might expect, incidents are reported much more often in parts of the world where reincarnation is part of the cultural heritage. Such cases are, however, also reported in countries where the majority of the population is not familiar with reincarnation or whose cultural heritage or religion is actually opposed to a belief in reincarnation (for example, Christians of Europe, the United States, and Canada).

Stevenson states that, though most Americans do not believe in rein-carnation—80 percent according to a Gallup poll (www.gallup.com)—many cases suggestive of reincarnation have been reported in the Unit-ed States. What I find most compelling is that 27 percent of the parents of children in these cases had little or no knowledge of the concept of reincarnation and only 16 percent were initially accepting of the idea. The remaining families (56 percent) had heard of reincarnation and felt some degree of openness to it as a perspective from which to view their children's experiences. The parents who said that reincarnation was not taught in their own religion often admitted that they initially scolded their child for claiming to remember a previous life. Some of these parents wrote to Stevenson in a tone of bafflement or even alarm be-cause nothing in their lives had prepared them for the experiences their child was having. This is, in fact, what happened in the first of the two case studies we look at below.

This case, involving a child in Louisiana, was recently researched and summarized by the psychiatrist Jim Tucker, an associate professor of psychiatry and neurobehavioral sciences at the University of Virginia. Tucker has taken over the reincarnation research that Ian Stevenson began at the UVA Division of Perceptual Studies.[16]

IN THE U.S. SOUTH: INITIAL SKEPTICISM

James Leininger was about four years old when he first came to Jim Tucker's attention.[17] The psychiatrist had agreed to be interviewed for an ABC News show with a segment on the past-life memories of chil-dren, which was to feature this story of a boy who apparently remem-bered being a World War II pilot whose plane was shot down in the Pacific, near Japan. Though the show never was broadcast, in prepara-tion for it Tucker watched footage of James's parents describing how, when he was two, their son had begun to have frightening nightmares about a plane crash. By the age of three, he was saying that he had been a pilot who took off in flight from a boat and whose plane was shot in the engine by the Japanese military; he said that his plane had crashed into the Pacific Ocean and this is how he had died. Tucker notes that at the point when Andrea and Bruce Leininger were being interviewed by the news reporter, they had no idea whether or not what young James was saying had any historic validity. It was obvious to them that their son was telling the truth. He was, in fact, having these dreams and spontaneous recollections. What they didn't know is whether or not the events had actually happened.[18]

Tucker contacted the Leiningers and asked if they would be willing to be interviewed by him for a scientific study. The couple agreed to let the psychiatrist study their son's case but put off the interviews until they'd had a chance to write and publish their own account of their son's story. The book they wrote, *Soul Survivor: The Reincarnation of a World War II Fighter Pilot*, was published in 2009. Tucker began his interviews several years later. I am taking my own information on this case wholly from Tucker's account because I trust that his research protocols are impeccable.

Tucker had the Leiningers begin their account with their son's nightmares, and his comments about a plane crash, which started when he was almost two. Tucker writes:

> The first noticeable incident in their story occurred when James was twenty-two months old. The family was living in Texas at the time, and Bruce took him to the Cavanaugh Flight Museum outside of Dallas. Before that, James would point at planes that flew overhead, but at the museum, he became transfixed. He kept wanting to return to the World War II exhibit. He and Bruce ended up spending three hours at the museum because James was so fascinated by those planes, and they left with a few toy planes and a video of the Blue Angels, the Navy's flight exhibition team.[19]

The Leiningers said that when James would play with the toy airplanes he would crash them into the coffee table saying, "Airplane crash on fire." A few months later, James began having nightmares.

> Andrea would find James thrashing around and kicking his legs up in the air, screaming "Airplane crash on fire! Little Man can't get out!"
>
> This was not just a one-time nightmare. James did the same thing night after night, multiple times a week. I talked with his aunt, Andrea's sister, after my trip to Louisiana. She emphasized several times just how disturbing these nightmares were to witness. . . . She saw a lot of them and said they were like watching someone in terror, fighting for his life.[20]

Once when Andrea was reading her son a bedtime story, he began to tell her about his dreams while re-enacting them. He said, "Little Man's going like this," kicking his legs up. And then he said, "Can't get out." When this happened, Andrea went to get her husband, who had been saying his son's nightmares were nothing more than typical childhood dreams. Bruce then asked the boy what had happened on the plane.

> James said it crashed on fire. Bruce asked him why, and James said it got shot. Bruce asked him who shot his plane. James, a little over two at the time, appeared exasperated and exclaimed, "The Japanese!" . . .
>
> Along with saying that night that he flew a Corsair, James also said he had flown off a boat. When Bruce asked if he remembered the name of the boat, James said, "*Natoma*." Bruce replied, understandably, that *Natoma* sounded Japanese. James, looking perturbed, said no, it was American.
>
> Afterward, Bruce searched online for the word *Natoma*. After some effort, he found a description of USS *Natoma Bay*, an escort carrier stationed in the Pacific during World War II. Fortunately, he printed out the information and kept it, so we have a record of it. Each page of the printout has the name of the website as the footer, along with the date the pages were printed, 8/27/2000. Thus, we know that Bruce was searching for *Natoma* when James was twenty-eight months old.[21]

Tucker adds that unless a person thinks that this story is an elaborate fraud—with Christian parents living in Louisiana creating a fake past-life narrative that their own friends might view with disdain—it is difficult not to accept that this two-year-old boy did give his parents the word *Natoma* as the name of his ship.

About a month after this incident, the Leiningers asked James if anyone else was in his dream. The boy said, "Jack Larson." So his father began looking for a Jack Larson. Bruce thought his son was referring to himself as Jack Larson, and so he looked for someone of that name in the U.S. Navy who had died in World War II.

> He said he wasn't thinking James's dreams were memories of a past life. When Andrea's mother eventually suggested that, Bruce's initial response was, "That's bullshit."

... Bruce's strong natural tendency to discount the possibility of past lives may also have contributed to his failure to understand what now appears to be the clear message of James's statements. Andrea's sister confirmed that for years Bruce resisted past lives as an explanation for James's behavior, because the idea conflicted with his Christian faith.[22]

When the boy was about two and a half years old, he climbed into his father's lap while Bruce was looking at a book, *The Battle for Iwo Jima, 1945*, that he planned to give to his own father. On a page with an aerial photograph of the base of the island, the toddler pointed to the picture and told his father, "My airplane got shot down there, Daddy."[23]

Bruce had found a listing for the *Natoma Bay* Association online, and at this point he called one of the contacts. The man said that the ship had been at Iwo Jima and that he remembered a pilot named Jack Larson but didn't know what had happened to him. Now, Bruce had confirmed three points from his son's story: there was a ship named *Natoma Bay*; this ship had been at Iwo Jima; and Jack Larson had been a pilot on it.

Bruce continued to look for further verification, and it was this that prompted him in September 2002 to attend the first *Natoma Bay* reunion. At the reunion, he learned that Jack Larson was still alive, and that only one *Natoma* pilot had been killed in the Iwo Jima battle: James Huston. James Huston was from Pennsylvania and was twenty-one at the time. Tucker writes:

> The aircraft action report filed after the event notes the following: heavy antiaircraft fire put the planes under fire from both sides of the harbor. James Huston's plane was apparently hit by the fire as he approached the harbor entrance. None of the other pilots saw him hit, but his plane suddenly careened into a 45-degree glide and crashed in the water. It exploded and burned and by the time two of the other pilots could get to the area, no wreckage of the plane was still afloat. Only a greenish yellow spot on the water marked where the crash had occurred. This happened on March 3, 1945, four days before *Natoma Bay* completed its work in the Iwo Jima operation.[24]

One person who was not in attendance at the reunion was Jack Larson, so Bruce Leininger arranged to visit Larson at his home in Arkansas. Larson said that he remembered very well the day that James Huston was shot down, though he said he hadn't seen the moment when the plane was hit. He was, however, able to describe other events of that day in detail. One of the points Bruce had wanted to verify was James's repeated claim that his plane had been hit in its engine. Bruce found a website concerning the events at Chichi-jima, the actual spot where James Huston's plane had hit the water, and so he posted a question about the fatal plane crash. A few months later, a man from another ship, the USS *Sargent Bay*, called Bruce to say that he had seen Huston's plane get hit. Tucker writes:

> His plane had been hit that day, too, on its second run. On its first one, he had seen a fighter from *Natoma Bay* take "a direct hit on the nose," as he had written in an informal memoir.
>
> Bruce talked to three other men who had seen Huston's plane get hit, and they all told the same story. One of them said Huston's plane was very close to his, and he and Huston actually made eye contact just before Huston's plane was hit in the engine and quickly engulfed by flames.[25]

Each of these accounts verifying what young James had described had been documented in an interview before Bruce Leininger ever heard the name James Huston.

In summing up the evidence suggesting that young James Leininger held memories of events that happened in James Huston's life more than fifty years before, Tucker writes:

> In that interview, Bruce reported that when their James was two, he had nightmares about a plane crashing on fire and being unable to get out. Andrea said that one day, as James was playing in their sunroom, he told her, "Mama, before I was born, I was a pilot, and my airplane got shot in the engine and it crashed in the water, and that's how I died." Andrea also states on the segment that James had said his plane took off from a boat and that it was shot down by the Japanese. . . . James also said that Jack Larson was there when his plane crashed. The aircraft action report for the day Huston was shot down includes a drawing of the paths each pilot took; Larsen's plane is shown next to Huston's.[26]

As researchers customarily do in studies of cases suggestive of reincarnation, Tucker created a grid showing the statements and behaviors of

James Leininger as they compared to the details known about the life of James Huston (see table 9.1).[27]

One day Andrea Leininger asked her son if Little Man (his name for himself in his dreams) had sisters or brothers. He replied that he had one sister named Annie and another named Ruth. James said that Annie was four years older than he was, and Ruth was four years older than Annie. This all was true for James Huston's family. Annie was still alive, so Andrea contacted her. Annie sent two photos, with James Huston standing in front of a Corsair.

One evening a while later Andrea went into James's bedroom carrying a glass of wine.

> James looked at the glass and said his father had been an alcoholic. His father would get drunk on liquor and tear up the house. When he was thirteen, the family had to put his father in the hospital for six weeks. His mother had to work as a maid during that time, and Ruth, his older sister, was "mortified." When their father got out of the hospital, Anne moved away.[28]

Table 9.1.

James Leininger	James Huston
Signed drawings "James 3"	Was James Jr.
Flew off *Natoma*	Pilot on *Natoma Bay*
Flew a Corsair	Had flown a Corsair
Shot down by the Japanese	Shot down by the Japanese
Died at Iwo Jima	The one *Natoma Bay* pilot killed in the Iwo Jima operation
"My airplane got shot in the engine and it crashed in the water and that's how I died."	Eyewitnesses reported Huston's plane "hit head-on right on the middle of the engine."
Nightmares of plane crashing and sinking in the water	Plane crashed in the water and quickly sank
Jack Larson was there	Jack Larson was pilot of plane next to Huston's

Tucker notes that Andrea hadn't yet met James Huston's sister, though the two women had spoken on the telephone. There is no way James could have known these things about his previous family from any inter-action in his current family. Andrea called Annie to verify the boy's account, and Annie acknowledged that what he had said was true.

> Her father had indeed gone into rehab. Ruth, who was working as a society columnist for the local paper, was definitely mortified when their mother had to work as a maid in the home of a family Ruth had written about. Anne, uncomfortable with their father when he re-turned, moved to their grandparents' home for her last year of high school.[29]

As Tucker's study shows, some of the information James Leininger knew was obscure and technical. When he was about two, his mother bought him a toy plane and in showing it to him, told him there was a bomb underneath it. He told her that it was not a bomb, but a drop tank. She later learned that it was, in fact, a drop tank. When James was four and being filmed for an ABC show, he told the crew that Corsairs always got flat tires. The crew went to a historian and he confirmed that, because these planes hit the ground hard when they landed, Cor-sairs often got flat tires.

Tucker's study also shows James knowing information that was ob-scure and personal—for instance, this anecdote:

> When James was six and a half, he attended his first *Natoma Bay* reunion. . . . Andrea reports that she and James were stopped in the hotel hallway by Bob Greenwalt, a *Natoma Bay* veteran who had talked to Bruce on the phone but hadn't met any of the Leiningers. He asked James, "Do you know who I am?" James replied, "You're Bob Greenwalt." When Bruce asked him later how he knew that, James said he recognized Greenwalt's voice.[30]

Young James Leininger also had a number of behaviors that could be most easily explained in light of the experiences of James Huston who—and I'll mention this once again in order to underscore the point—had lived fifty years previously. For instance, Tucker writes about the year James Leininger was four:

He used an old car seat and pieces from various objects to create a play cockpit in the closet of Bruce's home office. Bruce would hear him pretending to be a pilot, and James would come tumbling out, pretending to parachute after his plane had been hit.

When James was four and a half he and his parents visited some of Andrea's family in Dallas. They went to a community pool, where James and his cousin began playacting. James pretended to shoot at airplanes and talked about shooting "the Japs." After a short time, Andrea called him over and told him he shouldn't say that. She said the war was over anyway and we beat the Japanese. James was momentarily stunned and then became ecstatic, jumping up and down and screaming in celebration. . . . It was embarrassing for the adults but funny, and it was another demonstration of the emotional connection that James, like the children in many of our cases, had to the events he appeared to remember from long before.[31]

The next case I examine is similar to a large number of cases suggestive of reincarnation in another way: the children who remember a previous life appear to have birthmarks related to the mode of death they experienced in that previous life. These malformations, such as skin anomalies, occur in about 35 percent of the subjects that have been studied. Stevenson notes that in cases of this type in which a deceased person has been identified whose life details clearly matched the child's statements, there is nearly always a very close correspondence between birthmarks on the child and wounds that correlate with the death of the person whom the child remembers.[32] This study also exemplifies the extreme care taken by investigators in determining the authenticity of each case.

Interestingly, this case is part of a study that Dr. Antonia Mills,[33] who is now at the University of Northern British Columbia, carried out as an independent investigator, in order to determine if, following Stevenson's research methods, she would reach conclusions similar to his regarding cases suggestive of reincarnation, a project that Stevenson himself initiated. The account below comes entirely from Mills's research.

IN NORTH INDIA: BIRTHMARKS RELATED TO MODE OF DEATH

The child in this case—Toran, nicknamed Titu—was the youngest child of Shanti Devi and Mahavir Singh of the village of Bad, which is near Agra in India. The family lived in a traditional single-story cement house. Titu's father and his family had agricultural land near Bad, which they farmed. Mahavir Singh also taught chemistry at a school in Agra. Mills, from an interview with Shanti Devi, writes:

> Titu began talking when he was a year and a half, earlier than the rest of her children. Shortly thereafter Titu told her, "Tell my grand-father to look after my children and my wife. I am having my meals here and I am worried about them." When his mother asked, "Who are you?" Titu said, "I am from Agra. I don't know how I came here."
>
> At an early age Titu also began saying, "Mummy, please don't go out in these clothes. I feel embarrassed by them. My wife had beauti-ful saris." Titu made a number of other complaints. He said, "Your house is dirty. I will not stay. My house is very big," and "My sisters-in-law are educated," and "My brothers had beautiful shirts which you have not seen." When he was expected to walk or go on a bus, Titu would say, "I used to go by car. I will not go on foot or in a bus."[34]

Mills writes that once when Titu was very young, his family took him to a wedding in Agra. Enroute, Titu announced, "I have a shop in Sadar Bazaar." His parents said they paid no attention to his comment at the time. Mills writes:

> As Titu grew older he would cry almost every day, wanting to "go home." He commonly referred, as he continues to do, to his parents as "Guloo's mother and father," rather than calling them his own. He frequently asked to go see "my brother Raja Babu and my sister Susheela," particularly when scolded. Titu complained to his father, "You go every day to Agra but you don't bring any news of my family."
>
> One day in April 1987, Titu was crying very bitterly as his father once again left for Agra without him. A friend of Titu's eldest brother took him on his lap, and Titu said, in his brother's hearing, "My father doesn't take me. Can you take me there? I have a shop of

transistor radios, and I was a big smuggler and *goonda* [someone who uses force to get his way]. I am the owner of Suresh Radio."

After this, Titu's eldest brother and his friend sought out the Suresh Radio shop, which turned out to be in Sadar Bazaar in Agra. They had never been to the shop before. They told Uma Verme, the widow of the owner, what Titu had been saying. They learned that Suresh Verme, the owner of Suresh Radio (and a noted smuggler on the black market) had been shot dead August 28, 1983, in his car. He was about 30 years old. [35]

Uma Verme told her late husband's family about this visit, and his parents and three of his brothers went to see Titu and his family in April 1987.

When Titu saw the party approach, he was very excited. He recognized Uma Verme, Suresh's father and mother, and two of the three brothers. He correctly described a trip he had taken to Dolpur with Uma and the children, whom he called by their nicknames, Mono and Tono, and the *chatt* and *kulji* they had eaten. Titu asked why his children had not been brought. When queried Titu correctly described how he [Suresh Verme] had been killed, saying, "While I was near my house, three people stopped me. One shot me and then they ran off. I did not see their faces." When asked where he was shot, Titu said, "They came from the left side and after shooting ran away." Titu described Suresh's home and some of its unique features, such as its shape, the placement of lamps, and a room "which remains locked."

Titu accompanied the Vermes as they went to the road and noted that they had not brought his car. "This is not my car. My car was white," he said. He played the tape deck in the car, although he had not previously seen one, and insisted on driving the car, which he did with Raja Babu's help, working the brake, gas and clutch pedals. When the party left, Titu wanted to go with them and threw his shoes at his mother Shanti Devi saying, "I am not yours. You are not my mother." [36]

One of Suresh's brothers returned later with his two sisters. When Titu saw Suresh's sister Susheela, he said, "Susheela Gigi" meaning "sister Susheela" and when asked which of them was his eldest sister, he said that neither was. This turned out to be correct, as Suresh had a third sister, who had not come, and she was the eldest. That afternoon he was taken to Suresh's radio shop. Mills relates the encounter:

> Titu said, "This is my shop." Inside Titu said, "This showcase was not here; who got it constructed?" Indeed the showcase he was indicating had been built and installed after the death of Suresh. Titu identified a large, garlanded photo of Suresh on the wall as himself. He also identified the cash drawer (which looks like any of a number of drawers behind the counter in the shop), and recognized the manager of the shop by name. Titu was then taken to the home of Chanda Babu Singh Bharity, Suresh's father. He said it was not his house [kothi]. This was interpreted by Mahesh to mean Titu did not recognize the house, while other members of Suresh's family interpreted this statement, I think correctly, to mean that it was not Suresh's home. Suresh Verme and Uma Verme had lived in their own modern house [kothi] which was the one Titu had described to Uma Verme earlier in the day and to which he apparently expected to be taken.
>
> At Chanda Singh Bharity's home, Titu told Suresh's mother, "I am just passing through with these people who do not have a T.V., a car, a video. I will run away to you." When Titu's father, Mahavir Singh, tried to take him home to Bad, Titu hugged Suresh's father, and fought Mahavir Singh and tore his shirt. Chanda Singh said, "Son, go. I will come see you."[37]

The day of this visit, Suresh's relatives became aware that Titu had a small round birthmark on his right temple that appeared to be similar to the wound where the bullet entered Suresh's head when he was killed (you can see a photo from Mills's research article in figure 9.1).

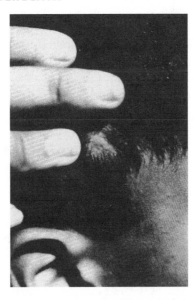

Figure 9.1.   Birthmark observed on the head of Titu, which corresponds to the site of the bullet entry in the postmortem report regarding Suresh Verne. Reprinted with permission from A. Mills, "A replication study: Three cases of children in Northern India who are said to remember a previous life," *Journal of Scientific Exploration* 989, 3:168.

Suresh's family also noticed a number of small birthmarks on the back of Titu's head and suggested that these could be the spots where the bullet left the head. Suresh's mother and wife also saw that Titu had an additional birthmark at the crown of his head that was like one Suresh had all of his life. Later, Mills visited the hospital where Suresh had been declared dead and looked at his postmortem report. The report said that the bullet had entered on his right temple—the very place where Titu had the circular birthmark. The report also said that the bullet left the skull at a point behind Suresh's right ear. Mills writes:

> After noting this, I returned to Titu and examined behind his right ear and found that Titu's skull is pushed out at the site indicated as the bullet exit site. Titu's parents had noted this deformity of the skull, but had not associated it with Suresh's death. Titu had not mentioned the mode of death of Suresh until asked by Rajvir Babu Verme at their first meeting. This is noteworthy, as 77% (p < .05) of the subjects in solved cases in India mention the previous personality's mode of death, and 98% (p < .05) when the mode of death was violent.[38]

Titu's parents were struck by similarities in the personalities of Titu and Suresh, both of whom were active, daring, fiery individuals. Mills noticed these very traits in Titu and reports that she saw him beat a boy with a sugarcane frond once when he became frustrated. She says that Suresh's father also told her that his son had not been afraid to fight. She writes:

> In 1975 eight *goonda* or "hit men" took Suresh and put him in their car. He kicked one and jumped through the window into the river, swam across and came out the other side, thus escaping. Within the year before his murder, Suresh went to recover two cars presumably stolen by the same man who had previously stolen his car (the man later accused of Suresh's murder). Suresh was fired upon but jumped from the car and caught one of the gunmen by the neck.[39]

After relating the details of Titu's case, Mills evaluates its strength as a case suggestive of reincarnation. She says that Titu had made fifteen statements or acts before meeting the people who were his alleged previous family that were later verified and thirty-one verified statements after meeting Suresh Verme's family. Mills notes that before the families met in April 1987, they didn't know each other. She also adds that though Titu's father didn't remember hearing of Suresh Verme's murder, she found that an account was published in one of the newspapers that he typically read. Thus, Mahavir Singh could have been subconsciously aware of the murder. She also notes that the correspondence of Titu's birthmarks to the entry and exit wounds of the bullets that killed Suresh is specific and direct and has no alternate explanation.

Mills goes on to address the question of the authenticity of this case and the others she had investigated:

> The question is whether the cases represent evidence that something paranormal is taking place or whether the cases are the result of conscious deceit (fraud), or unconscious self-deception and/or cultural construction. Infrequent cases of deception and self-deception have been reported by Stevenson, Pasricha and Samararatne (1988). . . . Before undertaking this investigation in India, I was prepared to find that some, perhaps all, of the cases I would investigate would be hoaxes perpetrated for any number of reasons by the participants, such as a desire of the child and/or its family to identify with a higher caste. This was my first experience in a caste society.

The investigations did not substantiate these suppositions. . . . In 3 of the 10 cases studied, the subject was born into humbler circumstances . . . or lower caste than the previous personality. Three of the cases showed no substantial caste or socioeconomic difference . . . , while in 4 of the cases the child was born in a higher caste than the previous personality.[40]

Mills writes that there are a number of reasons that this case might be discounted by people skeptical of the possibility of reincarnation. It could be hypothesized, for instance, that the child had multiple personality disorder (MPD). One proposed cause of MPD is a splitting of the child's personality as a result of the traumas of abuse. Neither Titu nor any of the other children Mills investigated appeared, however, to have characteristics of multiple personality disorder. There was no evidence of pathology either within the personalities of any of the children or their families. All the subjects appeared to be normal, other than that they had a conviction that they were, or had been, someone else. In other words, they did not appear to feel covertly or overtly rejected by their parents or to form a separate personality to deal with the disturbing events of abuse. In fact, Mills notes, the most characteristic aspect of these children's personalities was the consistency between the personalities of the past and present life.

A second alternative explanation to reincarnation for the child's showing past-life memories, Mills writes, is that this behavior could possibly help the child gain extra attention from parents.

> The hypothesis that children unconsciously develop what are interpreted as past-life memories seems to me to be counter-indicated by four factors: (1) it presumes that a very young child is aware that indicating a past-life identity would give it positive attention; (2) it presumes that a child gets only positive reinforcement for claiming to remember previous lives; (3) it presumes that the distress the child feels at separation from the apparent past-life family is feigned; and (4) it does not account for the child's apparently accurate knowledge of people and places about which the child has no normal means of knowing. It again presumes that the child is not getting adequate attention. I found no indication that the children were motivated by a need for compensatory attention.[41]

A third alternative explanation to reincarnation, Mills notes, is that possibly the children's remembering previous lives could be an artifact of a culture in which the parents interpret their children's fantasies as past-life memories. She says there was certainly some cultural interpretation happening in the cases she studied. Mills adds, however, that the best evidence for a paranormal process is in those circumstances when the child and the child's parents do not know anything about the previous personality before they met. She said that half the cases she studied fell within this category.

> On a continuum from most to least contact, Titu's case falls towards the end of no contact. The two families did not know of each other, although Titu's father may have read of the murder or heard about it from an acquaintance of Suresh's who lives in Titu's village and forgotten it. Nonetheless it is difficult to explain why Titu would identify as the owner of Suresh Radio on the basis of these possible sources of communication. If a motive could be found, it would not explain the correspondence of Titu's birthmarks to bullet entry and exit sites on the body of Suresh. [42]

Fourthly and finally, these cases suggestive of reincarnation have been criticized by some skeptics who say that it is only coincidence that a person who corresponds to the child's description exists. Mills notes that it "exceeds the bounds of credibility to imagine that it is mere coincidence" since there is direct verification that the specific facts noted in the cases in her article occurred. Mills concludes:

> I found no evidence that the cases I studied are the result of fraud or fantasy or could be explained on the basis of projection or assumption of an alternate identity in response to complex family dynamics. While the cultural acceptance of the concept of reincarnation and the category of children remembering a past life influenced the parents' interpretation of the child's behavior, it cannot be credited with causing all aspects of its occurrence, such as the high degree of accuracy of the statements these children make about an actual deceased person when that person is unknown to them and their relatives. The alternate normal explanations rest on the presumption that the existence of a previous personality fitting the child's description is a product of coincidence. The consistency and similarity of the child's personality with the personality reported for the previous per-

sonality is also significant. In the cases where there are striking birth-marks on the subject which relate to wounds on the previous person-ality or phobias related to the mode of death, the possibility of coinci-dence diminishes even further.

Like Stevenson I conclude that while none of the cases I studied (or the 3 cases cited) offer incontrovertible proof of reincarnation or some related paranormal process, they are part of the growing body of cases for which normal explanations do not seem to do justice to the data.[43]

CONCLUSIONS

When I first began reading about cases of reincarnation, like Mills, I was somewhat skeptical that I would find strong evidence for a person's consciousness and his or her mind's characteristics or personality sur-viving death of the body. And like Stevenson, early in his career, I thought it unlikely that one could accumulate evidence that might be suggestive of reincarnation in certain individuals. However, after read-ing the researchers' careful summaries of these cases, and many others, I am surprised to find myself quite convinced by the data they present.

In my opinion, researchers studying cases of the reincarnation type raise significant questions regarding the origin and nature of consciousness. As Stevenson notes, each of these cases may have a few flaws. Perhaps a child mispronounces a word. Perhaps he does not recall all of the names of his previous relatives. Perhaps he makes some error of memory. In the vast majority of cases, however, the high number of correct statements is re-markable and unlikely to be the creation of human imagination or chance occurrence. There may, indeed, be instances of fraud, but in most of these cases, there is nothing for an individual to gain from making such a claim.

I will echo a point that Stevenson and others have made repeatedly: whether the survival of some part of an individual after death is possible needs to be examined, not in a piecemeal way, investigating one case at a time, but as a whole. The strength of the evidence exists in the conver-gence of data from many cases, and many different types of cases, and cases from many cultures all leading to similar conclusions. Any single case might be considered weak if the reader questions whether an ob-servation may have been mistaken or an event may have occurred by chance, but when a reasonable investigator looks at thousands of such cases showing similar results, a more compelling explanation is required. In a book describing Stevenson's work, Dr. Emily Kelly, a colleague of Stevenson's at UVA, makes a significant point regarding the Western perspective on reincarnation:

> Modern society is deeply divided over the question of survival after death. Many people, on the basis of religious faith or personal experience or both, believe in survival or at least take the idea seriously. Many others, on the basis of what current scientific orthodoxy tells us, dismiss the idea outright or at least consider it highly unlikely. Perhaps the most important lesson to be taken away . . . is that there is a larger body of empirical observations relevant to the question of survival, and that no one should come down firmly on either side of the issue without considering that evidence seriously. As Ian himself put it, "The only improper stances are denial that there is any evidence worth looking at or assertion that what we have will suffice."[44]

As a scientist, I agree with this statement and feel it gives both a reason to work with the data and an approach for doing so in an unbiased way. As a meditator, I feel such attention is long overdue.

10

AWARENESS AND HEALING

In 2006, after meditating for more than three decades and performing studies on the physiological effects of both sitting meditation and tai chi, a form of moving meditation, I decided it was time to share what I was learning with science students. I wanted to expand my neuroscience teaching at the University of Oregon to include a class on complementary and alternative medicine as part of the science curriculum. Besides meditation, the class would explore such traditional forms of healing and relaxation as acupuncture, homeopathy, hypnotism, and therapeutic touch. I found it compelling that these forms of healing have been used in many cultures for thousands of years—and continue to be used in those cultures today. I was also intrigued by research Western scientists had done on these modalities. One study suggests that in recent years Americans have made more visits to providers of alternative and complementary therapies than they have to primary care physicians and nurses.[1] And there have been many studies done on the efficacy of these alternative therapies. It seemed to me that an introduction to such research would be excellent training for the pre-med students who are many of the UO undergraduate science majors.

Predictably, when I proposed this class to my department chairman, he was unmoved by my enthusiasm. "A class of this sort will have very low enrollment," he told me. "If you're determined to teach it, you should offer it to freshmen from all majors." The implication was that no serious science student would be interested in this sort of frivolous subject matter.

I talked him into an experiment: I would teach one term of complementary and alternative medicine to UO's human physiology students—the science students most directly concerned with healing modalities. I was elated when, within the first few days of registration, the course was already full and had a respectable waiting list. Teaching the class was, however, another matter entirely.

Once I began presenting material on complementary and alternative medicine, I found that young science students were, if anything, more conservative than my colleagues. We were discussing such modalities as acupuncture (where a practitioner places needles into strategic points in the patient's body to realign and activate energy along certain meridians), hypnosis (where the practitioner puts the patient into a mental state in which he will be receptive to suggestion), and homeopathy (where a medicine has been distilled and diluted to the point that the original substance—the presumed healing agent—is no longer present in the solution).

When put like that, it all sounds flakey. There is, however, evidence to support these modalities, and I was presenting that evidence in the class—double-blinded, placebo-controlled, randomized trials showing clinical proof that such treatments do cure illness.

A number of students were interested, but many remained skeptical, and a few were clearly unsettled or even infuriated by what was, for them, a challenge to scientific truths. I remember one solidly built young man with a round, serious face, who glared at me as he threw down his verbal gauntlet in response to the homeopathy results: "This. Is. Not. Science."

"My father is a biochemist," he added. "Science is my family tradition. We give people medication when we know the mechanism by which that medication works. If there is no mechanism, there is no science." It was as if I were attacking the very foundation of his world.

Homeopathy is always particularly difficult for the students. I invited practitioners from these modalities to share the benefit of their experience with students, and in a later class a homeopathic doctor was verbally accosted by a young woman, who was practically sputtering with fury as she said, "How could you possibly say that this thing could work when there is not one molecule left of the actual substance!"

The doctor was unfazed. "Western medicine doesn't yet have a mechanism to explain this," he told the girl. "Is that a reason not to use it?"

I've taught this class seven times, and now I know to begin the first session by asking for a show of hands: "How many of you consider yourselves skeptics in relation to complementary and alternative medicine?" Two-thirds of the students typically raise their hands. I tell them, "My goal in this class is that by the end of the term you will be open to more than just cutting, bandaging, bone-setting, and pharmaceuticals as means of curing disease."

And then I set about doing just that, presenting the results of studies at least some of which I will cite in this chapter and the next. The class is always a rich and rewarding experience. These students may be skeptics, but at least they're open to taking the class. With them, I have a chance. They might have a traditional view of medicine, but they are willing at least to take in another perspective. And for some, the class opens a door to new possibilities.

At the end of the term, the young woman who was so upset by homeopathy stopped me one day at a coffee shop to give me a hug and say, "It was my favorite class." I didn't ask her why, but I think it's because she was challenged by it on all levels.

Before going into our discussion of these complementary and alternative methods, I want to acknowledge that there is one criticism traditional science uses to dismiss the validity of the research that shows them to be effective: It's just the placebo effect.

Briefly stated, the "placebo effect" is the positive response patients have to a neutral element they have been told has healing power. That's where we will start this discussion, because not only does the placebo effect *not* invalidate the success of complementary and alternative modalities; the placebo effect itself is a clear demonstration of the power of consciousness to heal.

PLACEBOS

The concept of "placebo" goes back to the thirteenth century or earlier, a time when mourners would be hired for funeral processions; these professional mourners were called placebos ("to please") to describe their inauthentic grief. The term began to be used medically in the eighteenth century to describe treatments with no curative properties that were designed to make a patient comfortable. These early negative connotations no doubt came forward to current times in the stigmatized notion of the placebo effect.[2]

So what *is* a placebo effect? A "placebo" (or its opposite, a "nocebo") is "an intervention that has no direct physiological consequences but nevertheless improves (or worsens) a person's health."[3] This is the most prominent paradox of Western medicine: the effect of the placebo is acknowledged even though, within the framework of materialistic science, it cannot be explained. The placebo effect demonstrates that simply believing (a mental condition) that a medication will improve your health is enough to bring that about (a physical condition). The nocebo is where you think your health will be compromised by something inert, and it is.

Here we return to the premise of Roger Sperry, who hypothesized that our thoughts, rather than simply arising from the physical mechanism of the brain, can actually change the form of the brain. In terms of operations of consciousness, this is what would appear to be happening when a thought—*this will heal me*—enters one's mind and brings about a physical healing that is unconnected with the properties of the substance thought to be a healing agent. In other words, this is consciousness operating top-down (the thoughts affecting the body) rather than bottom-up (the body giving rise to the thoughts).

The existence of such a phenomenon "poses a serious challenge to much of the ideology of biomedicine . . . [that] disease is a mechanical phenomenon."[4]

A classic case study of the placebo/nocebo effect took place in the 1950s with a Mr. Wright, who had lymphatic cancer. According to his physician,

> Huge tumor masses, the size of oranges, were in the neck, axillas, groins, chest and abdomen. The spleen and liver were enormous. The thoracic duct was obstructed, and between 1 and 2 liters of milky fluid had to be drawn from his chest every other day. He was taking oxygen by mask frequently, and our impression was that he was in a terminal state, untreatable, other than to give sedatives to ease him on his way.[5]

Wright asked his doctor to put him on a new drug, Krebiozen, which he'd heard was effective against precisely the kind of tumors he had. Though Wright wasn't eligible to be part of the study evaluating the drug—he had a life expectancy of possibly two weeks rather than the three to six months required—he begged the doctor to be part of the study, and the doctor finally agreed. Klopfer says:

> Injections were to be given three times weekly, and I remember he received his first one on a Friday. I didn't see him again until Monday and thought as I came to the hospital he might be moribund or dead by that time, and his supply of the drug could then be transferred to another case. What a surprise was in store for me! I had left him febrile, gasping for air, completely bedridden. Now, here he was, walking around the ward, chatting happily with the nurses, and spreading his message of good cheer to any who would listen.
>
> Within 10 days he was able to be discharged from his "death-bed," practically all signs of his disease having vanished in this short time. [6]

Apparently Krebiozen was a miracle drug! Unfortunately, that was not the case, and a few months later, Wright happened to read an article detailing the negative results in a medical study of Krebiozen: it had failed to cure cancer in all the testing clinics. Shortly thereafter, Wright's tumors returned. The doctor, who noted the placebo effect that seemed to be at work, gave his patient what he called "a new super-refined double strength product." In fact, the doctor was injecting Wright with water. Once again, Wright's tumors disappeared and he was symptom free for two months.

And once again, Mr. Wright encountered negative press on Krebiozen. Two months after his second injection, he read a study by the American Medical Association—the definitive and final statement on the drug—in which the AMA declared Krebiozen to be worthless as a medication to fight cancerous tumors.

> Within a few days of reading the report, Mr. Wright was re-admitted to the hospital. His faith was now gone and his last hope vanished, and he succumbed in less than two days. [7]

It was at some point after this, in the 1970s, that the issue of placebos began to be discussed extensively in medical circles. The topic came up because evidence-based practice became the driving force for health care, and the medical community faced the need to prove that the efficacy of a medication—any medication—was greater than the placebo effect. Thus, the double-blind, randomized, controlled, clinical trial was introduced: both the medication in question and a placebo were tested, and neither the doctor nor the patient knew which was being administered at any given time. The inert placebo was the control condition against which every medication had to be tested.

Discussing the use of placebos in modern medicine, Emily Kelly, a psychologist at the University of Virginia and coauthor of the book *Irreducible Mind*, writes:

> Placebo's "odd" place, therefore is that, on the one hand, it has been so thoroughly accepted by the medical community that it is now an obligatory factor in the experimental design of studies of the efficacy of medical treatments; and yet on the other hand, there has been virtually no effort until recently to understand the "enigma" of the placebo itself and its apparent conflict with the biomedical model.[8]

Kelly notes that an experiment in 1978 began to change the view of some scientists regarding the nature of the placebo effect.

Jon D. Levine, Newton C. Gordon, and Howard L. Fields reported a double-blind study in which forty post-dental-surgery patients were given a placebo as a painkiller. An hour later, seventeen were randomly chosen to receive another placebo, and the remaining twenty-three were given naloxone, a substance that blocks the analgesic effect of endogenous opiate-like substances such as endorphins. Those given the naloxone reported significantly more pain than those given a second placebo, leading the authors to hypothesize that because naloxone undid the analgesic effects of the placebo, the original placebo effect had been the result of a natural opiate release.[9]

This suggests that believing you are receiving pain medication activates pathways that block pain and releases natural pain-relieving opiates within your body. Thus the belief you are taking the medication can have a similar effect to taking the medication itself. Let me repeat this: The belief you are taking the medication can have a similar effect to taking the medication itself. Again, the implication is that our thoughts can create our reality—top-down.

Later studies have added to the evidence that placebos can produce highly specific and objectively measureable physiological changes. One experiment shows that subjects, given a placebo they believed to be a pain reliever, changed activity within specific pain pathways—reducing activation of a number of the brain areas (the thalamus, insula, and the anterior cingulate cortex) associated with the feeling of pain.[10] A second placebo/painkiller study shows that, with the placebo, there is less activity in the brain's opioid (pain control) system.[11]

Another excellent area for assessing the power of placebos is antidepressants, which have been prescribed by the medical community in increasing quantities in recent years. In the United States, antidepressants were the third most commonly prescribed drug from 2005 to 2008 and the most frequently prescribed drug for people between the ages of eighteen and forty-four. Almost one out of every four American women in their forties and fifties takes antidepressant drugs.[12] Yet how do these drugs compare to placebos in improving mental states? A review of many randomized controlled trials in which patients were given either an antidepressant or a placebo showed that much of an antidepressant's power is due to the placebo effect. This means that the patients receiving an antidepressant experienced only a little more relief than the patients on the placebo. The authors concluded from their review of nineteen studies, comparing effectiveness of antidepressants and placebos in controlled clinical trials, that approximately 75 percent of the effectiveness of the antidepressants is due to a placebo effect.[13] The study's author, Irving Kirsch, a psychology professor at Hull University in the United Kingdom, writes,

> Most meta-analyses suffer from publication bias, which can happen when pharmaceutical companies withhold unsuccessful trials from publication. To circumvent this, we used the Freedom of Information Act in the U.S. to obtain the data on all clinical trials submitted to the Food and Drug Administration (FDA) for the licensing of the four new generation antidepressants. The results of our meta-analysis showed that people got better on medication, but they also got better on placebo, and the difference between the two was small. In fact, it was below the criterion for clinical significance established by the National Institute for Health and Clinical Excellence (NICE), which sets treatment guidelines for the National Health Service in the UK. Clinical significance was found only in a few relatively small

studies conducted on patients with extremely severe levels of depression.[14]

Even patients with serious movement disorders like Parkinson's disease
have responded to placebos, not only improving significantly their motor function but also experiencing certain side effects, such as nausea,
associated with the drug the placebo replaced. In one study on Parkinson's patients, the authors found that a placebo injection resulted in an
increase in the release of endogenous dopamine that was comparable to
the effect of L-Dopa, the drug most often prescribed for Parkinson's.[15]

As a motor-control neuroscientist, I have done quite a bit of research
on Parkinson's and motor control and was amazed to find that, even
here, the placebo effect is in place. Not only did these Parkinson's
patients' mind/belief system increase the release of dopamine, the
neurotransmitter whose function is drastically reduced by Parkinson's;
not only did they improve their motor skills; but they also experienced
unrelated side effects. This is a powerful and specific effect of the mind
on the body.

So, we have looked at the power of the patient's belief in a placebo.
There are many other factors that can be extrapolated and measured:
the power of the doctor's warmth and support,[16] the power of a patient's belief that they are being given pain medication,[17] and the power
of the doctor's belief in the procedure,[18] to name just a few.

I am especially interested in the power of the doctor's expectations
to influence the outcome of experiments related to placebos and pain
medication. This becomes apparent in a double-blind experiment,
when neither physician nor patient knows which therapy is being administered. In one double-blind study of postoperative dental pain, patients in each of two groups were told they would be given a drug that
would increase their pain, decrease their pain, or have no effect. In
each of these groups, a number of doctors were told that there was no
chance they were giving their patients an active pain medication. So,
these doctors were manipulated as well. The researchers found that the
placebo effect was significantly reduced in the group in which the doctors thought that no pain therapy was being given. Since the patients
weren't aware of the information that had been given to the doctors,
this suggests that the placebo effect also works through the physician.

In other words, altering the doctor's beliefs can change the outcome of the patient's well-being, which in this case was measurable by pain relief.[19] This is actually a significant point since it suggests that the power of the caregiver's belief can influence the patient's health without the patient even knowing what the caregiver's belief is!

Taking this point one step further, if the attitude of physicians interacting with patients can affect the outcome of a therapy, doesn't it follow that the attitude of researchers conducting studies can have an effect on their data? The researchers also bring the full weight of their ideas about a study—whether conscious or subconscious—into their interactions with patients. This factor alone may account for some of the differences in the findings from studies conducted by different researchers, some believing the method under consideration to be effective and others not.

Prescribing physicians may participate in the placebo effect by the way they administer medications, but they themselves often discount the significance of placebo research. As Kirsch observes, doctors are most likely to notice that the medications they prescribe work—and so they tend not to ask further questions. Kirsch writes:

> Clinical experience shows that antidepressant drugs work, in the sense that patients get better when given medication. So do our meta-analyses. Patients given antidepressants in the clinical trials showed substantial and clinically significant improvement, as did those given placebo. Physicians do not generally prescribe placebos to their patients. Hence they have no way of comparing the effects of the drugs they prescribe to placebos. When they prescribe a treatment and it works, quite naturally they ascribe the cure to the treatment. But the history of medicine is replete with cures that were "known" to work by doctors and their patients. These apparently effective treatments, that we now consider to have been placebos, include dolphin's [sic] genitalia, lizard's [sic] blood, crocodile dung, pig's [sic] teeth, putrid meat, frog's [sic] sperm, powdered stone, human sweat, worms, and spiders. That is why placebo-controlled trials are required in order to demonstrate drug efficacy. When the administration of a drug is followed by improvement, the improvement might not be due to the drug's chemical composition. Placebo controlled trials are used to separate the drug effect from such factors as the placebo effect, spontaneous remission, and regression towards the mean.[20]

Kelly points out that we have no idea how expectations in the patient's or doctor's mind can possibly affect a patient's physiological well-being:

> Even if we assume that expectation is the fundamental factor [in the placebo effect], a remaining question is how these expectancies then generate the corresponding responses. . . . Most scientists today take a "neuralist" [mechanistic neurophysiological] view that ". . . treats subjective phenomena (the conscious mind) as products of nervous system activity. . . . This approach avoids the problem of how subjective 'mind' could act on the objective and physical body."[21]

The correlation between subjective awareness and physical healing is evident, yet traditional scientists do not even attempt to track the connection. Kelly says,

> We observe that there are mental events and physical events, and few would argue that they are not somehow related. No one, however, can say how. How, for example, does "a person's belief in a sham treatment . . . send a message to his or her pituitary gland to release its own endogenous pharmaceuticals?"[22]

This is a question that medical science cannot answer within the materialist framework.

It is my perspective that this research on the placebo effect adds to the evidence included in the previous chapters on top-down influences, showing the clear and reproducible effects of higher levels of consciousness (in this case, the mind) on the nervous system and other systems in the physical body. I explore a variety of hypotheses about how this might occur in chapter 12.

Now we look at a few of the modalities I present in the class Complementary and Alternative Medicine. We won't be exploring meditation, hatha yoga, tai chi, and qi gong here—though these are the areas with which students have the greatest ease; unlike their grandparents, they're quite accustomed to thinking of exercise as a part of medicine. I feel that healing and hypnosis are most pertinent for us here, for in these modalities the patient is directly affected by the intention of the healer. From my perspective, this is conscious awareness in action. We'll look first at hypnosis and then, in chapter 11, at long-distance healing.

THE EFFICACY OF HYPNOSIS

So I could have firsthand experience of the subject matter in my alter-native medicine class, I made appointments with practitioners of most of the modalities discussed in the textbook I'd chosen. One of the most intriguing was hypnosis, which seems to produce miraculous results. "Miraculous," of course, is as far as you can get from traditional sci-ence—and yet because in a number of studies the inexplicable has irrefutably taken place through hypnosis, scientists have to accept that this method has at least some efficacy.

Hypnosis still carries connotations of mesmerism and mental telepa-thy from its rather murky beginnings in the late 1700s, when the Ger-man physician Franz Antoine Mesmer was putting suggestible subjects into trance and curing them (by telling them they were cured) of such ailments as psychosomatic blindness, paralysis, convulsions, and "other hysterical conditions." Mesmer's theatrical manner probably did much to undermine acceptance by the medical community of his startling results. The medical community did, however, seize upon the modal-ity's pain-relieving capacities, and one surgeon renamed it neuro-hyp-nosis, by which he meant "sleep of the nerves."[23]

By this time it was the early 1800s, still before the development of chemical drugs for anesthesia. In those days, physicians who wanted to counteract the severe pain of surgery had nothing more than a couple of shots of strong alcohol. The patient having a surgical procedure under those circumstances had an equal chance of dying or surviving, the main cause of death being neurogenic shock. So, at the time 50 percent of surgery patients died from extreme pain.

After reading accounts of Mesmer's technique, the Scottish surgeon James Esdaile used his own style of hypnosis in more than three thou-sand surgeries in Bengal, India, between 1845 and 1851, with no re-ported patient pain. Esdaile was able to reduce the death rate to about 5 percent. Hypnosis did more than eliminate the perception of pain; the doctor noted that his patients also showed no physiological signs of the experience of pain—no changes, for instance, in their pulse rates.

Once chemical anesthesia was introduced in the mid-1800s, hypno-sis was abandoned by most doctors in favor of the more conventional, more easily explained, and more easily administered anesthetics. It's possible that one reason hypnosis didn't take hold as a standard medical procedure was the lengths to which Esdaile had to go in order to put his patients under.

The patient would sit in a darkened room, wearing only a loincloth, and Esdaile would slowly pass his hands over the patient's body, holding them about an inch above the body. The doctor went from the back of the head to the pit of the stomach, breathing gently on the patient's head and eyes all the while. Sometimes it was necessary to perform this process repeatedly for hours each day, and for ten or twelve days at a stretch, before the patient was sufficiently hypnotized for surgery. Ultimately, Esdaile had to delegate the hypnosis to assistants so he could save his energy for surgery.[24]

Esdaile's thoroughness is probably what allowed him to hypnotize all of his patients, while current methods of hypnosis work exceptionally well for only one out of ten in the population, moderately well for eight out of ten, and not at all for another one in ten.[25] Still, hypnosis is studied currently for pain relief, and a 2014 meta-analysis that reviewed twelve clinical studies, including six randomized controlled trials, showed that hypnosis has a significant and reliable effect on reducing pain.[26]

Researchers are also attempting to determine just how hypnosis reduces pain. To test whether hypnosis acts by increasing the release of internal opioids (pain suppressants), in two studies subjects were given naloxone (an opioid antagonist). The drug had no effect; hypnosis reduced pain in both groups: those who were given naloxone and those who were not.[27] Another study showed that the physiological mechanism by which pain is reduced seems to vary, depending on the subject. For some subjects the physiological changes occurred in the anterior cingulate cortex (the brain's decision-making center) and for others it was in the somatosensory cortex (where we perceive touch).[28]

So, the same technique (hypnosis) brought about the same result (pain reduction) but by using different neural pathways in different subjects. It seems that with hypnosis, the subject's own mind has the ability to choose where in that subject's physiology the experience of pain will be blocked—either the emotional center (the anterior cingulate cortex) or a sensory center (the somatosensory cortex).

It is these physiological effects of hypnosis that I find most compelling, and none more so than the power hypnosis has demonstrated as a cure for skin conditions. The experience of pain is a subjective phenomenon, and changes in neural activity in a particular part of the brain are fairly subtle effects. The skin, however, is both the largest and the most visible of the body's organs; any disease or cure involving the skin is observable and measurable.

The first cases I'll mention involve a condition so common and menial that it might at first seem amusing: the removal of warts. These usually small, viral growths have been a human concern since ancient Greece, but not until the 1800s were they known to be contagious and not until 1949 were they shown to be caused by a virus. Over the years, folklore remedies for warts were such diverse techniques as bathing the wart under the moonlight, rubbing the wart with a cut potato, and using the warty limb to kick the father of an illegitimate child.[29] The modern medical approach to wart removal usually involves plastering with salicylic acid, freezing with liquid nitrogen, or burning with cantharidin.

Hypnosis, however, is even more effective. Typical of the studies I found is one that compared hypnosis to other modalities for treating warts, including a standard medical treatment, a placebo treatment, and a no-treatment group. The hypnosis group showed the best cure rates of all.[30] The authors conclude:

> These results replicate and extend those of earlier controlled experiments, and support the hypothesis that psychological factors can substantially influence the course of at least some virally produced disorders.[31]

So, as a cure, hypnotic suggestion turned out to be stronger than psychological suggestion (the placebo) and, even more significantly, stronger than chemistry.

Because warts can undergo spontaneous remission, an earlier study was designed to test whether or not this was inflating the success rate being attributed to hypnosis. In three studies patients who had warts in several places on their bodies were given the hypnotic suggestion that only certain of the warts be removed. That is exactly what happened.[32] In discussing one of these experiments, Kelly notes:

> In Dreaper's case, when treatment was begun the intention was to remove all warts, which were on both sides of both hands. When they began to shrink, however, he suggested to the patient that she allow one wart to remain, as a control; and "after ten months' treat-

ment the only wart remaining was the suggested one" (p. 308). Attention was then directed to the remaining wart, and it too disappeared after two months.[33]

As a neuroscientist, I find this selective cure to be extraordinary. When
I think about how most mind–body modalities work, I picture the entire
nervous system relaxing and, then, the entire physical system being
brought into a healthy balance. This is something entirely different.
This case demonstrates that with hypnosis the mind can direct the
immune system to combat a viral invasion specifically, operating in
particular areas of the body and not in others.

And that's just with warts. In regard to skin health, hypnosis has
taken on much bigger challenges than this.

Ichthyosis, also called fish skin or fish scale disease, is a genetic
condition that creates a black, horny layer of skin, often over much of
the body. The affected skin is hard and tends to crack and bleed. The
disease, which is present from birth or early childhood, is quite painful,
both physically and also emotionally. Ichthyosis is on the skin, for all to
see, and because it isn't at all attractive, the people who suffer from this
condition experience social ostracism and a sense of shame. At this
point, it has no medical cure. In a few cases, patients with ichthyosis
have responded to hypnosis. One of the first ichthyosis cases to be
improved by hypnosis is described by Mason:

> The patient was a boy aged 16 who suffered from congenital ichthyo-
> sis. The lesion consisted of a black horny layer covering his entire
> body except his chest, neck and face. . . . To the touch the skin felt as
> hard as a normal fingernail and was so inelastic that any attempt at
> bending resulted in a crack in the surface, which would then ooze
> blood-stained serum. . . . The condition was worst on the hands, feet,
> thighs and calves. . . . The hands were thickly covered with a rigid
> horny casing which cracked, fissured, and became chronically in-
> fected. This not only rendered them useless for work, but caused
> him great discomfort.[34]

This patient had been to several hospitals, but no treatment had helped
him. He was referred to a plastic surgeon who, two separate times,
removed the affected skin from the boy's hands and grafted skin from
his apparently normal chest onto his hands—to no avail. Within a

month of each of these surgeries, the grafted skin had returned to its tough, rigid state. The surgeon recommended not trying again. After this, the boy was treated by a hypnotherapist.

> The patient was hypnotized and, under hypnosis, suggestion was made that the left arm would clear. (The suggestion was limited to the left arm so as to exclude the possibility of spontaneous resolution.) About five days later the horny layer softened, became friable, and fell off. . . . From a black and armour-like casing, the skin became pink and soft within a few days. . . . At the end of 10 days the arm was completely clear from shoulder to wrist.[35]

Later the boy's right arm was treated and then both of his legs, in exactly the same way and with the same results. Figure 10.1 shows a photo of the right arm both before and eight days after the hypnosis. Drawing from a table that charts his observations of the boy's improvement from hypnosis, Mason indicates that before the treatment, the arms were only 20 percent clear of the disease; and the hands, thighs, legs, and feet were either completely or heavily covered. After treatment, the arms were 95 percent cleared, the palms completely cleared, the thighs 70 percent cleared, and the legs and feet 50 percent cleared. There was no relapse over a period of four years, during which the boy was observed by the doctor, and in fact his condition continued to improve.[36] Kelly writes:

> Mason's first case report prompted numerous letters to the editor of the *British Medical Journal*, many of them skeptical and dismissive. One of the correspondents, however, who had himself actually seen Mason's patient, had this to say, "It is surprising that it [congenital ichthyosis] should respond to any kind of treatment; that it should respond to hypnotic suggestion demands a revision of current concepts of the relation between mind and body."[37]

Other physicians have also treated patients with ichthyosis in this way and have found varying degrees of improvement, from 90–100 percent remission to more modest amounts and also, in many patients, no effect.[38] It is possible that the differences in remission reflect the degree to which the patients were hypnotizable. For example, in a pair of patients, a father and his son of four years, the father was 90 percent

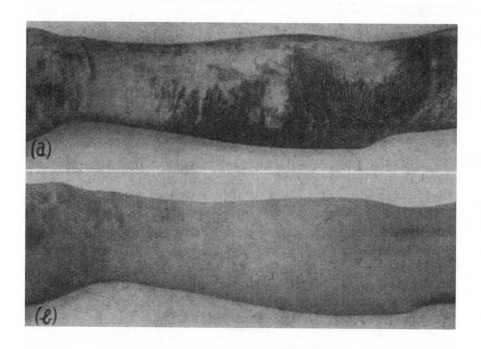

Figure 10.1.   A photo of the right arm of a boy with ichthyosis both before (a) and eight days after (b) hypnosis treatment was begun. Before the treatment, the boy's arms were only 20 percent clear of the disease. After treatment, the arms were 95 percent cleared and the palms completely cleared. Reproduced from A. A. Mason, "A case of congenital ichthyosiform erythroderma of Brocq treated by hypnosis," *British Medical Journal* 2 (1952): 423, with permission from British Medical Journal Publishing Group Ltd.

cured, while his son, who was inattentive and distractible, was only improved by 30 percent.[39]

A more recent set of studies looking at the effect of hypnosis on skin conditions involves allergic reactions, which are hypersensitivity of the immune system. Many randomized controlled clinical trials have shown hypnosis to have significant effects compared to controls.[40] Earlier research related to allergic reactions tracks the specificity of responses that hypnotic suggestion can create.[41] In this study, two Japanese physicians used hypnosis to affect the allergic skin reactions of thirteen Japanese boys to lacquer and wax trees. Five were given the suggestion, described below, when hypnotized, and eight were given it in the waking state. They were each touched on both arms: on the first arm they were touched with the lacquer or wax tree leaf (to which they were allergic) but told it was a chestnut tree leaf (to which they were not allergic); on the second arm they were touched with the chestnut tree leaf, being told it was a lacquer or wax tree leaf. Here is what was reported:

> Four of the five hypnotized subjects and seven of the eight non-hypnotized subjects developed dermatitis in response to the inert substance that they thought was the allergic agent, and conversely showed no reaction to the real allergic agent that they thought was inert. The other two subjects showed an allergic response to both substances, including the inert one.[42]

These results indicate, the physicians note, that allergic reactions have a psychological component, since one can both suppress and induce a reaction with suggestion. Kelly, in reviewing the article asks, "But what known mechanism can selectively turn on the allergic response in one arm while simultaneously turning it off in the other?"[43] The question underscores one of the most important aspects of this study. We could imagine that reducing the stress in a person's life might improve their mental and physiological function by improving, for example, the immune system in general. But for a skin condition to occur in response to an inert substance and not to an allergic agent defies our normal scientific understanding of effects of the mind on the body.

The conventional scientific community discounts the sorts of studies we have been looking at in this chapter by a trick of wording. Kelly notes that most scientists argue that

> understanding the "how" of psychophysiological interactions presents no problem because the "psychological" parts of these interactions are themselves ultimately biological, involving nothing more than patterns of electrochemical activity in the central nervous system. "Thoughts" and "emotions" simply represent certain aspects of this biologically unitary mind-brain system, while "warts and allergic responses" represent others, and there is thus no particular problem in understanding, at least in principle, how the former might produce or influence the latter. Indeed, to suggest anything different is automatically viewed with horror as threatening a return to outmoded forms of dualistic thinking.[44]

My interpretation of this passage is that science calls the "hypnotic suggestion" simply a neural input. There is a certain amount of handwaving in this label and no explanation of how a mental image or idea can remove a viral wart or congenital skin scales, or can create a blister on otherwise healthy skin. This is the real question: how is a mental image translated into a physiological reaction that can be physically transforming? The scientific community has not yet come up with an adequate answer.

I have been more than willing to experience such modalities myself. After reading the studies recounted above, I was especially interested in trying hypnosis. I found a local hypnotherapist online and decided to ask her to help me with weight control. I'm not overweight per se, but throughout my adult life, I've struggled with what I consider to be ten extra pounds. I used to laugh with a colleague of mine about how each of our grant proposals or articles would bring on an additional five pounds—weight we had to work to lose once the grant or paper was accepted.

The hypnotherapist operated out of a clinical building, and her office looked to me like any other clinical office. She had me sit up in a recliner for the forty-five minutes we spent discussing my therapeutic goals; she put the recliner down and gave me some headphones when we started the hypnosis. I was supremely comfortable in the chair, and as I listened to the therapist speak, I could hear flute music interspersed with birdsong. The therapist led me verbally down a woodland path into a clearing; at one point she told me I was wearing a heavy backpack, which I could now take off so I would be able to move more freely. Later, she told me to visualize my "new self"—and then to step into that image.

That exercise was quite powerful for me. I could actually see standing before me an image of myself as a slimmer and more vibrant "me"—and I loved the sensation of stepping into that identity. I felt fully present, and I was also relaxed—so relaxed that when the therapist told me I could begin to become aware of the chair underneath me, I didn't want to. I knew the session would end soon, she would ask me to open my eyes, and some part of my mind resisted. This was when I realized that I had gone deep in this session—deeper even than I usually do in meditation. Typically, I don't hesitate to come out of meditation; I am usually ready to move on to the next project of my day.

I found my initial reaction to hypnosis gratifying. I lost the ten pounds in ten weeks. Though it has been a year and they're still gone, it is too soon to know if I have removed those ten pounds long term. But I have noticed a shift in my attention, away from cravings for my favorite foods and toward other, more playful ways of enjoying myself: playing the piano, cuddling my kittens, taking a walk. So, yes, my behavior has changed. In the hypnosis session, I was introduced to another "flavor" for my life. Rather than pushing myself to be productive and perform well (nine at least on a scale of one to ten), I began to make more space for myself to be at ease. And it is *this*, I find, that is making a difference in the way I eat.

In the weeks before the hypnosis, I would wake up thinking that I would be going on vacation soon, I needed to lose some weight in preparation, yet when three o'clock came around, my stress levels would be so high that I would eat as I always had. The next morning, I'd wake up thinking, *I have to lose some weight!*

Now, I would say I still have to make an effort to eat correctly, but a bigger issue than eating is being addressed. I'm more relaxed and playful. I work at an intensity of seven rather than always shooting for a ten. And my desire to eat has gone down as well.

It wasn't just one session that had this effect. I promised myself that I would listen to the tape that was made for me by the hypnotherapist, and so I am revisiting that powerful visual image of myself as I would like to be, every day for about thirty minutes. This is a practice for me, and the practice is solidifying these beneficial changes at a deep level.

Of course, what I'm experiencing—relaxation and a healthier attitude toward eating—is nothing like the disappearance of ichthyosis, which is a genetic disease. But I wonder if these two "cures" don't have a similar root. They are, actually, both based on strongly visualizing a shift in one's condition. And this strong visualization, through the power of the mind or consciousness, can—at least in some cases—make the visualization a physical reality.

11

THE HEALING INTENTION

I could simply say the term "energy healing" to a group of UO science majors and watch their faces freeze. In the Complementary and Alternative Medicine class I've offered for the past several years, students always have had the greatest difficulty with energy-based healing. These same students have no trouble accepting that various forms of exercise—tai chi, hatha yoga, even just walking—can accelerate healing and ward off disease. But the idea of one person transmitting energy that heals another? Initially, most of these scientists-in-training are not simply reluctant to learn about such modalities; they're *opposed* to learning about them.

As a trained neuroscientist, I can understand this response. A neuroscientist might say, "Of course, encountering someone's anger can cause measurable stress for another person." But the scientist thinks this anger—this emotional energy—will have an effect on the other person only if it's physically apparent to him. It is quite a leap for a scientist to consider that the unperceived energy of one person might have an effect on the physiology of another. And this is, in fact, the claim of energy healing: that subtle energy transmitted from the one person has actually improved the physiological function of the other.

From the scientist's perspective, it is virtually impossible to verify such a premise. A human being is a highly complex system. When our bodies change, there are infinite numbers of factors involved. Each of us has countless components to our physiology as well as our mindset, our emotions, our lifestyle, our environment—*all* of which influence our health. How could we possibly extract the effect of one factor—say, the intention of a spiritual healer—from the others? We have to take into account a subject's stress levels, mood, diet, belief system, intentions, environment, and so on. This is why such a study is extremely difficult to carry out with what is considered to be scientific validity.

To be absolutely certain of the effects a spiritual healer has on a person's health, a researcher would have to keep all the other factors that might influence that person's life absolutely static. How could you possibly do that? You couldn't. And even if you *could* isolate persons so that most of these factors are stable—where subjects, for instance, would receive no touch from another human being, where they would not be affected by changes in the weather, where they would receive no news from the world around them—such an antiseptic and isolated environment would not provide an ideal setting for energy healing.

So, the researchers interested in studying such subjects began by turning their attention to a simpler question: if human intention is directed toward a system that is simpler than another human being, will the intention itself affect a change in that system? In other words, can a person have an effect on a system, whether animate or inanimate, simply by thinking about it? This sort of mind-to-body—or mind-to-object—influence, it turns out, can be verified. It has been verified. This phenomenon, called distant intentionality, has been explored extensively in scientific literature, yet the research is still at the margins of Western neuroscience.

DISTANT INTENTIONALITY

Distant intention is, at its core, a person attempting through thought alone to affect the physiological processes of another organism or the physical condition of an inanimate object. There is no physical interaction, not even a verbal cue. This is a wholly mental process based on personal intention, and—here we see why most neuroscientists want nothing to do with distant intentionality—it is the foundation of all energetic healing. The person engaged in distant intentionality is, in effect, saying, *I'm paying attention to you and, in this way, trying to change something in you.* If the person is a healer, the basic message is only slightly different: *I'm paying attention to you and, in this way, trying to heal you.*

Early distant intention research measured whether a person could alter the pulses made by a random event generator, an electronic machine the size of a toaster oven that was programmed to pulse a random series of numbers just above and just below a hundred. The numbers would come at a rate of a thousand per minute. The subject, sitting in front of the machine, was simply instructed to "think high" or "think low" in an attempt to raise or lower the numbers from the mean.[1] These experiments were done in the 1960s through the 1980s by Robert Jahn and his colleagues at the Princeton Engineering Anomalies Research Laboratory (PEAR) and were replicated later by PEAR researcher Dean Radin and others.[2]

By 2003, at least 516 experiments published in 216 articles by 91 different first authors explored the ability of persons to influence the random event generator output. The cumulative results were strong: distant intentionality was shown to be a measurable, verifiable factor. In a review of all of these studies, Radin and Roger Nelson,[3] also from PEAR, reported that the effects of distant intentionality were small but statistically significant ($p < 10^{-16}$). Figure 11.1 is a graph that tracks the effect of a person's intention on the output of a random event generator, taken from many studies over time. When compared to the baseline (BL), it's easy to see the impact of the participants' intention to increase (HI) or decrease (LO) the count.[4]

"Significant" is a statistical term meaning that the results of the test have a very high probability of being caused by something other than random chance. To my mind these data are unequivocal. Even critics who have assessed the experiments agree that the equipment, protocol, and data processing techniques were appropriate and that, thus, the findings must be valid.[5] The results are, however, largely ignored. When he closed his research laboratory in 2007, Jahn said that after twenty-eight years of work, there was no reason for PEAR to continue running these experiments. "If people don't believe us after all the results we've generated," he said, "then they never will."[6] I hope he's wrong.

In light of this distant intention research, what astonishes me is that no one is asking what I see as the key question: how does a person alter

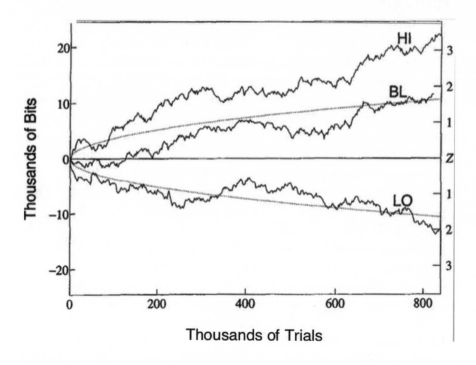

Thousands of Trials

Figure 11.1. The cumulative effect of personal intention on the output of the random event generator, over time. The baseline (BL) is the standard by which to measure the cumulative effect of subjects trying to increase the output (HI) and the effect of subjects trying to decrease the output (LO). The curved lines are the confidence intervals for statistical significance at the .05 level. Reprinted with permission from R. G. Jahn, B. J. Dunne, R. D. Nelson, Y. H. Dobyns, and G. J. Bradish, "Correlations of Random Binary Sequences with Pre-Stated Operator Intention: A Review of a 12-Year Program," *Journal of Scientific Exploration* 11:351 (1997).

the output of a machine by the power of thought? How can the human mind actually accomplish such a feat?

In more recent distant intention experiments, Radin introduced a modification of an experiment that is well known within the realm of quantum physics: the double-slit. In the double-slit[7] light is shone through a screen with two slits onto a second screen. The pattern of light that appears on the second screen will be different depending on whether light moves as a particle or a wave. If light moves as particles, it will go through the slits in straight lines and make two slit-shaped lines of light on the second screen. If light travels in waves, it will refract as it goes through the slits and what appears on the second screen will be a series of lines produced by the action of waves, one upon the other.

When Thomas Young performed the double-slit experiment in 1801, his results seemed to prove conclusively that light travels in waves. In the early 1900s, however, Einstein and others found evidence that light also travels as discrete particles or quanta, called photons. Scientists began to ask how light, which is recognized as particles, could also show wave-like behavior. What was it that produced the interference pattern Young originally saw? In 1909 G. I. Taylor performed the experiment again, but with such weak levels of light that one photon would pass through the slits at a time. The interference pattern was still there, which was surprising. How could one particle interfere with itself? In time, when quantum mechanics theory began taking form, the answer became clear.

One of the most mysterious aspects of quantum theory is exemplified by the paradoxical results of the double-slit experiment. Quantum theory predicts that the wave of a photon should indicate the probability of finding that particle at a particular point along that wave. It's as if the photon's wave function followed all its possible paths simultaneously, including the probability of going through both slits in a double-slit apparatus. Yet when the photon's position is measured, it is only detected in one place. When the photon is measured, its wave-function collapses and the photon is detected as a point. Yet when the experiment is repeated again and again, the photons begin to aggregate in some regions (places of constructive interference) and not appear in others (places of destructive interference), with the classical wave interference pattern building up over time. So, depending on how you decide to measure a particular phenomenon, in this case light, you can see it as individual particles, having collapsed to a specific point in space, or as waves. In other words, you would find what you expected to find.

This is the experiment that all amateur quantum physicists love, the one that demonstrates that we, the subject, do indeed create our own reality. We do this by paying attention to it and by intending that it be a certain way.

What interested Radin is the question of whether a subject's intention could induce a photon to move through one slit as opposed to the other. He wanted to apply distant intentionality to this great paradox of quantum physics, which Pasqual Jordan, quantum physicist and winner of the Max Planck Medal in 1942, describes in this way:

> Observations not only disturb what has to be measured, they produce it. . . . We compel [the electron] to assume a definite position. . . . We ourselves produce the results of measurement.[8]

Radin felt that the double-slit experiment was a way to explore the possible role of consciousness in the physical world. As he explains,

> The double-slit experiment . . . is based on two assumptions: (a) If information is gained—by any means—about a photon's path as it travels through two slits, then the interference pattern will collapse in proportion to the certainty of the knowledge gained; and (b) if some aspect of consciousness is a primordial, self-aware feature of the fabric of reality, and that property is modulated by us through capacities we know as attention and intention, then focusing attention on a double-slit system may in turn affect the interference pattern. The first assumption is well established. The second, based on the idea of panpsychism, is a controversial but respectable concept within the philosophy of mind.[9]

Radin set out to determine if subjects could, by their intention, shift the photon's nature—either wave or particle—within the double-slit experiment. The subjects were told to direct their attention toward a double-slit apparatus inside a sealed box. They were told to imagine the two tiny slits and to try to mentally block or to mentally push the beam to go through one slit or the other. Remember, as a wave, the photon would go through both slits. Because in previous experiments Radin had found that people who meditated might be better at performing this task than the people who didn't, he divided his subjects: those who meditated and those who didn't. The subjects performed six variations of the experiment to try to rule out various confounding effects. Their results are shown in figure 11.2.

The meditators were, on average, successful in influencing the path of the photons and significantly more successful than those who didn't meditate. The figure shows the cumulative effect (the z score, which tells the degree that the results are different than the mean in the control condition) across all the sessions of the six experiments with both those who meditated and those who didn't. In one of the experi-

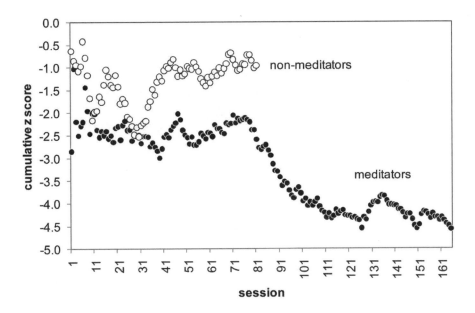

Figure 11.2. **Graph showing the abilities of meditators versus non-meditators, by their intention, to shift a photon's nature—either a wave or a particle, within the double-slit experiment. The figure shows the cumulative effect (the z score, which tells the degree that the results are different than the mean in the control condition) across all the sessions of the six experiments with both those who meditated and those who didn't. Note that the meditators were significantly more successful than non-meditators. Quoted by permission of Physics Essays Publication, from** *Physics Essays,* **Volume 25, Nr. 2, pp. 157–171 (2012).**

ments, an electroencephalographic (EEG) marker was placed over the left occipital lobe to measure any attentional variable. For those who wish more detail here, the variable measured was alpha band (8–12 Hz) event-related desynchronization (ERD), which is a neural correlate of focused attention, most detectable over the occipital lobe. There was a decline in the variable, indicating a correlation between increased focus and the subject's ability to influence the photons' path.[10]

In summation, Radin points out that the theoretical literature in quantum physics discusses at length the possibility that observation affects the results of experiments and, therefore, the role consciousness plays in creating reality. Yet there have been few experiments performed to test this possibility.

> [T]he reason is not surprising: The notion that consciousness may be
> related to the formation of physical reality has come to be associated
> more with medieval magic and so-called New Age ideas than it is
> with sober science. As a result, it is safer for one's scientific career to
> avoid associating with such dubious topics and subsequently rare to
> find experiments examining these ideas in the physics literature. In-
> deed, the taboo is so robust that until recently it had extended to any
> test of the foundations of quantum theory. For more than 50 years
> such studies were considered unsuitable for serious investigators. [11]

He adds that there are, however, more than a thousand articles focusing
on the interface between mind and matter within the literature of parapsychology. A number of these articles—including those from Radin's
own laboratory, the Institute of Noetic Sciences—have appeared in
highly respected journals such as *Science, Nature,* and *Neuroscience
Letters.* Radin also discusses some of the practical challenges that arise
in an exploration of human intention and attention.

He points out, for instance, that attention itself is variable. The ability to focus varies greatly from one individual to another and, within the
same person, from one day to the next—and, I might add, from one
time of day to another. Radin also notes that the outcomes can be
altered when the subject's beliefs are challenged by the nature of the
experimental task. [12] Such variations are apparent in the studies on placebo effects and hypnosis discussed in the previous chapter, and also in
studies examining healing intentions. It was to avoid these pitfalls that
Radin focused his experiments on conditions that were easily controlled, having his subjects interact with a random event generator or
with interference patterns of photons.

There are, of course, other distant intentionality studies that look at
the influence of attention on living systems and even on other human
beings. Studies have been done, for instance, to examine the effects of
intentionality on the growth of bacteria, fungi, and yeast under blinded
conditions. [13] This research has shown that bacterial growth can be ac-
celerated or decelerated depending on the instructions given to the
subject taking part in the experiment. [14] As for the effect of distant
intentionality on other human beings, there is much to say.

THE EFFECT ONE PERSON HAS ON ANOTHER

Often when I am in a public space like a subway or an airport, I find it interesting to watch people—some call this "people watching." I try to imagine who these strangers are, what stories they carry. Recently in the Portland airport while waiting for a plane, I was watching a man who was sitting across the aisle from me, reading. He had an interesting angular face and was wearing a fedora, and I was letting my mind play with these details when suddenly this man turned from his book and looked straight at me with a bit of a glare. I looked away. I wondered if there was some way this man could feel my attention, even on a subconscious level, and if this is what had prompted him to look up. He did seem to be reacting to some subtle input because he had looked up from his book with the expression of annoyance already on his face—as if he knew, at least on some level, that he was being watched. There is, in fact, a growing body of research that suggests that watching someone, even though that person cannot see what you're doing—even when that person's eyes might be trained on a book—can bring about a physiological response that causes him to respond.

Here is another application of distant intentionality. In such an experiment, researchers try to determine whether or not there is a relationship between the specific intention of one person (called the agent) and a change in the physiology or behavior of a second person in a remote location (the receiver).

An experiment might be set up with receivers sitting in a soundproof chamber and being continually monitored so that any arousal is measured on their skin, through their electrodermal activity. In such a test, some of the agents would be able to observe (and even stare at) their receiver on a closed-circuit video system, and some of the agents would not. The skin resistance of the first set of receivers would then be compared with that of the second. If distant attention has no power, then there should be no difference between the arousal of these two sets of receivers. None of the receivers would have had any external indication that they were being watched.

In a variation on this theme, the receiver's electrodermal activity is relayed to the agent, who then attempts through his or her intention either to heighten the receiver's reaction, to calm them, or to do nothing. The experiment typically consisted of trials of thirty to sixty seconds apiece, with a single session consisting of about twenty of these trials.[15]

In a third variation, the receivers are asked to focus their attention on a candle. Whenever they notice their mind wandering, they are to press a button and then return their attention to the candle. The agent, who is again in a different location, views the receiver through a monitor. Whenever the word "help" appears, the agent focuses their attention on a similar candle and keeps an intention that their partner will do the same. When the word "control" appears, the agent lets their mind go to other subjects.

In a set of three meta-analyses of the various studies done in these three related areas, the German psychologist Stefan Schmidt[16] calculated that all research showed almost the same effect of distant intentionality. When averaging the results of these sixty-two different studies Schmidt found a small but significant effect size of about .1 standard deviation from the control condition.

It is true that, like the results related to the random event generator and the double-slit manipulation, these effects are small. Once again, however, the point is that the effects are, statistically speaking, significant. These results show that mental intention *can* influence the physiology or behavior of a second person. Schmidt concludes his study of the studies with this observation:

> If the data reported here are not due to some artifact in the design of distant intention experiments, it may be concluded that under some circumstances persons can intentionally interact or connect from a distance with each other, although this effect may be very limited in size and power. . . . Overall, if the data of this study hold true, this might have some implications for the areas of nursing and health care, distant healing, as well as group meditation practice.[17]

What strikes me with these distant intention experiments is that they typically measure the effect of subjects with no training in a healing practice. The results of these distant intention experiments are reliable and repeatable, and I wonder if their effects might not be even greater if the agents used were people skilled or practiced in relaying their intentions.

There are clearly similarities between energy healing and the distant intention research we've been looking at. According to one study, the very definition of energy healing is "any purely mental effort undertaken by one person with the intention to improve physical or emotional well-being in another."[18] Another study defines such healing as "the intentional influence of one or more persons upon another living system without utilizing known physical means of intervention."[19]

Energy healing encompasses prayer vigils, faith healing, and various types of therapeutic touch—Reiki, jin shin jitsu, acupuncture, and so much more. In fact, all forms of therapy involve an intention by the therapist. There is no measure for the power of this intention, but we do know that the therapist's intention has power. In the last chapter we discussed research showing that a medical doctor's belief in the efficacy of a treatment has an effect on the outcome of that treatment for the patient.

One of the first studies of intention in energy healing that I encountered was by Jeanne Achterberg, formerly a professor at Southwestern Medical School in Dallas. Perhaps because she was also a pioneer researcher in mind–body medicine and served in the U.S. government's first Office of Alternative Medicine, Achterberg performed a controlled experiment to determine the extent to which one could, in a laboratory setting, measure the effects of a healer's distant intention upon a receiver's brain processes. It was an ambitious undertaking, to say the least.[20]

Achterberg chose to study eleven practitioners from different healing modalities. All subjects were respected in their own tradition, each was regarded as a successful healer, and each had practiced healing for about two decades. The healers were asked to choose their own partners, receivers with whom they felt bonded. Previous work had indicated to Achterberg that people who feel a mutual connection tend to have a stronger physiological effect on each other.

In this study, the healer was in a magnetically shielded control room, and the receiver, in a separate room, was lying inside a functional magnetic resonance imaging (fMRI) scanner. The healers were instructed to start and stop their distant intention healing at random points in time. A session involved twelve two-minute intervals of sending a healing intention. When asked to send this intention, the healers were told to connect with the receiver in whatever ways were customary in their own healing practice. The receivers were asked to relax as much as was possible in the scanner environment.

The study outcome revealed that the healers' intention was, in fact, registered by the fMRI as changes in the receivers' brain activity during the transmission periods as compared to the rest periods. There was significant activation in at least two areas of the receivers' brains: the frontal superior cortex (which is involved in information processing and decision making) and the anterior cingulate cortex (which involves decision making and executive control).[21] The anterior cingulate is also activated during both hypnosis and meditation.

There were, of course, limitations to this research study, and these were noted by the authors. As we've discussed, it was impossible to conclude that changes in the receivers' brains were caused *only* by the intention of the healers. Due to the requirements of the study, the healers were not alone in their control rooms; they were joined by a radiology technician, a nurse, and a researcher. So, three other people in the control room were also aware of the timing and conditions for beginning and ending the healing intention. An intention could have come from any of these people, though, of course, no one other than the healer was deliberately sending an intention. Also, there was no conceivable way to measure the healing abilities of each participant, so no correlation could be made between healing abilities and extent of influence on the recipient's nervous system activity. On the other hand, as the authors also pointed out, no biological processes are known that would account for the changes that occurred in the receivers' brain activity.[22]

There have also been a number of studies performed on the efficacy of various energy-healing techniques and, of these, I propose to explore one in particular: Reiki.

A CLOSER LOOK AT REIKI

Reiki is a form of therapeutic touch developed within the last century. Though its roots are in Japan and in Buddhist practice, Reiki healing is performed throughout the world and is not a spiritual practice per se. The etymology of its name gives some insight into the theory behind Reiki: the syllable *rei* (pronounced *ray*) can be translated as "spirit or divine wisdom" and *ki* (pronounced *key*) refers to the universal life force that's known in the Indian tradition as *shakti*. Reiki healing is said to depend on the movement of *ki* not from but *through* the Reiki practitioner into the person on whom he or she is working. (We explore this later.) Skeptics say that this life force is hypothetical, imaginary, and that any anecdotes regarding the power of Reiki to heal sickness or increase well-being can be attributed to the placebo effect or the simple influence of touch upon the body.

Reiki also has its proponents among healthcare professionals, and one psychologist, Dr. Adina Goldman Shore, performed a year-long study exploring the long-term effects of Reiki on psychological depression and perceived stress.[23] Shore was especially interested in learning if the results of Reiki therapy are due to the placebo effect, physical touch, or the practice's energy—*ki*.

The study was a randomized, blinded, controlled clinical trial. The forty-six participants were randomly assigned to one of three groups: a hands-on Reiki group, a distance Reiki group, or a distance placebo group. Since the intention to heal through Reiki practice can happen either with hands-on or from a distance, both of these modes were tested—and the placebo group, the control group, all were told they were receiving distance healing. Actually, the researcher reduced the placebo effect by leading the participants to believe that the placebo group would receive a mock hands-on Reiki session. So the hands-on Reiki group thought they might be receiving nothing, and the distance placebo group thought they were definitely receiving Reiki. In a humane gesture that I particularly appreciated, the researcher told all participants that if they received the placebo during the experiment, they would be offered Reiki sessions after the study was finished.

The participants received a sixty- to ninety-minute Reiki or placebo treatment every week over a six-week period, and the group was monitored for a year after the trial.

Prior to treatment there were no significant differences on the Beck Depression Inventory (BDI) among the three groups, which had mean scores of 11.8, 11.4, and 10.4—all in the range of mild to moderate depression. After the treatment period, however, both the hands-on Reiki and distance Reiki groups showed significantly reduced symptoms of psychological distress (mean BDI scores of 4.7 and 3.1) compared to the placebo control group (BDI: 8.5). What I find compelling is that the significant differences in depression and self-perceived stress for the Reiki groups were still present a year after the treatment ended.

Let me repeat that: *a year after the treatment ended.* The author notes that the scores for the groups that received Reiki treatment continued to improve throughout the course of the year even though there were no further treatments.[24]

In a separate study, Shore performed a qualitative analysis, using questionnaires and interviews, to learn about the participants' experiences during their Reiki sessions.[25] I found this article especially intriguing because it gives first-person accounts—the subjective viewpoint that one finds only rarely in scientific journals. For this follow-up analysis, Shore chose only from the Reiki groups (not the placebos), and she selected the seven who'd undergone the greatest change and the seven who'd made the *least* change as a result of the study. She notes that except that low responders said they were more skeptical of the treatment, there were no other differences between the two groups. And in spite of their skepticism, five of the seven low responders felt they had received significant benefits from the treatment. Shore reports that, altogether, 79 percent said they felt calmer and more at peace, and 57 percent felt kinesthetic experiences of increased energy movement or flow in their bodies. As to *ki* being "imaginary," Shore quotes three of the subjects:

> In the words of one participant, "I mean I can actually, literally feel it when I'm getting treatment. I can feel the energy coming." Another participant described the energy as "tangible because you can feel it." In the words of another participant, "The experience of energy for me is kinesthetically real."[26]

Since the original article by Shore explores the effects of Reiki on depression and stress, I was also interested to see the participants' experiences of the effects of the treatments on their emotional health. For example, Shore notes:

> Furthermore, the theme of heart, experienced by 50% of reporting participants, was described as an increased experience of an open heart, love, and forgiveness.
>
> Similarly, 50% of interviewed participants reported the theme of emotion, an experience of greater emotional health from an emotional release during or as a result of treatment. It is best described in the words of a participant, "It [the Reiki] opened me up more to

my emotions, allowing me to emote and clear away and cry, release emotions." Nearly half of the participants (49.9%) reported the sensation of vibration in their physical bodies during treatment and 42.9% reported lightness, a physical sensation of floating. A typical sensation described by Reiki recipients was, "I feel that I'm being lifted up on a whale's back and being lifted up to the light."[27]

Some participants (35.7 percent) described their Reiki sessions as powerful, some (35.7 percent) said their attitudes had become more positive, and others (28.6 percent) reported physical sensations such as warmth, improved balance, or even increased joy as a result of the treatments.[28] When asked what she took from her experience of this energy work, one participant replied:

I think that it's the awareness of energy; it's something that we, that all of us are capable of having. It's a matter of becoming in tune with it. I do believe we naturally are able to perceive energy within ourselves and other living things, but a lot of our culture is focused on the mind and the intellect. So . . . this is a sensitivity that can be learned and I feel that, with it, the quality of one's life can improve.[29]

Asked the same question, another participant described her experience of energetic healing as

Very relaxing and blissful. . . . I think it's important to know that for me, as a participant in this study, the Reiki treatments have really made a significant change in my life and how I view my life. And I think it's important for anybody who might read about this to have an open mind about just trying it, you know. . . . There were times when I was quite skeptical about it and I just did it anyway. And what I've gotten back from it is . . . a lot more than I would have thought, but I had the open-mindedness to just try it anyway, and so that's what I would recommend.[30]

Another woman responded to the same question by saying,

I believe that . . . we store experiences, traumas, pain, and positive things in our bodies as energy. And that they continue to affect us through our lives if we don't move them, release them, address them, and that this [energetic healing] is a truly deep and effective way to

move beyond that. It . . . jumpstarts or accelerates your movement in
life by removing blocks.[31]

I have given quite a bit of space to these firsthand reports from the
Shore study because I believe they show the varied and often profound
effects of energy treatments—in this case, Reiki—on a person's emotional health and sense of well-being. I believe this tells us much more
than the study's statistics about how this six-week treatment influenced
forty-six lives in the long term. I say "long term" because the BDI scale
was still showing significant improvement when participants were examined again a year after treatment and also because the interviews
quoted above were done a year after the study was completed.

In another study, researchers from the Yale University School of
Medicine[32] noted that Reiki has been shown in a number of studies to
have significant benefits, including reduction of anxiety and perceived
stress. They also noted that its physiological effects have been less well
explored. As Reiki is an ongoing clinical program offered at the Yale
teaching hospital in its cardiac section, the researchers looked at whether these Reiki sessions were associated with a change in heart rate
variability for patients recovering from acute coronary syndrome. The
changes were compared between three groups: a group that received
Reiki treatments, a group that received meditative music therapy
(which is known to improve relaxation and thought to reduce heart
rates and blood pressure), and a resting control group.

The outcome was that the Reiki group showed a significant improvement in heart rate variability from the baseline, which did not change in
the resting control group, and slightly improved in the music group.
This increase in heart rate variability indicates increased autonomic
function and vagal activity. The authors note that the magnitude of the
effect on heart rate variability was similar to that of pharmaceuticals,
such as propranolol, used to improve autonomic function. These
changes in the patients who were given the Reiki treatment were also
associated with increases in positive emotional states and decreases in
negative states, with smaller changes occurring in the music group and
the least changes in the resting control group. The physician researchers from Yale recommended that "Reiki be incorporated into standard-
ized hospital care to provide therapeutic benefit."[33]

This was one of many studies that have now explored the effects of Reiki, therapeutic touch, and other forms of energy healing on a variety of factors related to health and well-being. A number of reviews of these studies have been performed, to look at the overall effect of Reiki in healthcare. One recent review of Reiki studies[34] found twelve randomized controlled trials that had been conducted on a variety of health conditions, including anxiety, depression, and stroke recovery. The review noted that nine of the twelve trials demonstrated positive results from the Reiki treatments. The authors were also appropriately cautious and advised that trials on Reiki treatment are still in an exploratory mode and that many more carefully planned blinded, randomized controlled trials need to be performed in order to more clearly evaluate the efficacy of Reiki in treatment.

After reading a number of these Reiki studies, my curiosity was aroused—and for me curiosity is a siren call! To answer my questions—and as a way to prepare for teaching my class on alternative approaches to healthcare—several years ago I made an appointment for a session with a Reiki practitioner. I saw her in an office that looked like many other private healthcare settings I've been in—it was clean, comfortable, and unobtrusive, with a peaceful feeling about its decor.

The practitioner, a woman in her middle years, asked me first if there were any areas of concern I had about my health or well-being. I had none, but I explained that I knew that there was room for improvement in my overall physical, mental, and emotional functioning. It turned out I was right about that. This woman spent about an hour with me, placing her hands for varying periods of time over various parts of my body, from head to toe. I found the experience relaxing, and by the time I left her office, I felt that my mental state *had*, in fact, changed. I felt noticeably relaxed and expansive—by which I mean I felt connected to what was around me. This peaceful state lasted for the rest of the day.

Did this one Reiki session change any of my physiological processes? I don't know. I was, however, sufficiently intrigued by the effects of the session to make an appointment with another practitioner—an RN in Seattle—whom friends had told me about. This woman left me feeling not only peaceful but also "seen" in some surprising ways. Though I can think of no way that she could have heard of these personal details before our session, she spoke of my relationship to my mother, my father, and my first spiritual teacher—all of whom were deceased.

After this second Reiki session, I registered for a three-day Reiki training workshop in Seattle. My goal for the workshop was not to become trained as a Reiki practitioner. I was still curious. I wanted to learn more about this modality, and watching a training was a way for me to study it. The operative word here is "watching." I saw myself not as an intuitive but as a scientist, and so it seemed to me that Reiki was an activity I would watch, not one I would ever be able to do.

For the first day of this workshop, the teacher went through Reiki's history and theory and the practical details of how to give a Reiki session. One of the points that impressed me was the assertion that in a Reiki session, it is not the practitioner who is creating or even moving the *ki*, the healing energy that goes into the subject. Before beginning, practitioners ask that the Reiki energy flow through them at the highest level possible that is beneficial to the practitioner and the client, and then attempts to be in tune with that power, allowing the *ki* to flow through unimpeded.

At the end of the day, the teacher had us meditate and then she "initiated" each of us into Reiki practice by performing an energetic transfer that is part of every Reiki training. The transmission is supposed to affect the students' hands, which she had instructed us to hold palm up on top of our thighs as we sat in meditation. When the teacher finished my initiation, I felt a palpable energy, like a weight, remain in the palms of my hands, which were still on my thighs. This sensation lasted for most of the rest of the session, as I continued to meditate.

The next morning I found out I would not be continuing to merely observe. The next step in our training, the teacher explained, was for us to perform Reiki on each other. She told us to each choose a partner. In the flurry of partner finding, I became quite anxious. How could I possibly "do" Reiki? I'm a scientist—not an intuitive, not a psychic, not a healer! When the pleasant young man who was my partner asked which of us should go first, I said, "Please, you go first!" I added, "I don't know what I am doing."

This man had, in fact, taken other Reiki workshops, and even though he wasn't what you would call an aggressive or assertive person, he wasn't at all shy about placing his hands on my abdomen, my forehead, the crown of my head, my shoulders, my back, and so on. As he did this,

Reiki began to seem natural to me, familiar even—and I suddenly knew, with conviction, that I *could* do this. When the young man had finished his practice session on me, I stood up, and began to practice on him. I placed my hands on his abdomen, his forehead . . . and as I worked, I went into a profound meditation, a moving meditation in which I felt grounded and at peace.

While I was doing this Reiki session, the teacher watched me for a time. Later, she said, "You're very organized in your Reiki treatment." I thought she was making a little joke about my academic approach, and I touched her arm lightly and smiled. "No," she said, "I'm serious. You were good."

As I thought about this exchange afterward, I was struck by the similarities between the energy of healing and the energy I'd been in touch with all these years in meditation, the energy that was awakened for me with *shaktipat*. We've been discussing the healing intention. *Shaktipat* occurs through the intention of a spiritual master to awaken energy and is often associated with a higher awareness in an aspirant— and thereby initiates a spiritual "healing." Shore describes energetic or spiritual healing as "the transference of a universal all-pervading life energy,"[35] and it is my experience that there are parallels between the processes of initiation of students by a spiritual master and of the physiological healing that is done by a healing practitioner. The spiritual "healing" may happen on a more profound level than does physical healing, but they are both healing nonetheless.

It seems to me that there is, indeed, a universal energy at work and that this energy can respond to human intention.

So, let us move from subjective experience and return once again to the objective realm of Western science. What do scientific studies have to say about the intention to heal? The studies I have cited do give evidence that the intention of one individual can influence the brain activity of a second individual, even at a distance and with no sensory communication between the two.

Clearly, the effects of energy healing are just beginning to be explored clinically. In such research, as was mentioned earlier, it is difficult to separate the effects of energy healing from all the other influences on the patient's health and well-being. Additionally, as all the researchers in these studies have concluded, any results that tend to

establish the efficacy of energy healing do not fit within Western science's current deterministic and materialist model of brain function.
Herein lies the paradox.

Although a large body of clinical evidence supports the proposition
that the mind can affect physiological processes, both within one's own
body and in the body of another person, the current scientific models
do not accommodate such findings. The evidence demonstrates healing
power of placebo, hypnotic suggestion, and distant intention. How do
such events occur? Traditional science cannot explain it, and thus most
research papers describing such a result say, simply, that it cannot be
explained by current scientific theory.

Is there truly no theory to account for this reality?

12

RESEARCH INTO CONSCIOUSNESS

At a point when it seemed I'd finished the research for this book, I discovered *Irreducible Mind: Toward a Psychology for the 21st Century*, a book by a group of scientists and philosophers that covers such topics as near-death and mystical experiences, hypnosis, and cases suggestive of reincarnation.[1] Finally! A compendium of evidence that consciousness exists independently of the neuronal activity of the brain. I read this book from cover to cover, all eight hundred–plus pages, repeatedly interrupting my husband or Skyping friends to say, look at *this!*

I wanted to meet these scientists. I wanted to talk with them. I wanted to learn what had prompted them to create this summary of research—their own and other people's—on mind–brain, top-down influences on our physiological processes. Fortunately, four of the six authors of *Irreducible Mind* are based at the University of Virginia in the Department of Psychiatry and Neurobehavioral Sciences' Division of Perceptual Studies. Feeling tentative, I sent an email to the main author, psychologist Edward F. Kelly, to introduce myself as a neuroscientist, to describe my own book, and to ask about visiting them at UVa.

He responded the following morning, "Thanks for making this contact, and by all means do come! Let's try to coordinate well in advance so that we can all be here." His tone was warm and receptive, which, in my experience, is not the norm in the scientific community, at least not among neuroscientists. Many of my colleagues seem distant when another scientist expresses interest in their research. It's almost as if they're saying, "Have we been introduced?"

So, Ed Kelly not only invited me to come to UVa at a time when almost everyone on his team would be present (I was disappointed that a key team member, Emily Kelly, was out of town) and arranged for me to have individual meetings, he also picked me up at the airport in Charlottesville and took me out to dinner. I didn't need to steer the conversation with Kelly; almost immediately he began talking about his work—his interest in it, his orientation to it, his introduction to it—and this had been the reason for my trip.

KELLY: SUBTLER LEVELS OF CONSCIOUSNESS

I was particularly interested in how Ed Kelly first became interested in these research topics that never would have been introduced to him through his academic and professional training—topics considered outside the bounds of traditional science. Kelly did his undergraduate work in psychology at Yale. I found out later that he studied under a Yale National Scholarship and graduated Magna Cum Laude and Phi Beta Kappa. He earned his PhD in psycholinguistics and cognitive science at Harvard. So, it certainly wasn't a lack of academic rigor that led him to an interest in the paranormal!

"It came up while I was in graduate school," Kelly said. "I got a call one day from my mother, who said that a female relative had become a medium."

A "medium" is someone who "mediates" between conscious reality and the spirit world, allowing a spirit to speak through them. Ed's mother asked if he would "check this out." She figured that since he was a graduate student in psychology, he would know all about mediums. He didn't.

> So I went over to the library to see what I could find out. Here I was, working in William James Hall, and I had no inkling of William James's enormous interest in these subjects. It was not a part of William James that anybody [at Harvard] talked about. There were probably five hundred people in that building; I don't think there were ten who actually knew anything about this and most of *them* wouldn't have wanted to discuss it. We still had Edwin G. Boring, B. F. Skinner, guys like that, on the faculty.[2]

Boring and Skinner were renowned reductive psychologists from Harvard. After reading James's writings, Ed Kelly called his mother and told her that it all sounded pretty benign to him. He then talked to his relative and learned that she was part of the Spiritual Frontiers Fellowship, a PanChristian group that held services in members' homes. At the center of the service was a medium who relayed messages important to that community. That was his relative.

Kelly read about a thousand pages of his relative's automatic writing—writing she did while in a mildly dissociated state—and found it sufficiently interesting that he wanted to see her "in action."

> I find it extremely hard to understand how anyone can do this, but she would essentially step aside, fully conscious, while something else expressed itself through her. It must be a very hard trick to learn how to do. . . . I went to one of their services, and there were two things about it that really struck me.
>
> First of all, she basically replicated what William James had described. He talks somewhere about how there is a remarkable sort of homogeneity about this stuff. So much so that you can't help suspect that it was all written by the same person. So there typically will be an Oriental wise man, an American Indian, a Christian saint. My relative had all these things. They had emerged successively in the course of her mediumship. So, that was interesting.
>
> The other thing was that there were a couple of physiological things that got my attention. First of all, when Wu Sung [the Oriental wise man] for example, came on board, her face would undergo an extraordinary transformation. Her eyes would stretch out and take on an Oriental cast. I didn't think anybody could do that voluntarily. That was really interesting. The other thing was that she is just sitting there, talking in a low-key way in a session that lasts half an hour. At the end of it she jumps up, goes into the kitchen, and slugs down about a quart of orange juice. What was that all about? It was like she'd been playing full court basketball for two hours.[3]

Kelly started reading on the subject of experimental parapsychology, mainly articles in the *Journal of Parapsychology*. The journal had begun as an extension of the famed Parapsychology Lab, founded at Duke University in 1935 by J. B. Rhine, a botanist who was exploring telepathy and clairvoyance—which he termed "extra-sensory perception" or ESP—among the undergraduates. After his retirement in 1962, when the lab was closed, Rhine founded his own Institute for Parapsychology across from Duke's East Campus.

Ed Kelly, who was exploring what to do after graduation, began a correspondence with J. B. Rhine about a position at his institute at the same time he applied for other professional positions. Kelly received a lucrative offer from a San Francisco company to work in an area related to his dissertation topic, "A Dictionary-Based Approach to Lexical Disambiguation."

Kelly was pondering which direction his career should take when a highly regarded visiting professor gave a lecture to the Psychology Department. The thrust of his talk was that even people who are knowledgeable and sophisticated about statistics will modify their opinions in response to new evidence much more slowly and conservatively than they rationally could, or should. Kelly found himself not much interested in this lecture, but that night it precipitated a vivid dream in which he was, once again, listening to this professor speak.

> In this dream, I'm standing next to a river, looking over at this guy, [the visiting professor], talking about what rotten Bayesian estimators we all are, and for some reason I look over my shoulder. I can see that the riverbank is eroding, and hidden in it are gilt-bound volumes. The title I can see is something bizarre like *The Blake*. . . .
>
> I woke from that dream and thought, *Well, there's the answer.* These things are more important than decision and stress and estimation of probability.[4]

Kelly wasn't the sort of person who remembered dreams, but this particular dream, as he said, "just knocked me over." To him, *The Blake* meant the poet William Blake, whose writings—ignored during his own lifetime—are now celebrated for their mystical undercurrents. So, *this* was the direction Kelly's work was to take: subtle, parapsychological, and psychical research. For him, academic linguistics would be a dead end. He saw that the job in California would give him a comfortable life, but this had no interest for him—no more than the visiting professor's lecture.

> My heart was somewhere else. The next day I wrote to JB and said, "I'll give it a go."[5]

At this point, Kelly was exploring meditation, to which he'd been introduced at a public lecture on Vedanta at Harvard. He went to the lecture on the invitation of one of the secretaries at a project he worked on. She asked him if he'd like to attend a lecture on campus one evening, and Kelly, exhausted though he was at the time, thought, *What the hell.* He went. The speaker was visiting from the Ramakrishna Society in the United Kingdom, and there was quite a crowd. The originally scheduled room was too small, and even the second room, which Kelly described as "enormous," became filled to capacity.

> So, I was already quite amazed. Eventually this little guy comes in and goes to the stage, and he starts talking in this flawless Oxford English, giving an exposition of Vedanta. He went on for about an hour. I didn't take in very much, but I was increasingly impressed that this guy had an absolutely stunning presence. There was just something about him—he was a tiny guy, maybe five foot three! Somehow he just seemed to get bigger and bigger.
>
> I came out thinking, *I've got to get over there and find out what this is all about.*[6]

The next day Kelly located the Ramakrishna Vedanta Society in Boston, and visited the organization's chapel in Back Bay.

> It was a simple place: a whole bunch of pictures of religious figures—not just Indian religious figures, but Islamic, Christian—a simple altar with flowers on it and a sign saying, "Truth is One. Men call it by various names." I was impressed. I bought a few books from their bookstore. They had a little sign there—the swami used to say this all the time—Please steal these books.[7]

Kelly began to frequent the Vedanta Society and also to meditate on his own, about an hour in the morning and again at night. After about a year of this, one day he had a memorable meditation experience:

> I was just sitting there doing my normal thing—focusing on my breath and trying not to let anything else come in [to my awareness]—and I realized that I . . . the entire room, basically . . . How can I say this? The relationship between me and the room was the relationship I normally experience with my own body. I was the size of the room. My being was the size of the room. The experience was

absolutely clear and distinct. And the moment I realized it had happened, it went away. I snapped back to my normal size. I wondered,
What was that all about?[8]

A few years after this, Kelly had another striking subtle experience
when, standing on the back porch of the house where he'd spent his
childhood, he felt for a moment a synthesis of everything he had ever
experienced in that place. In that one instant, he took in his surroundings in a way that cannot happen physically: not 180 degrees, not even
360 degrees but encompassing every past perceptual experience into
one "hyperconscious moment." His initial reaction was, *Wow! That was
great!* and then he thought, *These guys are really onto something!*

By "these guys," Kelly meant meditators, people who explore what
goes on at the levels of reality beyond the physical. As he put it,

> I registered the fact that things can go on in meditation that exceed
> our expectations about what is possible—and our knowledge of what
> things are. I flagged that for future reference.
>
> Then, you know, I got right back into the daily thing of the ex-
> periments, the unfolding of my career in these areas.[9]

So, these are the kinds of experiences that prompted Edward F. Kelly, a
Yale and Harvard graduate with sufficient acumen to become a leading
academic researcher, to step away from the prevailing neuroscientific
paradigm in experimental psychology. He wanted to explore the scientific backwater of parapsychology. Following his work with J. B. Rhine,
an appointment at Duke, and work at other institutes in the area, Kelly
moved to the University of North Carolina and from there, in 2002, to
the University of Virginia, where, as a research professor, he could
devote himself full time to investigating the paranormal topics that most
interest him. He has, for instance, explored mystical experience and
out-of-body experiences with his colleagues in research cited in chapters 7 and 9. In fact, Ed Kelly and his team at the Division of Perceptual
Studies have brought together and discussed the meaning of much of
the scientific evidence I've presented in the last half of this book. With
this in mind, I was fascinated to visit their offices and labs, which I did
the following day.

THE DIVISION OF PERCEPTUAL STUDIES

The Division of Perceptual Studies (DOPS) is located in downtown Charlottesville, housed in a modern glass and brick building with two floors dedicated to the offices, conference room, library, and neuroimaging lab. DOPS was founded in 1969 by Ian Stevenson, whose work in cases suggestive of reincarnation we speak of in chapter 9. Stevenson had been chair of the UVa Medical School's Department of Psychiatry and stepped down to take an endowed professorship that would allow him to do full-time research into studies in parapsychology, especially cases suggestive of reincarnation on which DOPS was founded.

I met with four of the five professors, beginning with a group discussion in the elegant library/conference room, which was lined with wooden bookshelves holding one of the most complete libraries on paranormal research in the United States. When I walked in, I was struck by the thought, *How wonderful it would be to spend weeks reading the books in this room! I would learn so much about research on mysticism and consciousness.*

A few weeks before I had sent a preliminary manuscript—the chapters leading up to this one—and in our meeting, I spoke about the topics covered by this book and heard from various DOPS researchers about the pertinent research they are doing currently. Then I met individually with a few of the scholars who had contributed to *Irreducible Mind*.

As with Ed Kelly, what interested me most was the stories these scientists couldn't include in their impeccable scientific extracts—the human stories that came out of their research and, ultimately, the personal stories that led them to an interest in these paranormal topics in the first place. These scientists, though rigorous in their experimental approach, were open to examining perspectives beyond those normally considered within traditional material science. I found our conversations fascinating.

GREYSON: NEAR-DEATH EXPERIENCES

Bruce Greyson was dressed in a shirt and tie, ready for his work in the UVa Medical School's outpatient psychiatric clinic later in the day, and his office was lined on two sides with serious metal filing cabinets in grey and beige. The cabinets are filled, he said, with individual cases of near-death experiences he has yet to analyze and publish.

I began by asking this working psychiatrist how it was that he, with his traditional medical training, developed an interest in something so far outside the scientific box as near-death experiences.

"I don't think I'm outside the scientific box," Greyson said. "I'm just expanding the box a little."

It was an answer that exemplifies the perspective of the UVa team. Greyson further said that he couldn't point to a specific personal experience that led him into paranormal research—though an interest in anomalies was very much a part of his childhood.

> I grew up in a scientific atheistic household. My father was a research chemist, and he was a pure materialist. When I finally went into my psychiatric training, I happened to mention to him one day about the unconscious, and he said, "The what?" It was beyond his understanding that there could be unconscious processes. But even though he was a strict materialist, he was always interested in anomalous findings that challenged science.
>
> I remember when I was a small boy, he showed me how South America and Africa could fit together. And at that point Wegener's theory of continental drift was a very controversial idea. It was crazy. But my father loved it. And it turned out to be true. . . . He liked to explore things that weren't explainable. And try to bring them into the scientific—which meant changing science, but staying within the materialistic worldview.
>
> That is what I grew up with: I was always interested in these anomalous things. [10]

As an undergraduate studying psychology at Cornell University, Greyson happened upon some parapsychology journals at the library. He'd never heard of parapsychology, and he was fascinated by what he read.

> Here were rigorously done experiments with people leaving their bodies and guessing [the correct] cards and seeing into the future—and the research was at least as rigorous as the stuff we were doing with our rats in their cages. So, I took the journals to my professors and said, "What about this?"

> To my shock, they had nothing bad to say about them. They just said, "I'm not interested in that. Those aren't interesting questions." So it wasn't that the research was being declared invalid; it just wasn't important. They weren't interested. Which made me all the more interested. [11]

Greyson said he would walk away from these conversations with his professors, wondering, *Why is this so threatening to you?* He kept looking into it on his own. He went on to the State University of New York's Upstate Medical University at Syracuse, a school with a liberal elective policy. He arranged to spend a month doing research with Ian Stevenson at the University of Virginia.

> I fell in love with Charlottesville, and got deeply involved in the fact that there was good research going on in this stuff. And it opened my eyes. In a lot of ways Ian was a good mentor—because he was so conservative, so very careful with what he would say.
> There was a physicist here . . . who taught a class called "Science and Religion." She would often have Ian guest lecture and Jim [Tucker], and [later] I would guest lecture in her class. She used to get so frustrated with Ian for not saying that we have proven reincarnation. She would say, "Look, put a p value on this. We are happy with a p of .05 in physics. You are way beyond that." But Ian would never say that. [12]

After taking an elective with Ian Stevenson, Greyson went to the UVa Medical School for his residency and, in 1975, joined the Medical School faculty and began directing the psychiatric emergency center. One of the medical interns that year was Raymond Moody, whose groundbreaking book on near-death experiences, *Life after Life*, had been printed by a small publisher in Georgia and had received virtually no public attention. Shortly after Moody began his residency, Bantam Books picked up *Life after Life*, and the book sold three million copies in the first year.

> Moody comes to me one day and says, "I'm getting lots of letters from people who've had this experience, and I don't have time to deal with them."
> I started reading the letters, and every one was the same. They were saying, "You mean I'm not the only one?" Some of them were

in their 90s, people who'd had experiences when they were teenagers
and had been keeping them secret all their lives. I couldn't put these
down. I've always been interested in the unexplainable, the paranormal. I was running the emergency service where people were dying
all the time, and here was the combination of death and the paranormal. So I took the box to Ian, and said, "Let's do something with
this."

We started writing to these people. And that was the start of it.[13]

At this point Ian Stevenson had been collecting accounts of near-death
experiences for at least a decade, but they didn't have a name then and
so they were scattered throughout his files—some called out-of-body
experiences, some called death-bed visions. Greyson helped Stevenson
sort through his files and find the near-death experiences. This was the
beginning of Greyson's NDE work, and though he also spent several
years working at the University of Michigan and in Connecticut, he
eventually came back to collaborate with Stevenson at UVa.

Greyson said that, as a psychiatrist, he frequently deals with patients
who tell him about bizarre and abnormal experiences. The spiritual
experiences reported by people near death may also be bizarre and
abnormal, but they are of a different order.

> Psychotic experiences make people terrified, more indrawn. The
> spiritual experiences make them expand, make them more produc-
> tive.[14]

And just as psychotic experiences are a phenomenon that requires scientific attention, near-death experiences occur, Greyson said—people
do have them—and for this reason alone, these experiences need to be
studied.

> These are things that definitely happen to people, and if you are a
> scientist you can't just push them aside and say, "I'm not going to
> look at that." You need to address it, learn more about it. I think this
> is part of our world, and scientists need to explore it.[15]

Greyson said that, as a scientist who has *not* had a near-death experience, he finds himself most affected by the accounts other scientists
give of their own near-death experiences—Eben Alexander, for instance, from chapter 8.

They are just blown away by it and struggle to try to make sense out of it. You can see in people like him [Alexander], why science doesn't want to let go. He can't deny it, yet he wants to try to make sense out of it.[16]

One case that was especially powerful for Greyson was from social worker Kimberly Clark Sharp,[17] who described in a book Greyson co-edited an account of a scientist who'd had a heart attack.

He and his wife were both hard scientists in the medical school. He had an NDE with his heart attack, and he asked Kim to help him talk to his wife about it. The three of them are sitting in the room. The man is telling the story, and he can't bear to look at his wife because he *knows* what she is going to think.

When Kim finally looks over at the man's wife, her mouth has dropped open. She says, "Stop a minute. Stop a minute."

She says to the man's wife, "What is going on with you?"

She says, "This happened to me ten years ago. I was afraid to tell anyone about it."[18]

With tears in his eyes, Greyson added,

We hear this over and over again. People have these experiences—they can't deny them—but they don't know what to do with them.[19]

At one point Greyson had said that he often chokes up when he speaks of people's near-death experiences. I asked him if the transformation of patients who've had NDEs hadn't also benefitted him, both as a human being and as a doctor. Nodding, he reminded me that Kenneth Ring speaks of this in his book *Lessons from the Light*, where he describes the near-death experience as a benign virus with powerful secondhand effects.

I felt I may have received some of those effects myself.

GROSSO: MYSTICISM

Michael Grosso and I spoke in the parapsychology research lab—a large room with a number of computers, one of them with a sign: Psi Practice Machine. I laughed at the idea of parapsychological drills, and then turned to a bulletin board where there was an example of a similar subtle skill: a spoon with the end of its bowl bent backward 45 degrees and the accompanying explanation "via psychokinesis." Someone, perhaps a visiting expert, had bent that spoon, using only the mind.

Grosso, as befits his current position—writer and retired teacher— was dressed in jeans. He coauthored the chapters on mysticism and genius in *Irreducible Mind,* and I could tell from our conversation that he has a passion for these subjects. In fact, he practically cut his teeth on them. From a Catholic background, Grosso had experiences of extrasensory perception as a child, experiences his mother not only acknowledged but talked about having herself.

Grosso's earliest experience of ESP involved a dream he had involving another child, a boy who lived on his block but whom, as Grosso put it, "I did not know and did not hang out with."

> I had a vivid dream . . . [in which] I saw this kid, Johnny, and he said, "Do you want to play handball?" This was completely out of my experience, because we never played handball [together]; we never hung out.
>
> The next morning I have breakfast, I step out onto the sidewalk, and there is Johnny, and he says, "Do you want to play handball?" First time.
>
> I was maybe eight, nine years old when this happened, and it stood out in my mind because the dream was so vivid and then I step outside and there's the kid—a virtual stranger. That was the only time we ever, ever played together. [20]

Years later, working on a PhD in philosophy at Columbia University, Grosso found that he couldn't talk about experiences of ESP, not to his professors and not even to his friends. One day in a conversation with a fellow graduate student, Grosso casually mentioned that he'd had this experience of ESP as a child. His friend's reaction was immediate and strong.

> He looked at me outraged and said, "But that is impossible. That would imply dualism!"
>
> That penetrated. That stuck in my mind. First of all the idea that this guy was telling me that my experience is impossible, I found outrageous and ridiculous. At the time I was reading R. D. Laing on the politics of experience, and the whole notion of the destruction of

an experience bothered me. It wasn't just the denial of my experience but the idea that his ideology—an assumption on his part—should be introduced in such a casually destructive way. That was a turning point.[21]

Shortly after, and also after receiving his degree, Grosso walked down the street from Columbia to the American Society of Psychical Research, which was also in New York City but might as well have been on another planet. Walking in cold, he had a two-hour conversation with the head of the Parapsychology Foundation—Karlis Osis, "a lovely man"—and when he got home that day, Grosso wrote a paper on Plato and the out-of-body experience.

I had written my dissertation on Plato. He defines philosophy as the practice of the soul separating from the body. I said, "That is what an out-of-body experience is." So, I put it together.[22]

Over the years, Grosso has taught courses in both philosophy and psychic phenomena, and this is, as he describes it, his life's work. He considers himself extremely fortunate to have grown up in a household where people spoke of ghosts and psychic experiences and where Padre Pio—a monk who lived most of his life with stigmata—was a fixture.

Padre Pio's books were lying around the house. Oddly enough, I still have some of those books. I had that great advantage, growing up: I never doubted my sanity. . . .

I actually taught a course in psychic phenomena. It was a very popular course. At one time, I had three sections. The students who took this course had stories, and one I'll never forget. A student came up to me after class one day and said, "My psych professor told me that if I took this course with you, it was going to ruin my life."

I asked him, "So, has your life been ruined?"

"No, not at all. That's why I'm telling you this."[23]

Grosso said he knew this psych professor, who wasn't especially angry or malevolent—just someone "thick-headed, with a shut mind." The message this man was putting out could have had an impact on Grosso's career, he said, "but it had no effect at all on my students."

TUCKER: REINCARNATION

Jim Tucker, who is associate professor of psychiatry and neurobehavioral sciences at UVa, looked every inch the child psychiatrist in his white shirt and tie. He is the team member now pursuing the research on cases suggestive of reincarnation, a topic that might never have come into his career path except for his wife. Tucker, a lapsed Southern Baptist, said he was respectful of the spiritual side of life while having nothing to do with it himself.

When he finished his psychiatric training, he went into private practice—by his description, "a typical practice," and then he met the woman he would marry.

> She was open to things like reincarnation and psychic abilities and areas that I had never explored. That got me curious and then . . . That's the official version. The slightly unofficial version is that my relationship with my wife opened me up in a way that is hard to put into words.
>
> A group of us were talking yesterday about how when people have had transcendental experiences, with meditation or whatever, they then see the world differently than people do who have not had that. Just having the relationship and being with her helped me be present. . . . It opened me up in a way that I hadn't been open before. [24]

With this burgeoning sense of openness, Tucker read one of Ian Stevenson's books on his cases suggestive of reincarnation and then noticed a newspaper article saying that Stevenson and Bruce Greyson had just received a research grant to look at the effects of near-death experiences on the lives of the people who'd had them. Tucker decided to call and see if they needed help interviewing patients—"just as a sideline hobby," he said, "along with my private practice, which was, frankly, not completely fulfilling." He added that most of his patients would improve, and some would improve quickly, but he saw one patient after another and the phone messages kept piling up. "It was a bit like being on a wheel." [25]

At this point Tucker had no real interest in reincarnation, but he was very much interested in the possibility of whether or not there was life after death. Ian Stevenson, however, then in his eighties, saw in Tucker another possibility: a potential successor. Stevenson invited the younger man to go on a trip to Asia to work with one of their colleagues on a few cases and, as Tucker put it, "one thing led to another." Tucker continued working as a child psychiatrist but he began to spend much of his energy investigating the possibility of reincarnation—and his view of consciousness no longer echoed his psychiatric training. He told me that it "makes sense" to him that the brain transmits rather than produces consciousness—"that consciousness originates from elsewhere."[26]

In the last chapter of his book, *Return to Life: Extraordinary Cases of Children Who Remember Past Lives*, Tucker writes extensively about the concept that consciousness has its origin separate from the brain's neuronal function. There he describes the world we live in as "a shared dream." By "dream," he means it is the creation of the mind. Tucker writes:

> I don't think there is our [material] world and then the *real* spiritual world. Our world is as real as it gets. It is created by Mind, but that is also true for other worlds. Existence grows out of consciousness.
> . . . I think we each have a larger part of us that transcends the individual dream—the individual lifetime—and continues to take part in creating other dreams, other lifetimes or worlds. . . . A larger aspect of each of us would carry over from one lifetime to the next.[27]

In the database Stevenson and Tucker collected, they coded for six personality or behavioral features (for example, attachment to wealth, generosity, criminality, etc.). They found that there is a statistically significant correlation between the presence of specific features in the previous personality and those the child exhibits in his current situation.

For Jim Tucker, the term "mind" is another way of saying consciousness—and in this respect, I was struck by the similarity between his views and those of Kashmir Shaivism, the philosophy I describe in chapter 6. In both cases, consciousness is seen as the substratum of everything.

After I finished my interviews with the scientists in the division, I was given a tour of the research laboratory and was able to be a subject in one of their experiments. The test I did was something like the one performed at Princeton to determine an individual's ability to change random number generator outcomes through the exercise of personal intention. While I found it fascinating to sit in a shielded room, staring at a black box, and creating an intention for the output of that box to shift, when the results of my session were computed, it was shown that this particular skill of parapsychology is not one that I possess.

I guess I'll stick to analyzing parapsychology—which is quite enough for me!

13

THE CONSCIOUSNESS–BRAIN
INTERFACE

Coming to the final chapter, we're left with many of the same questions we raised early in the book: *What is the interface between consciousness—or the mind—and the brain? What is the nature of the interaction between the mind and the brain?* Throughout this book we have been looking at the psychic and paranormal experiences individuals have reported having, experiences that from the bottom-up, materialist view of this mind–brain relationship—actually from their perspective, a brain–mind relationship—could not have happened.

These events *could not have happened*, and yet again and again we have seen researchers following rigorous scientific methods who demonstrate that such events did happen. The response of traditional science to this paranormal research is to ignore it. Because I am one of the individuals who have had such experiences, I am committed to finding another approach.

So, how do we map out an expanded scientific framework, a perspective that takes into account the otherwise inexplicable experiences that I and untold millions have had—in meditation, near death, of past lives, in silent communication with other minds, as a recipient of energy from healers, and on and on?

This entire area of experience, an anomaly to traditional science, is often brought together under the term "psi," short for "parapsychology"—"psychology" being the study of the mind and "para" meaning "beyond" or "abnormal." In this final chapter we explore parapsychology: how paranormal experiences might—possibly—be accounted for within a scientific model.

Nothing I say in this section is new. I have drawn on the research of many reputable scientists, including neuroscientists, quantum physicists, psychologists, and physicians as well as philosophers and spiritual seekers. My aim is to integrate and also to elucidate for myself and others the nature of consciousness. As a neuroscientist, I wish to adopt an understanding of the mind that encompasses my experiences of meditation.

When I employ the term "mind," I am including both the *Oxford English Dictionary* definition, "the element of a person that enables them to be aware of the world and their experiences, to think, and to feel; the faculty of consciousness and thought," and also those aspects of awareness—consciousness—that appear, from research presented in chapters 7, 10, and 11, to be capable of existing separately from the neuronal processes of the brain even while they interact with these processing functions.

The fact that I need to add to the dictionary definition of the mind in order to include aspects that I feel are essential to consciousness underscores the frustration I have felt in continuously trying to bridge two disparate philosophical frameworks—and my need to come up with a worldview that encompasses my own subjective reality. I have come to think that one way of understanding superconscious mental operations is to see the brain and its sense organs not as the source of all mental experience but as a filter. In other words, the brain and sense organs act as a filter for what we experience. This perspective, known for the last hundred years as the "filter theory," brings together some significant philosophical tenets shared by various mystical traditions over thousands of years.

THE FILTER THEORY

The filter theory was originally suggested in the late nineteenth century by psychologists William James and F. W. H. Myers, whose work I discuss in earlier chapters. This theory was their attempt to elucidate the relationship between the physical world and what we might call extracerebral consciousness, that is, consciousness that appears to extend beyond the limits of neural activity. In a lecture on the subject of objections to human immortality, James had this to say about the nature of consciousness:

> Suppose, for example, that the whole universe of material things— the furniture of earth and choir of heaven—should turn out to be a mere surface-veil of phenomena, hiding and keeping back the world of genuine realities. Such a supposition is foreign neither to common sense nor to philosophy. Common sense believes in realities behind the veil even too superstitiously; and idealistic philosophy declares the whole world of natural experience, as we get it, to be but a time-mask, shattering or refracting the one infinite Thought which is the sole reality into those millions of finite streams of consciousness known to us as our private selves.
>
> "Life, like a dome of many-colored glass, stains the white radiance of eternity."
>
> Suppose, now, that this were really so, and suppose, moreover, that the dome, opaque enough at all times to the full super-solar blaze, could at certain times and places grow less so, and let certain beams pierce through into this sublunary world. These beams would be so many finite rays, so to speak, of consciousness, and they would vary in quantity and quality as the opacity varied in degree. Only at particular times and places would it seem that, as a matter of fact, the veil of nature can grow thin and rupturable enough for such effects to occur. But in those places gleams, however finite and unsatisfying, of the absolute life of the universe, are from time to time vouchsafed. Glows of feeling, glimpses of insight, and streams of knowledge and perception float into our finite world.[1]

This, in its essence, is the filter theory. And what the brain filters out, as James is saying, is consciousness itself—a supremely expanded consciousness. Consciousness is seen to be self-existent, a vast and limitless entity that exists beyond time and space. Certainly, consciousness is not produced by or dependent upon the brain. Consciousness can be experienced by human beings, but typically in only a limited form. And the reason for this limitation is the brain itself—acting as a filter, a partial barrier, to a full experience of consciousness.

Though most scientists in the late 1800s and early 1900s considered that consciousness was a product of brain activity, James, Myers, and others felt that this alternative point of view was equally plausible and that it, in fact, explained the occurrence of supernormal states of consciousness.[2]

I first encountered the filter theory in the book *Irreducible Mind,* where Ed Kelly explains it in this way:

> James pointed out that to describe the mind as a function of the brain does not fully specify the character of the functional dependence. Physiologists routinely presume that the role of the brain is *productive,* the brain generating the mind in something like the way the teakettle generates steam, or the electric current flowing in a lamp generates light. But other forms of functional dependence exist which merit closer consideration. The true function of the brain might for example be *permissive,* like the trigger of a crossbow, or more importantly, *transmissive,* like an optical lens or a prism, or like the keys of a pipe organ (or perhaps, in more contemporary terms, like the receivers in our radios and televisions).[3]

In this apt paraphrase, Kelly points out what I find most intriguing in James's approach not only to his topic but also to his audience. In his own sweet way, this venerable psychologist is pointing out how our worldview can limit the way we perceive and understand reality. Having come up with one solution to a question, we tend to think that this is its only answer. When we take this answer into our culture, we lose the ability to step outside the box we have created for ourselves to see another perspective.

The danger with the scientific approach, which involves the careful accumulation of a body of knowledge that is built, one fact upon another, is that scientists can become trapped by their own view of science itself—the body of scientific knowledge. Thomas S. Kuhn, possibly the most influential philosopher of science in the twentieth century, has this to say about the behavior of scientists who are adherents of any accepted scientific theory:

> By themselves, they cannot and will not falsify that philosophical theory, for its defenders will do what we have already seen scientists doing when confronted by anomaly. They will devise numerous articulations and *ad hoc* modifications of their theory in order to eliminate any apparent conflict.[4]

This is what was done with Newton's theory for decades when, in experiment after experiment, the results did not fit the generally accepted framework. That framework was patched, the formulas were modified, until, as Kuhn describes, a scientific revolution occurred. In this case, quantum mechanics emerged.

Throughout the course of research for this book, I have been disheartened to find how few of my colleagues in neuroscience are willing to question the materialistic paradigm. For support I found just a few scientists—whether they be in neuroscience, physics, psychology, medicine—who entertain the veracity of parapsychological experience. I must say that I have an almost familial sense of connection with those scientific colleagues who do.

The next step in considering the filter theory is to ask why the human organism might develop a means of limiting its sensory input. Why would the brain act as a filter to keep out a greater, conscious reality? The French philosopher Henry Bergson, a friend to James with an interest in psychology, the brain, and also paranormal phenomena, devised an answer. Though Bergson was no scientist, I am intrigued by his theory. He describes the brain's filter mechanism as an adaptive strategy to allow us to attend to the most relevant stimuli in our immediate environment. He sees the brain as a utilitarian function to support a successful normal life—as a means for us to optimize our physical survival. This filter mechanism of the brain allows into our consciousness only the information that is useful for our survival. In this way, we are not flooded with irrelevant information that would be both distracting and overwhelming in its content.[5] As another of the early proponents of the filter theory, the philosopher and author Aldous Huxley, writes:

> To make biological survival possible, Mind-at-Large has to be funneled through the reducing valve of the brain and nervous system. What comes out at the other end is a measly trickle of the kind of consciousness that will help us stay alive on the surface of this particular planet.[6]

If there is, indeed, a filter mechanism in place, the next question that comes up for me is what kind of interaction happens through that filter between the greater mind and the brain? William James uses a variety of verbs when he speaks of the processes of the brain in relation to consciousness. He sees the brain as "straining, sifting, canalizing, limiting, and individualizing" the vast consciousness that exists beyond it.[7]

I can see a translation of at least part of his description to the physical sciences. For instance, the idea of "limiting" and "individualizing" can be expressed by the action of the pigment within the visual system of the human retina, which is capable of receiving inputs from only a specific set of wavelengths. Thus, some people are "blind" to color or to certain colors, and all human beings perceive a smaller color spectrum than certain insects, like bees, which are able to take in the ultraviolet wavelengths that we're unable to see. The same is true of hearing, which often diminishes with age and which varies between species, with humans hearing lower wavelengths in the audio spectrum than do dogs and cats and not hearing the higher frequencies that our pets have no choice but to take in. This can also be said of the sense of smell, for which humans have 5 million olfactory receptors in the nose and dogs have 220 million.

There is a specifically limiting factor that we discuss in chapter 4, suggested by the experimental psychologist Daniel Broadbent in his filter model of attention. Simply speaking, Broadbent suggests that our brains have a limited ability to process the sensory information coming in, and so our attention selectively filters it—"filters" being his word.[8]

So, in all these ways, the neuronal apparatus of our brain can be said to "limit" or "individualize" what we perceive from the whole of what is available to be perceived.

The brain also "canalizes" information—it establishes particular canals or channels through which information flows—in that it employs sensors to perceive specific aspects of the energy spectrum. This is one way to think of the eye, the ear, the receptors of the skin, and so on. Further, each of us individualizes the sensory information we receive in that we are each attuned—through our habits, interests, and past experience, and also through the varied strengths of our sensory organs—to perceive certain aspects of the environment and not others. For instance, I notice whenever Pachelbel's *Canon* comes on the radio, whereas my friend, who isn't familiar with this piece of music, does not perceive it. Pachelbel's *Canon* is to me a delight and to my friend, merely background noise. I have another friend who smoked between her midteens and midtwenties and has had, ever since, a diminished capacity to perceive odors. A scent that might be overpowering to one person, this friend doesn't smell at all.

Where James speaks of the brain as "sifting" and "straining" the information that comes in, I think he might be referring to psi experiences. Many, probably most, of us have had an experience in which we've had a strong thought about a particular person and then, shortly after, that very person telephones or we encounter him or her somewhere. Another instance, less common but more carefully documented, is when someone has a strong image of a loved one or friend, and finds out later that it was in that very moment that the envisioned person died.[9] What such experiences demonstrate to me is that this kind of subtle information is available, and only in certain instances does the mind that sifts and strains information let it through to us.

The questions that most interest me, of course, are these that go beyond the physical senses and into the higher regions of consciousness that we have explored throughout this book, experiences of meditation, near death, with extrasensory perception, and so on. F. W. H. Myers, also a psychologist, speculates that there is a permeable boundary between our everyday awareness and these higher regions of consciousness, with the degree of permeability varying from person to person. This would mean that the psychophysical threshold an individual must cross—that is, the conditions under which it is possible for a particular mind to access levels of consciousness or capacities that are far greater than those of which that mind is typically aware—is different for various people.[10] I'd like to add, from my own observation, that this moving threshold can change for any one individual from one moment to the next. Some mornings when I meditate, I move from my filtered awareness quite easily into a state where I can feel the subtle energies moving inside me, a movement that is associated with feelings of exquisite bliss or love. On other mornings, I am struggling with that filter; it's all I can do to direct my focus to my breath or the mantra.

ANOTHER LENS FOR THE FILTER THEORY

While I was in Virginia, Ed Kelly recommended a book he'd recently read that draws some interesting parallels between a wide range of philosophical perspectives on mystical experiences. I read this book—

Mystical Encounters with the Natural World by Paul Marshall, a contemporary philosopher—and found it extremely helpful. Marshall had summarized these modern philosophers in a way that made their thinking accessible to me as a scientist, and he also showed the clear influence of Platonic and Indian philosophy on modern concepts of mind–body interactions. When I thanked Kelly for the reference, he arranged for me to meet Marshall on a teaching trip I took to Europe a few months later.

This is how I was able to sit down with this angular, unassuming, and quintessentially brilliant scholar in a café in Nottingham, England, to talk over our respective academic backgrounds and our shared interest in mysticism. Like me, he had been interested in experimental science at an early age. For me it was that gopher; for Marshall, at the age of thirteen, it was chemistry and a fascination with the idea that everything in the universe is made of about a hundred elements and they themselves of just a few elementary particles in various quantities and configurations. He said that he became a science-bore, "educating those around me," and did a lot of home experimentation "that was sometimes quite explosive and destructive towards home furnishings." He had understanding parents, he said. Even as a boy, however, his attention wasn't on hard science alone.

> At the same time I read about out-of-body experiences in my mother's women's magazines, and I thought, *This is interesting.* I tried to induce experiences like that in myself. I started engaging in deep relaxation before going to bed, in an attempt to induce these experiences. I did this for several months. [11]

Nothing happened, so the boy gave up his experiments—but he didn't let go of the habit he'd developed of deeply relaxing each night before going to sleep. With no particular goal in mind, he continued this deep relaxation and then, when Marshall was in his twenties, one night he had an out-of-body experience.

> One night while sleeping, I found myself looking down on my sleeping face, my eyes closed, about a foot above my face. There was a light in the room behind me, and I felt that if I looked into that light I would wake up. That's what happened. I found myself bending toward the light and woke up. So, I was surprised and yet I wasn't

surprised, because I'd been interested in this possibility many years before. I think those years of deep relaxation possibly were some kind of unthought-out meditative practice.[12]

Soon after this, he had a strong mystical experience while asleep. When he awoke, he "was able to recall in fragmentary fashion an experience of expansive knowledge, vision, unity, and love."[13] Marshall had done his undergraduate work in chemistry and physics, and at this point he embarked on several years of research in the philosophy of science and in religious traditions, attempting to come to an intellectual understanding of his experience. His research and contemplation of the mind–body question led him to write his first book, *The Living Mirror: Images of Reality in Science and Mysticism*. In it, Marshall proposes that experience cannot be reduced to material bodies and processes alone.

In his second book, *Mystical Encounters*, Marshall presents the filter theory in a philosophical context, speaking of it as "panpsychic idealism." In short, the term names a worldview that sees consciousness as existing in all aspects of the universe (panpsychism) and all these aspects as being a manifestation of consciousness (idealism). The first takes mind into all matter, and the second makes mind primary. Marshall writes:

> Panpsychism attributes mental properties, sentience, consciousness, protoconsciousness, feeling, or experience to the individual constituents or units of nature, the bits and pieces that compose the world.[14]

Marshall, probably more than any other commentator, makes clear how the filter theory can contain and explain mystical experience:

> The contents of ordinary consciousness are "selected" or "filtered" from the subliminal [extracerebral or transcendent] consciousness, but if the filtering becomes less efficient or changes its operation, previously excluded contents emerge [into awareness], giving rise to non-ordinary experiences, including mystical experiences.[15]

This means that when events disrupt an individual's normal brain processes, the shift can reduce the brain's filtering mechanism and, in this way, precipitate a state of expanded consciousness, a mystical experience.[16] It could be that this dynamic explains the opening up of extrasensory experience when a patient is near death, or the experience of expanded perception when someone is fasting or has been meditating or otherwise emptying the mind of thought for a long period of time.

But if access to higher consciousness is simply a matter of reducing one's "filter" so that one can take in more of a vast potential, then why do various people report strikingly different experiences of that potential? If a veil simply lifted to give one direct access to additional experiential knowledge, then that knowledge would be consistent, no? When scholars from any discipline examine mystical experiences and other telepathic and extrasensory phenomena, they note that there appears to be a spectrum of perceptions "typical" to the experience and reported by many, if not most, subjects. After an experience of expanded consciousness, subjects will often say that they felt supremely comfortable or felt they had come home; they talk about having expanded understanding; and they often report heightened sense perception, especially seeing colors more vividly. Other aspects of the experience seem to be affected by the person's memory or cultural context. For example, atheists might call their experience one of unity consciousness while a Christian or Hindu might call it God. In the same vein, it has been observed in scientific testing that telepathic experiences often have a central element of truth but may also include erroneous information.[17]

This would explain both the commonalities and the variations between the experiences of various mystics regarding the body's subtle terrain as it's perceived in meditation (some yogic texts say there are seven chakras; others list more) or the variations between near-death experiences according to the cultural background or the perceptual depth of the experiencers. To make this idea easier to grasp, Marshall came up with a model to show potential stages in the perception of mystical or extracerebral experiences. As you see in figure 13.1,[18] the perception starts in a transpersonal domain (extracerebral consciousness) and moves to the personal domain (ordinary consciousness).

Notice that in this model there are three points of selection to account for differences in the final reported experience—an individual's ability to take in a subtle experience, the way that individual "processes" or understands the experience, and the way he holds it in his waking awareness.

What most interests me in this model is its implication that there might be a worldview that supports both the experience of mystical phenomena *and* the experience of the workaday world. In his discus-

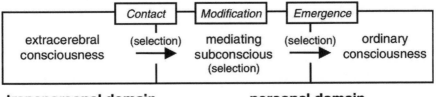

Figure 13.1.   A model to show potential stages in the perception of mystical or extracerebral experiences. The perception starts in a transpersonal domain (extracerebral consciousness) and moves to the personal domain (ordinary consciousness). P. Marshall, *Mystical Encounters with the Natural World*, Oxford, UK: Oxford University Press, 2005, figure 8.1, p. 240. Reprinted by permission of Oxford University Press (www.oup.com).

sions Marshall employs, of course, the terminology of his own academic discipline, religious studies, which views our topic as metaphysics, the study of the nature of reality. This whole book has been about metaphysics, but, because I approach our subject matter as a neuroscientist and yogi, I've never yet used the term. In metaphysics, one of the main issues involves the question of duality or even plurality—is there one fundamental entity in the universe, or are there two, or many? Are mind and body essentially one, or are they two separate entities? Are God and the universe separate, or are they essentially expressions of the same reality?

Paul Marshall suggests that a worldview that includes mystical phenomena would need to view mind/consciousness/experience as a part of existence.[19] Fundamentally, it's all one. In philosophical terms, this is called a "monistic" worldview, as opposed to a "dualistic" worldview, by which mind and matter are seen as separate entities. Marshall also indicates that a worldview that attributes mental capacities, like consciousness or experience, to all the components of the universe also supports mystical experience. Even rocks and the individual atoms in those rocks have a limited form of consciousness. This is "panpsychism."[20] Finally, Marshall notes that of all monistic philosophies, those that take mind to be more fundamental than matter have the most clear and extensive links with mysticism. These are called "idealist monistic" philosophies, and I was pleased to find that Kashmir Shaivism, the philosophy that I discuss in chapter 6 and which my own spiritual teacher felt was the closest to his experiential understanding of reality, is considered by Marshall to be the prime example of idealist monism. He says:

> The pre-eminent example of idealist ontology integrated with mystical soteriology is perhaps the "realistic idealism" of nondual Kashmir Shaivism, which is theistic as well as idealist. The spiritual practitioner realizes total immersion of self and world in the divine consciousness of the supreme deity Shiva.[21]

While I was at UVa, Ed Kelly reminded me that, in his later years, William James refined his theory of mind–brain interactions to include a concept of panpsychism similar to what had been proposed by many of India's ninth- to thirteenth-century philosophers—Vasugupta, Abhinavagupta, Kshemaraja, and others of the Kashmir Shaivism tradition. It is a similar framework to what the philosopher David Chalmers proposes in the twenty-first century related to solving the "hard problem" of how conscious experience could emerge from neural processing (see chapter 6). Chalmers's view is that there is some sort of consciousness in all aspects of the universe, down to the proto-consciousness of an atom or a subatomic particle.

Such theories of panpsychism suggest there is a basic level of "awareness," though it may be primitive, that is an essential part of even simple material objects.[22] Some scholars propose that this rudimentary consciousness evolves into more complex forms as organisms evolve in complexity. Kelly and his colleagues consider such frameworks to be bottom-up—to be saying that the mind comes out of the body—and they propose an alternative top-down interpretation that involves the co-evolution of mind and matter. Kelly suggests that the increasing complexity of organisms through evolution allows for a more complex expression of the powers associated with the vast consciousness that is at the foundation of the universe.[23] In other words, though the expression is increasingly complex, consciousness itself remains the same.

These ideas are similar to the concepts of Kashmir Shaivism that we explore in chapter 6. For instance, the names of God—of which there are many thousands—include Awareness (*Vimarsha*) and Consciousness (*Cit*). As well, consciousness is thought to take the form of every aspect of the universe. In other words, there is nothing in the world that is *not* consciousness. My first teacher often quoted a seminal teaching of Kashmir Shaivism that expresses this quite succinctly: "Nothing exists that is not Shiva."[24]

There is another aspect of panpsychism that strikes me as pure Kashmir Shaivism, one suggested by James, who feels that humanity has a higher conscious life apart from our brain processing and of which we are largely unaware. He writes,

> The drift of all the evidence we have seems to me to sweep us very strongly toward the belief in some form of superhuman life with which we may, unknown to ourselves, be coconscious.[25]

By "co-conscious," I think James is saying that we can be both at our own level of consciousness and also at the level of this "superhuman life." James suggests that this higher conscious life has a complex structure of its own, like a nested hierarchy of continually greater integration of the lower levels of consciousness.[26] This is similar to the way the *tattvas*, the levels of creation, are described by Kashmir Shaivism—and, incidentally, by most Indian philosophies, including Vedanta, Samkhya, and so on. We discuss *tattvas* in chapter 6, quoting a verse of the *Pratyabhijna-hrdayam* that describes infinite consciousness descending from its expanded state to become the mind. This descent is said to move through specific levels of decreasing subtlety—or increasing subtlety, if you view the progression, as James did, from material to subtle. The Shaivites see these *tattvas* not as causal—one creating the next, which creates the next, and so on—but as co-existing, co-enfolded, all eternal.

There is a Western concept that describes the philosophy of Kashmir Shaivism more fully than "panpsychism"—which is saying that the mind, or soul, is in everything—and that is "panentheism," which says that God is in everything. Panentheism is a term used by two contemporary scholars of philosophy and religion, Charles Hartshorne and William L. Reese, in their anthology entitled *Philosophers Speak of God,* in which they bring together writings from some of the world's greatest philosophers and theologians, including those of Kashmir Shaivism.[27] The editors use the term "panentheism" to describe a view they believe is foundational among these theologians. While "pantheism" sees the Divine as the same as the universe, "panentheism" means, literally, "all-in-God." In this view, the Divine interpenetrates every part of the material world and, in addition, timelessly extends beyond it.

The Divine is, thus, simultaneously immanent (interpenetrating the universe) and transcendent (beyond the universe). Kelly describes this view as follows:

> Panentheism's supreme being paradoxically absorbs into itself, or aspects of itself, the various ultimate polarities that previous theisms and pantheisms have projected onto their conceptions of God in a more one-sided manner—polarities such as eternal *vs.* temporal, being *vs.* becoming, spiritual *vs.* corporeal, simple *vs.* compound, necessary *vs.* contingent, absolute *vs.* relative, potential *vs.* actual, and one *vs.* many. Their panentheistic God is . . . conceived as both eternal *and* temporal, conscious, knowing of the world, and world-inclusive. . . . [It] fills the world, as in pantheism, but there is also something left over, as in theism. God thus is to the world roughly as we are to our bodies. . . . [28]

This is an excellent approximation of the Shaivite view. To explain the difference, I must come back to that verse my teacher so often quoted: "Nothing exists that is not Shiva." In true panentheism, nothing is left over. God is both our body and our awareness of our body.

In another, but similar, vein, the idealist philosophy of Timothy Sprigge[29] is one that Paul Marshall sees as a thorough, sophisticated, and appropriate framework for understanding what happens during a mystical experience. Marshall describes it in this way:

> The consciousness associated with the universe can be regarded as a "super-consciousness" that contains the universe, holding all the smaller consciousnesses, together in a unity. Ordinarily we are not aware of the unity, and we suffer from the illusion of separateness. [30]

In a mystical experience, the illusion of separation lifts; we experience not only the enormous relief of this but we suddenly have direct access to the object that is before us—we can perceive the object as it is in itself, independent of our own memories of it and concepts about it. Marshall terms this clarity "noumenal consciousness itself," adding,

> The mystic really does make contact with consciousness in the world at large. [31]

In figure 13.2, Marshall creates an image of how this tenet of idealist philosophy can be represented in terms of our understanding of reality. To avoid the "hard problem"—the leap a materialist perspective necessitates when stepping from the physical brain to the contents and experiences of the mind—Marshall suggests that we see everything as the contents of the great mind. In his diagram, he depicts two people seeing a tree and processing the image of the tree in their brains. Marshall's idea is that everything in the diagram—including each person's sense organs and brain and the tree itself—exists within the noumenal contents of the great mind.

Causal chains of events proceed within the mind, leading from the noumenal tree, through the noumenal sense organs, to the noumenal brain, where a representation of the tree is pieced together as a special kind of experiential content, a phenomenal (object of the senses) experience. Marshall says:

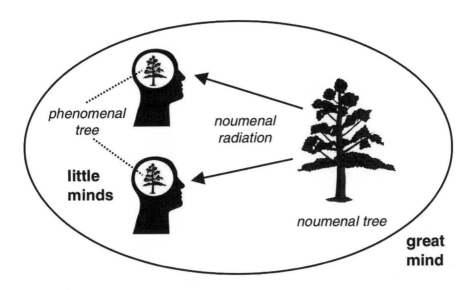

Figure 13.2. Diagram depicting two people seeing a tree and processing the image of the tree in their brains. Everything in the diagram—including each person's sense organs and brain and the tree itself—exists within the noumenal contents of the great mind. P. Marshall, *Mystical Encounters with the Natural World*, Oxford UK: Oxford University Press, 2005, figure 8.4, p. 264. Reprinted by permission of Oxford University Press (www.oup.com).

Thus, experience is not created by the brain, for the entire universe is experience. Rather, brains are special sites in the universe at which experience takes on phenomenal characteristics. . . . There is not just one great mind with its noumenal and phenomenal contents but a plurality of similar minds with their cosmic contents organized from centres of experience. In effect, each one of us is individually endowed with the great mind and its contents. . . . The minds differ by expressing the universe from their individual vantage points. They can do so because they are all manifestations of a common, unifying ground.[32]

The word "noumenal," which we use so rarely in modern culture, has a wonderful connotation of "thatness" or "suchness"—again, concepts we rarely encounter. Such a perspective demonstrates not only that we create our own worlds but *how* we create those worlds—by holding within ourselves a concept of what we experience that is specific to ourselves. We can do this, Marshall says, because we are each contained within the great mind.

Once again, I find an interesting connection between Western philosophical thought and Shaivite scripture. Marshall posits the existence of a great mind that contains the little minds of each one of us. He suggests that each little mind experiences the universe from its own vantage point, making of sensory experiences whatever it will. There are parallels between this view and verse 3 of the *Pratyabhijna-hrdayam*:

That [Consciousness] becomes diverse because of the division of reciprocally adapted objects and subjects.[33]

In other words, as Supreme Consciousness (Marshall's "great mind") contracts through the process of creation (the *tattvas* we discuss in chapter 6), all the individual little minds along with all the objects of the universe are created. The little minds are made of the same Consciousness as the great mind but exist at a lower *tattva*. Each little mind is limited to a single locus of being—and perceives the objects of the universe from its own perspective, as a subject. Thus each one of us in seeing a tree has a different experience and assessment of that tree— even though the tree and all of our little minds exist within the framework of one great mind. That is one level of the adaptation the *sutra* speaks of—the fact that each of us responds differently to a single object. The other, "reciprocal" level of adaptation is that the object itself can change because of the way a subject perceives it. Marshall doesn't hint at this reciprocity, but it has been demonstrated by research we discuss later in this chapter.

The simplest mystical experiences—a feeling of unconditional joy, a sense of profound connection—can occur, Marshall suggests, when the brain's filter has only moderately opened. There is simply a relaxation of the clear distinctions between oneself and others, so that the self and body are felt to be part of a greater stream of consciousness or being. This brings a sense of joy and clarity, yet the noumenal background of consciousness is not strongly felt. An experience of such profundity comes, Marshall suggests, with greater shift in the filter:

> In the more developed cases, the phenomenal stream begins to reveal its noumenal bedrock, bringing luminous transfigurations of phenomenal contents, more advanced feelings of unity, a growing sense of meaning and knowledge, significantly altered time-experience, and so forth. In the profoundest cases, the noumenal background comes to the fore, blotting out phenomenal experience, resting alongside it, or containing it.[34]

Once persons experience all-encompassing unity, knowledge, and vision, once they know eternity and universal love, they have, as Marshall puts it, "accessed the pellucid depths" of their own minds. The filters have come off.

We have spoken of ways in which current neuroscience research assumes a sort of brain process that acts as a filter and is always in effect, allowing only certain information to emerge into conscious awareness. There are some other ways that I find interesting as well. Our normal conscious experience happens in relation to a complex and mainly unseen background of neural activity, which allows automatic regulation of most physiological processes: blood pressure, blood sugar levels, and the like. What has been proposed by James, Myers, and many recent scholars is that conscious experience includes much, much more. In describing this phenomenon, Kelly uses a metaphor from Myers that I particularly love. Myers speaks of the vital bodily functions as an "infrared" extension of the spectrum of our everyday conscious experience. These are subconscious, below the lowest frequency—red—that we can perceive on the color spectrum. The more interesting and less frequently examined part of what is available to our experience, he calls the "ultraviolet" extension. This is the super-conscious level of experience, which he has chosen to represent by the higher than the highest frequency—violet—that we perceive on the spectrum.[35]

ACCESSING HIGHER LEVELS OF CONSCIOUSNESS

Two of the metaphors often used to describe gaining access to higher levels of consciousness are the lowering of a mechanical threshold (as in the locks of a canal) or the opening or closing of a valve (like the water tap). These may describe the mystical experiences of some, but Kelly thinks, for the most part, the images are simplistic. What happens, he suggests, is something much more complex,

> something more akin to an overall change in "permeability" or "tuning," which provides entryway or access to these normally inaccessible subliminal capacities and contents. *These "openings" clearly must be tied, in ways we presently do not understand, to functional states of the brain.*[36]

Kelly suggests that what might give individuals the capability to make incursions into higher levels of consciousness is an alteration in their brain function—an alteration through some not yet elucidated process of resonance between higher levels of consciousness and the brain.[37] He quotes Edward Carpenter, a British intellectual, mystical thinker, and social commentator and contemporary of James and Myers who had also had mystical experiences, describing a key that might access these regions beyond normal consciousness:

> Of all the hard facts of Science . . . I know of none more solid and fundamental than the fact that if you inhibit thought (and persevere) you come at length to a region of consciousness below or behind thought, and different from ordinary thought in its nature and character—a consciousness of quasi-universal quality and a realization of an altogether vaster self than that to which we are accustomed.[38]

The process Carpenter describes mirrors the mystical teachings from many traditions, including from India, and is considered crucial to opening the mind to higher levels of awareness. For example, in the first *sutras* of the well-known *Yoga Sutras* of Patanjali, written about two thousand years ago, it is stated:

Yogash chitta vritti nirodhah. Tada drashtuh svarupe avasthanam. [39]

I translate the *sutra* in this way: "Yoga is the stilling of the mind. Then the Seer dwells in his own true nature."

PANPSYCHIC IDEALISM VERSUS MATERIALISM

In considering the filter theory and the theoretical framework for it that's outlined above, one question I think could be asked is whether or not it explains human experience. By this I mean *all* of human experience, both our everyday experiences and the super-normal experiences of which there have been many reports. If you were to choose between the filter theory and the materialist framework, what I have been calling "bottom-up"—the idea that the brain produces all mental activity—which of them seems a better fit for humanity?

In the early 1900s William James noted that the filter theory and its general framework are compatible with the facts generally used to support the materialist model. For example, the act of thinking is, indeed, a function of the brain. The work summarized in chapter 4 on the consequences of a stroke, brain tumor, or traumatic brain injury indicates that without activity in the appropriate neurons, people typically have difficulty perceiving and understanding the world around them in an integrated way. The brain's role in thought does not mean, however, that the brain is the *only* source of thought. One proposal we have discussed is that when an individual's normal brain processes are disrupted—in a coma, near death, or in meditation—this very shift can reduce the brain's filtering mechanism and, in this way, allow the mind to have an extrasensory experience of the expanded consciousness that is always present, but is usually unperceived.

In explaining this filter theory, James said it was superior to the materialist model because it accounts for some data, clearly observable in psychical research, that are inexplicable if you hold that all consciousness arises from the brain.

Ed Kelly adds to this discussion the observation that the power of the filter theory is not its marked superiority in explaining any single phenomenon, but its creation of a coherent scheme for interpreting all of the observed phenomena. This panentheistic theory takes into account the lucid memory at a time of brain inactivity associated with near-death experiences, the accurate memories of another lifetime in cases suggestive of reincarnation, the inexplicable power and suddenness of mystical experiences, and in psychic experiences, the implied interconnections between individuals with no physical links. [40]

Only such a theory explains these events that have been demonstrated, these connections that have been shown, and, in case after case, have had no explanation on the physical level.

Earlier in this book I presented what I believe is extensive and carefully documented evidence to support the concept of a consciousness that exists beyond the bounds of brain activity. James writes that the existence of a consciousness beyond our ordinary state is seen in a number of contexts, including

> profound mystical experiences, in which the everyday self opens up, widens or expands, and becomes at least temporarily identified with some larger, wiser, and benign self hidden within. [41]

The mystical traditions are typically in agreement on two suppositions: first, that the greater consciousness is within us and, secondly, that through the mystical experience, we can recognize that this consciousness has been within us all along. In Kashmir Shaivism, "recognition" is a technical term for this realization, this remembrance; the name *Pratyabhijna-hrdayam*, a text I frequently quote, translates as *The Heart of Recognition*.

MIND–BRAIN INTERACTIONS AND QUANTUM MECHANICS

The theories of mind–brain interactions I've discussed so far, coming from the psychological and philosophical perspectives, are interesting— yet I can't help but feel they're incomplete. These are strokes with a broad brush, and as a neuroscientist, I want detail, not just metaphor but specifics. How does consciousness interact with the brain? The physicist Henry P. Stapp, whose groundbreaking work in quantum mechanics we explore in chapter 6, provides just such a model in his recent writings. He explores how quantum mechanics, which includes within its framework interactions of both the mind and the physical universe, accounts for mystical and psi phenomena whereas classical or Newtonian physics does not.

In his discussion of the inadequacy of Newtonian physics to explain mind–brain connections, Stapp quotes John Tyndall, a nineteenth-century physicist who recognized this problem about a century and a half ago:

> We can trace the development of a nervous system and correlate it with the parallel phenomena of sensation and thought. We see with undoubting certainty that they go hand in hand. But we try to soar in a vacuum the moment we seek to comprehend the connection between them. . . . Man the object is separated by an impassible gulf from man the subject. There is no motor energy in intellect to carry it without logical rupture from the one to the other.[42]

The dilemma—the vacuum that Tyndall laments—is created because Newtonian physics does not include in its description of the universe the concept of "mind." As I mention earlier, most neuroscientists deal with this omission by adhering to what Karl Popper describes as the stance of "promissory materialism." This is the belief that if one keeps at it long enough, the principles of Newtonian physics will lead to an understanding of the mind and consciousness. It has, however, not yet done so.[43]

Stapp asks whether

> given the postulated existence of these anomalous [psi] happenings, they can be comprehended within an appropriately elaborated version of contemporary quantum mechanics.[44]

One of the key differences between quantum and Newtonian physics is that to Newton's atom-based theories, quantum physics adds the observer. The original formulators of quantum theory often considered the boundary between the two parts of the theory to be located between the external measuring device and what is being measured. In other words, the way the observer decides to perform the experiment (what type of measuring device is used), will affect its outcome—will determine, for instance, whether light is observed as a wave or a particle. Stapp suggests that this boundary can be pushed toward the observer in order to include the observer's mental process. Stapp proposes that quantum physics' framework be expanded to include, specifically, the interface between the observer's mind and physical brain.

> The problem of reconciling these two disparate aspects of our understanding of the world thereby gets shifted to the place where it naturally belongs: the mind–brain interface. [45]

So, a key feature of quantum theory is that, instead of assuming that our perceptual realities are only a result of the physical properties of the universe and the sensory stimuli affecting the brain processes—that is, a bottom-up framework of mind–brain interaction—quantum theory considers that our mental processes allow us to dynamically participate in decisions related to our actions. Through top-down processing, we engage in the creation of our future. Henry Stapp says,

> The conscious mind probes and thereby influences the brain, rather than being controlled by it. . . .
>   This ontological separateness of our human mental qualities from the atom-based aspects of reality is also an essential part of John von Neumann's logically and mathematically rigorous formulation of quantum mechanics, both as spelled out by his words, and also as deduced from his analysis of the process of measurement. [46]

Von Neumann, one of the original formulators of quantum physics, postulated that the mental aspect of the discipline consists of the "free choices" the experimenter makes in choosing which actions to perform. According to Stapp, Von Neumann says that any observation we might make as human beings—including, of course, *all* scientific experiments—contains three distinct stages or levels, which he names processes 1, 2, and 3. At stages 1 and 3 certain choices are made.

> Each such choice picks out, in a way not determined by the quantum dynamical rules, some particular *possible* experience from a smeared out continuum of potential future experiences. [47]

Experience is created by what Von Neumann calls process 2.

According to realistically interpreted orthodox quantum theory, the world of tables and chairs and other atomically constituted macroscopic objects is considered to be fully quantum mechanical. But that means that, in spite of its classical material appearance, the macroscopic physical world is "really" a bundle of potentialities pertaining to what will appear to observers if someone *actually looks. Perceivable properties* become actual properties only insofar as perceptions actualize them.[48]

Observational activities—including the decision to make a particular observation, to perform an experiment, to ask a problem question, to notice certain behaviors—are all process 1. The specific responses given to these by nature are process 3. If the answer is yes, observers experience the physical property they are asking about, and

the quantum state of the universe "collapses" to the part of itself that is compatible with the existence of that physical property.[49]

If the answer is no,

it is accompanied by a reduction of the physically described state of the universe to the part of itself that definitely does not have the property in question, but with no associated experience.[50]

Stapp explains the mysteries of what is proposed to happen in a universe of quantum physics when we make a choice to observe a particular event, but ends with a question:

An essential feature of this process of observation is that the observer-chosen property is something that the system being observed definitely possesses *after* a positive response, but may not have possessed *before* the process was initiated. For example, the quantum state of an observed system before the observation [the observer's decision to observe is process 1] might be represented by a physical system that is spread out over a large spatial region, like a wave [process 2], whereas after the positive response the state might be confined to a tiny atom-sized region [process 3]. Such a "collapse of the quantum state" provides a resolution of the famous "wave-particle duality" problem. But it does so at the expense of requiring an instantaneous change over a large region of space at a single instant of time: most of the large region occupied by the "wave" that represents the system being studied suddenly becomes no longer occupied by that system. Thus if one tries to go beyond mere practical utility, puzzles arise pertaining to these sudden instantaneous collapses. Are they really happening in some objectively existing sense, or are they mere artifacts of our own theoretical invention?[51]

In this more recent work in quantum mechanics about the paradox of whether light—or a mass of electrons, for that matter—constitutes a wave or a particle, the answer seems to be clear: it depends on our question. It depends on what we're looking for. It depends on how we perform the experiment. Paradoxically, those electrons are typically a probability cloud until we ask a specific question about their location; then they collapse into a particular point in space.

Von Neumann calls the mental aspect of quantum theory—process 1, the observer—the abstract ego. This mental aspect could be considered the structure of our conscious experiences and is considered distinct from the atomically constituted physical world. Yet, Stapp postulates, each abstract ego has, according to the orthodox quantum theory, a dynamic link to its associated physical brain.

Stapp suggests that this connection between the observers' observational activities and their physical brain provides an answer to Tyndall's expressed problem of the lack of connection between brain and mind:

> Thus Tyndall's "impassible gulf" between "man as *object*" and "man as *subject*" was bridged by rigorous quantum mathematics. Von Neumann converted what had originally been offered as a mere practical tool into a rationally coherent putative description of a dynamically integrated psychophysical reality. . . .
>
> Thus quantum mechanics, in its orthodox form, is not simply a theory of a world made of atomic constituents. It is basically a theory of *"the multifold aspects of our experience"* and their connections to each other via atomically constituted physically described brains—which are, in turn, connected to each other via other parts of the atomically described world.[52]

Stapp reminds us that within quantum theory's framework, there is room not only for the elements of the physical world but also for the consciousness and intentionality that acts upon it.

Because of my own background and interests, I am particularly intrigued by this question of how the conscious mind exerts control over the material brain to carry out its intentions. The importance of right intention is something I seem to have been born knowing, and most of what I value in my life has come to fruition for me because I put forward the effort to make it happen. Not everyone I meet has this gift, and some people I know have developed the capacity over time. It's never made sense to me that focus and will power are functions of the brain, and Stapp has now offered a model for how the mind itself might be in control of such questions.

Stapp notes that, according to quantum theory, our minds can have effective control over our brain processing when process 1 is an either/or question and process 3 is limited to only one response. This can occur with an either/or question, according to the mathematical formulae, when the initial chosen answer—often the easiest to get right—is followed by a sufficiently rapid sequence of the same question. Stapp says

> in that case the observer becomes empowered, by his own free choices of what property to probe, *and when to probe it*, to hold stably in place a brain activity that otherwise would quickly fade away.[53]

This is known in quantum physics as the Quantum Zeno effect. For anyone interested in greater detail, in his writings Stapp goes through the logic and mathematics that support this conclusion.

You may ask how the Quantum Zeno effect might be applied in human terms. Stapp uses the example of our initiating an action, let's say, reaching for a glass. An accurate reach requires precisely timed activation of neurons in the brain with impulses being sent to the appropriate arm muscles. Carrying out this action successfully requires creating a stable neural processing state and sustaining that state until the end of the activation of the motor commands. Stapp adds:

> The role of the observer is thus to choose, on the basis of his or her mentally felt reasons and values, what to attend to, and how effortfully to attend to it. These choices effectively select from the huge mass of existing potentialities a sequence of classically describable observations that, to the extent that quantum effects are unimportant, will conform to the predictions of classical physics. If it is assumed that the intensity of the effort is positively correlated to the rapidity of the

probing actions, then the physical effectiveness of the mental intentions will, by virtue of the Quantum Zeno effect, be positively correlated to the intensity of the mental effort. One's mental self thereby
acquires responsibility for one's bodily actions.[54]

It seems to me that success in almost anything depends on having
enough interest in that endeavor to select the appropriate goal, to make
choices that take you toward that goal, and to keep on making such
choices. I experience this as a kind of hunger, a mental hunger. This
kind of self-effort seems to draw me toward the right people and situations, to set up the world around me in such a way that everything helps
me attain that goal.

Stapp is giving us another way that we, as individuals, create our own
reality. In addition to creating our world through our perceptions,
which we discuss earlier, we also do this as we choose one intention or
another. This is true whether we are focused on a particular outcome or
we have no focus or no intended outcome in mind. In *effortfully* attending to a goal, our actions are significant, of course, and so are our
thoughts. Stapp also postulates that the universe itself makes choices,
and that it is "not implausible that the probabilities of these choices
should be positively correlated with what living organisms" hold as their
goals.[55] He is saying that the universe also conspires to help us with our
intentions. If valid, this theory gives us incredible control over our destiny.

This theory of intention is in harmony with mystical writings from
most spiritual traditions. The Shaivites say, "Do the practice of Shiva to
become Shiva"—which means know "I am Shiva" and it will happen.[56]

As Stapp says, this is a very encouraging and auspicious worldview.
We can create a harmonious play of life for ourselves, and others, if we
take responsibility for a strong intention to help co-create that world.

A SCIENTIST CHANGES HIS WORLDVIEW

People can change their intentions. Allow me to introduce to you
Christof Koch. During the twenty-seven years he was a biology professor at Cal Tech, he spent much of his time in argument with scientists
and scholars like those cited throughout this book. Koch was a materialist neuroscientist, and he seemed to be wedded to the bottom-up per-

spective—that consciousness *must* be produced by the activity of neurons in the brain. Koch wrote about two hundred peer-reviewed articles on this and related subjects, not to mention separate chapters and books.

In "A Framework for Consciousness," an article he wrote in collaboration with the Nobel laureate Francis Crick and which was published in *Nature Neuroscience*, a highly regarded scientific journal, Koch puts forth a structure for how activity patterns in competing groups of neurons in the human brain could explain the neural correlates of consciousness.[57]

In other writings, he asks, "Is there any hope of moving from mere correlation to causation?" His answer is yes, and he delineates numerous potential experiments, including pharmacological interventions that have the ability to "selectively, transiently, reversibly, and delicately inactivate populations of neurons." This exercise was to demonstrate ways that the scientific community could step forward to produce proof that consciousness is produced by neuronal populations.[58]

Recently, however, Koch has changed his mind. In 2012 he published a scientific memoir in which he describes his reasons for moving, though somewhat tentatively, into the opposing camp. The book is entitled *Consciousness: Confessions of a Romantic Reductionist*, and in it Koch says,

> The pursuit of the physical basis of consciousness is the focus of my intellectual life—and has been for the past two dozen years.
>
> Francis Crick and I spent days sitting in wicker chairs in his studio, debating how living matter brings forth subjective feelings. We wrote two books and two dozen scholarly articles expounding on the need to link distinct aspects of consciousness to specific brain mechanisms and regions. We postulated a relationship between awareness and the rhythmic discharge of cortical neurons, firing every twenty to thirty milliseconds. We obsessed about the need for neurons to fire action potentials synchronously.[59]

In describing the gradual change in his understanding, Koch writes that over the years, he began to see that no matter what neural circuits he identified as critical for consciousness, there would still be a problem. He would never be able to account for how those neural circuits had actually created consciousness.

Koch's shift began in 1992 at a seminar in Zurich, Switzerland, when another neurobiologist, Volker Henn, posed a critical question to him:

> Suppose that all of Crick's and your ideas pan out and that layer 5 cortical neurons in the visual cortex that fire rhythmically and that send their output to the front of the brain are the critical neural correlates of consciousness. What is it about these cells that gives rise to awareness? How, in principle, is your hypothesis different from Descartes' proposal that the pineal gland is the seat of the soul?[60]

An evangelical on this topic, Koch replied to Henn with the usual promissory note that

> in the fullness of time science would answer this question, but for now, neuroscience should just press on, looking for the correlates of consciousness.[61]

Koch writes that for many years he pushed the question aside. It wasn't productive, he felt, and he wanted to move the neuroscience of consciousness forward. Finally, however, he realized that this fundamental question had to be answered. After years of theoretical contemplation and research and many conversations with another scientist and friend, Giulio Tononi, Koch now writes:

> I used to be a proponent of the idea of consciousness emerging out of complex nervous networks. Just read my earlier [book] *Quest*. But over the years, my thinking has changed. Subjectivity is too radically different from anything physical for it to be an emergent phenomenon. . . . The phenomenal hails from a different kingdom than the physical and is subject to different laws. . . .
>
> This point of view comes with a metaphysical cost many are unwilling to pay—the admission that experience, the interior perspective of a functioning brain, is something fundamentally different from the material thing causing it and that it can never be fully reduced to physical properties of the brain.[62]

I have to applaud Koch's courage and his integrity. He made this radical shift in perspective not because his life circumstances changed, not because he received some bolt from on high, but because he, as a scientist, saw that the current model could not explain the universe as he saw it. As I've been saying, this, to me, is science!

Koch now believes, as many philosophers have said over the last two thousand years,

> that consciousness is a fundamental, an elementary property of living matter. It can't be derived from anything else; it is a simple substance. . . . [63]

He says his new perspective is in resonance with the integrated information theory, which was formulated by his friend Tononi and which Koch calls an elaborate version of panpsychism. The integrated information theory proposes that, like an electrical charge is associated with, but not a product of, material objects, so consciousness is associated with, but not a product of, the brain. Koch writes:

> The hypothesis that all matter is sentient to some degree is terribly appealing for its elegance, simplicity, and logical coherence. Once you assume that consciousness is real and ontologically distinct from its physical substrate, then it is a simple step to conclude that the entire cosmos is suffused with sentience: it is in the air we breathe, the soil we tread on, the bacteria that colonize our intestines, and the brain that enables us to think. [64]

These are revolutionary statements from one who was a materialist neuroscientist, a science professor at one of the most highly regarded U.S. universities, and a member of a team of researchers that included the Nobel prize–winning Francis Crick, a leading materialist.

What I hope for *Infinite Awareness* is that other scientists who have questions about the prevailing materialist paradigm—whether these questions are based on personal experience or observation or just plain frustration with a model that doesn't explain all the data—will begin to give those questions air time, will write about them, and will design research projects to look into other possibilities. In this way, science moves forward.

As I read Koch's memoir and his reflections on the fundamental characteristics of consciousness, I remembered what Bruce Greyson, the researcher into near-death experiences, said when I asked him what had motivated him to operate outside the traditional scientific box.

"I don't think I'm outside the scientific box," he said. "I'm just ex-panding the box a little."

The scientific box *is* expanding, and it may be that in the not-too-distant future consciousness will be accepted as a primary phenomenon from which everything in the universe springs into being.

NOTES

1. THE MAKING OF A RENEGADE

1. Society for Neuroscience, "Dalai Lama Urges That Ethics Be a Guide in the Application of New Scientific Knowledge," NR-05-08 (11/12/05), accessed December 20, 2014, http://www.sfn.org/Press-Room/News-Release-Archives/2005/Dalai-Lama-Urges?returnId={0C16364F-DB22-424A-849A-B7CF6F-DCFE35}.

2. Ibid.

3. B. Carey, "Scientists Bridle at Lecture Plan for Dalai Lama," *New York Times*, October 19, 2005, accessed December 27, 2014, http://www.nytimes.com/2005/10/19/national/19meditate.html?pagewanted=all&_r=0.

4. Ibid.

2. TO EXAMINE A QUIET MIND

1. D. Chan and M. H. Woollacott, "Effects of Level of Meditation Experience on Attentional Focus: Is the Efficiency of Executive or Orientation Networks Improved?" *Journal of Alternative and Complementary Medicine* 13 (2007): 651–57; Y-Y. Tang et al., "Short-Term Meditation Training Improves Attention and Self-Regulation," *Proceedings of the National Academy of Sciences of the United States of America* 104, no. 43 (2007): 17152–56; Y-Y. Tang and M. I. Posner, "Training Brain Networks and States," *Trends in Cognitive Sciences* 18, no. 7 (2014): 345–50. doi: 10.1016/j.tics.2014.04.002, Epub 2014 May 7; D. Roberts-Wolfe et al., "Mindfulness Training Alters Emotional Memory Recall Compared to Active Controls: Support for an Emotional Informa-

tion Processing Model of Mindfulness," *Frontiers in Human Neuroscience* 6 (2012): 15, doi: 10.3389/fnhum.2012.00015, eCollection 2012.

2. W. Britton, "Why a Neuroscientist Would Study Meditation," *TEDx Talk*, accessed January 27, 2014, http://www.tedxtalks.ted.com/video/TEDx-BrownUniversity-Willoughby.

3. M. A. Killingsworth and D. T. Gilbert, "A Wandering Mind Is an Unhappy Mind," *Science* 330, no. 6006 (2010): 932.

4. Britton, "Why a Neuroscientist Would Study Meditation."

5. W. James, *The Heart of William James*, ed. R. Richardson (Cambridge, MA: Harvard University Press, 2010), 101.

6. S. W. Lazar, "How Meditation Can Reshape Our Brains," *Ted-Talk*, March 14, 2012, accessed February 1, 2014, http://tedxtalks.ted.com/video/TEDxCambridge-Sara-Lazar-on-how.

7. S. W. Lazar et al., "Meditation Experience Is Associated with Increased Cortical Thickness," *Neuroreport* 16, no. 17 (2005): 1893–97.

8. Lazar, "How Meditation Can Reshape Our Brains."

9. Ibid.

10. L. Freeman, *Mosby's Complementary and Alternative Medicine*, 3rd ed. (St. Louis: Mosby, 2008).

11. Chan and Woollacott, "Effects of Level of Meditation Experience on Attentional Focus."

12. H. L. Hawkins, A. F. Kramer, and D. Capaldi, "Aging, Exercise, and Attention," *Psychology and Aging* 7, no. 4 (1992): 643–53.

13. T. D. Hawkes, W. Manselle, and M. H. Woollacott, "Cross-Sectional Comparison of Executive Attention Function in Normally Aging Long-Term T'ai Chi, Meditation, and Aerobic Fitness Practitioners versus Sedentary Adults," *Journal of Alternative and Complementary Medicine* 20 (2014a): 178–84.

14. T. D. Hawkes, W. Manselle, and M. Woollacott, "Tai Chi and Meditation-Plus-Exercise Benefit Neural Substrates of Executive Function: A Cross-Sectional, Controlled Study," *Journal of Complementary and Integrative Medicine* 11 (2014b): 279–88.

15. F. Travis, "Autonomic and EEG Patterns Distinguish Transcending from Other Experiences During Transcendental Meditation Practice," *International Journal of Psychophysiology* 42 (2001): 1–9; F. Travis et al., "Patterns of EEG Coherence, Power, and Contingent Negative Variation Characterize the Integration of Transcendental and Waking States," *Biological Psychology* 61, no. 3 (2002): 293–319.

16. E. Schroedinger, "Why Not Talk Physics?" in *Quantum Questions: Mystical Writings of the World's Great Physicists*, ed. K. Wilber (Boston: Shambhala, 2001), 83–85.

17. M. Orchin et al., "Atomic Orbital Theory," *Wiley Online Library* 27 Jan doi: 10.1002/0471713740.ch1 (2005).

18. J. Jeans, "In the Mind of Some Eternal Spirit," in *Quantum Questions: Mystical Writings of the World's Great Physicists,* ed. K. Wilber (Boston: Shambhala, 2001), 129.

19. Ibid., 137.

3. AN UNACCOUNTABLE ENERGY

1. L. Sannella, *The Kundalini Experience: Psychosis or Transcendence?* (Lower Lake, CA: Integral Publishing, 1987), first published in 1976, 38.

2. Ibid.

3. I. Tweedie, *Chasm of Fire* (Shaftesbury, UK: Element Books, 1979), 62, 130.

4. G. Krishna, *Kundalini: The Evolutionary Energy in Man* (Berkeley: Shambhala, 1971), 11–12.

5. G. Krishna, *Living with Kundalini* (Boston: Shambhala, 1993), 1–3.

6. Krishna, *Kundalini: Evolutionary Energy*.

7. W. James, *The Varieties of Religious Experience: A Study in Human Nature* (New York: Simon & Schuster, Inc., 1997), first published 1902, 29.

8. Ibid., 210.

9. Ibid., 220–22.

10. Ibid.

11. Sw. V. Tirtha, *Devatma Shakti (Kundalini): Divine Power* (Varanasi, India: Swami Shivom Tirth, 1962), 58.

12. Sannella, *The Kundalini Experience*, 7.

13. J. Vøllestad, M. B. Nielsen, and G. H. Nielsen, "Mindfulness- and Acceptance-Based Interventions for Anxiety Disorders: A Systematic Review and Meta-Analysis," *The British Journal of Clinical Psychology* 51, no. 3 (2012): 239–60.

14. H. J. H. Kuijpers et al., "Meditation-Induced Psychosis," *Psychopathology* 40, no. 6 (2007): 461–64.

15. Ibid.

16. S. Sethi and S. C. Bhargava, "Relationship of Meditation and Psychosis: Case Studies," *The Australian and New Zealand Journal of Psychiatry* 37, no. 3 (2003): 382.

17. G. Hansen, *Ugeskrift for laeger* ["Schizophrenia or Spiritual Crisis? On 'Raising the Kundalini' and Its Diagnostic Classification"], *Weekly Journal of the Danish Medical Association* 157, no. 31 (1995): 4360–62.

4. CONSCIOUSNESS, VIEWED AS BOTTOM-UP

1. E. Kandel, J. Schwartz, and T. Jessell, *Principles of Neuroscience*, 4th ed. (New York: McGraw-Hill, 2000).

2. Ibid.

3. Ibid.; E. Kandel et al., *Principles of Neuroscience*, 5th ed. (New York: McGraw-Hill, 2013).

4. M. Gazzaniga, *The Bisected Brain* (New York: Appleton-Century-Crofts, 1970).

5. J. E. LeDoux, D. H. Wilson, and M. S. Gazzaniga, "A Divided Mind: Observations on the Conscious Properties of the Separated Hemispheres," *Annals of Neurology* 2, no. 5 (1977): 417–21; E. Schechter, "The Switch Model of Split-Brain Consciousness," *Philosophical Psychology* 25 (2012): 203–26.

6. Kandel et al., *Principles of Neuroscience*.

7. H. P. Stapp, *Mindful Universe: Quantum Mechanics and the Participating Observer* (Heidelberg: Springer, 2007).

8. H. Bazner and M. G. Hennerici, "Painting after Right-Hemisphere Stroke—Case Studies of Professional Artists," in *Neurological Disorders in Famous Artists*, pt. 2, ed. J. Bogousslavsky and M. G. Hennerici, *Frontiers of Neurology and Neuroscience* (Basel: Karger, 2007) 1–13; F. Brown, *Reynold Brown: Fine Art Paintings* (website), accessed January 23, 2015, http://www.franzbrown.com/reynoldbrownart/reynoldbrown/reynold0501_Fine-art_1970-1976.htm.

9. J. Moran and R. Desimone, "Selective Attention Gates Visual Processing in the Extrastriate Cortex," *Science* 229, no. 4715 (1985): 782–84; G. G. Gregoriou et al., "Long-Range Neural Coupling through Synchronization with Attention," *Progress in Brain Research* 176 (2009): 35–45, doi: 10.1016/S0079-6123(09)17603-3.

10. O. Sacks, *The Man Who Mistook His Wife for a Hat* (New York: Touchstone Books, 1998).

11. Ibid., 9.

12. Ibid., 10.

13. Ibid., 12.

14. Ibid.

15. E. F. M. Wijdicks, "Minimally Conscious State vs. Persistent Vegetative State: The Case of Terry (Wallis) vs. the Case of Terri (Schiavo)," *Mayo Clinic Proceedings* 81, no. 9 (2006): 1155–58.

16. L. Verrier et al., "An Intensive Massed-Practice Approach to Retraining Balance Post-Stroke," *Gait and Posture* 22 (2005): 154–63.

17. J. D. Schaechter et al., "Motor Recovery and Cortical Reorganization after Constraint-Induced Movement Therapy in Stroke Patients: A Preliminary Study," *Neurorehabilitation and Neural Repair* 16, no. 4 (2002): 326–38.

18. H. U. Voss et al., "Possible Axonal Regrowth in Late Recovery from the Minimally Conscious State," *The Journal of Clinical Investigation* 116, no. 7 (2006): 2005–11; Wijdicks, "Minimally Conscious State vs. Persistent Vegetative State," 1155–58.

19. B. Libet, E. W. Wright, and C. A. Gleason, "Readiness-Potentials Preceding Unrestricted Spontaneous Pre-planned Voluntary Acts," *Electroencephalography and Clinical Neurophysiology* 54, no. 3 (1982): 322–35.

20. B. Libet et al., "Time of Conscious Intention to Act in Relation to Onset of Cerebral Activity (Readiness-Potential): The Unconscious Initiation of a Freely Voluntary Act," *Brain* 106 (1983): 623–42; B. Libet, "Do We Have Free Will?" *Journal of Consciousness Studies* 6 (1999): 47–57; B. Libet, "Cerebral Physiology of Conscious Experience: Experimental Studies in Human Subjects," in *Neural Basis of Consciousness*, ed. N. Osaka (Amsterdam: John Benjamins, 2003), 66.

21. Libet, "Do We Have Free Will?" 51.

22. Libet, "Cerebral Physiology of Conscious Experience," 67.

23. Libet, "Do We Have Free Will?" 55.

24. Ibid.

25. Ibid.

26. Ibid.

27. Ibid., 56.

5. THE TOP-DOWN PERSPECTIVE

1. R. Sperry, *Science and Moral Priority: Merging Mind, Brain and Human Values* (New York: Columbia University Press, 1983).

2. D. Dennett, *Consciousness Explained* (London: Penguin, 1991), 228.

3. Sw. Prabhavananda and C. Isherwood, *How to Know God* (Hollywood: Vedanta Press, 1953), 103.

4. R. Sperry, "Mind-Brain Interaction: Mentalism, Yes; Dualism, No," *Neuroscience* 5, no. 2 (1980), 195.

5. Ibid.

6. Ibid.

7. R. W. Sperry, "Changing Priorities," *Annual Review of Neuroscience* 4 (1981): 1–15.

8. Sperry, *Science and Moral Priority*.

9. Sperry, "Changing Priorities," 1–15.

10. Sperry, *Science and Moral Priority*.

11. J. C. Eccles, *How the Self Controls Its Brain* (Berlin: Springer-Verlag, 1994).

12. F. Beck and J. C. Eccles, "Quantum Aspects of Brain Activity and the Role of Consciousness," *Proceedings of the National Academy of Sciences of the United States of America* 89, no. 23 (1992): 11357–61.

13. J. M. Schwartz, H. P. Stapp, and M. Beauregard, "Quantum Physics in Neuroscience and Psychology: A Neurophysical Model of Mind-Brain Interaction," *Philosophical Transactions of the Royal Society of London*, ser. B, 360, no. 1458 (2005): 1309–27; H. P. Stapp, *Mindful Universe: Quantum Mechanics and the Participating Observer* (Heidelberg: Springer, 2007).

14. Schwartz, Stapp, and Beauregard, "Quantum Physics in Neuroscience and Psychology," 1315.

15. D. J. Chalmers, *The Conscious Mind* (New York: Oxford University Press, 1996), 202.

16. Ibid.

17. F. Crick and C. Koch, "Toward a Neurobiological Theory of Consciousness," *Seminars in the Neurosciences* 2 (1990): 263–75.

18. Chalmers, *The Conscious Mind*, 208.

19. Ibid.

20. Ibid., 210.

21. Ibid.

22. Ibid., 230.

23. Ibid., 231.

24. Ibid.

6. OR IS CONSCIOUSNESS
ON A CONTINUUM?

1. C. U. M. Smith, "The 'Hard Problem' and the Quantum Physicists. Part 2: Modern Times," *Brain and Cognition* 71 (2009): 54–63.

2. D. Bohm, *Wholeness and the Implicate Order* (London: Routledge & Kegan Paul, 1980), 175.

3. Ibid.

4. Ibid., 178.

5. D. Pratt, "David Bohm and the Implicate Order," *Sunrise Magazine* (February/March, 1993), Theosophical University Press, accessed January 31, 2015, http://www.theosophy-nw.org/theosnw/science/prat-boh.htm.

6. Bohm, *Wholeness and the Implicate Order*, 150.

7. Pratt, "David Bohm and the Implicate Order"; Bohm, *Wholeness and the Implicate Order*.

8. Bohm, *Wholeness and the Implicate Order*, 190.

9. Ibid., 191.

10. Ibid.

11. B. Miller, *Yoga: Discipline of Freedom: The Yoga Sutra Attributed to Patanjali* (New York: Bantam, 1995), 42; Sw. Hariharananda Aranya, *Yoga Philosophy of Patanjali* (Albany: State University of New York Press, 1981), 110; G. Feuerstein, *The Yoga Sutra of Patañjali: A New Translation and Commentary* (Rochester, VT: Inner Traditions, 1989), 58.

12. J. Singh, *Pratyabhijnahrdayam: The Secret of Self-Recognition* (Delhi: Motilal Banarsidass, 1991).

13. P. Muller-Ortega, author's notes from class at yoga institute (2000).

14. Singh, *Pratyabhijnahrdayam*, 46.

15. Ibid., 59.

16. J. Singh, *Siva Sutras: The Yoga of Supreme Identity* (Delhi: Motilal Banarsidass, 1979).

17. Ibid., 6.

18. Ibid., 16.

7. AWARENESS WITHOUT A BRAIN

1. K. Clark, "Clinical Interventions with Near-Death Experiencers," in *The Near-Death Experience: Problems, Prospects, Perspectives*, ed. B. Greyson and C. P. Flynn (Springfield, IL: Charles C. Thomas, 1984), 243; K. Ring and M. Lawrence, "Further Evidence for Veridical Perception During Near-Death Experiences," *Journal of Near-Death Studies* 11 (1993): 223–29.

2. Ring and Lawrence, "Further Evidence for Veridical Perception During Near-Death Experiences."

3. A. Kellehear, *Experiences Near Death: Beyond Medicine and Religion* (New York: Oxford University Press, 1996).

4. Ibid., 125.

5. Ibid., 126.

6. S. Parnia and P. Fenwick, "Near Death Experiences in Cardiac Arrest: Visions of a Dying Brain or Visions of a New Science of Consciousness," *Resuscitation* 52 (2002): 5–11.

7. P. van Lommel et al., "Near-Death Experience in Survivors of Cardiac Arrest: A Prospective Study in the Netherlands," *Lancet* 358, no. 9298 (2001): 2039–45.

8. P. van Lommel, *Consciousness Beyond Life: The Science of the Near-Death Experience* (New York: HarperOne, 2010), 137.

9. S. Parnia, K. Spearpoint, and P. B. Fenwick, "Near Death Experiences, Cognitive Function and Psychological Outcomes of Surviving Cardiac Arrest," *Resuscitation* 74, no. 2 (2007): 217.

10. Lommel et al., "Near-Death Experience in Survivors of Cardiac Arrest," 2044.

11. Parnia, Spearpoint, and Fenwick, "Near Death Experiences, Cognitive Function and Psychological Outcomes of Surviving Cardiac Arrest," 218.

12. S. Parnia et al., "A Qualitative and Quantitative Study of the Incidence, Features and Aetiology of Near Death Experiences in Cardiac Arrest Survivors," *Resuscitation* 48, no. 2 (2001): 154.

13. Ibid., 155.

14. B. Greyson, "Incidence and Correlates of Near-Death Experiences in a Cardiac Care Unit," *General Hospital Psychiatry* 25 (2003): 275.

15. Parnia et al., "Aware-Awareness During Resuscitation—A Prospective Study," *Resuscitation* 85, no. 12 (2014): 1799.

16. Ibid., 1803.

17. Ibid.

18. E. F. Kelly et al., *Irreducible Mind: Toward a Psychology for the 21st Century* (Lanham, MD: Rowman & Littlefield, 2010), 384.

19. Greyson, "Incidence and Correlates of Near-Death Experiences in a Cardiac Care Unit"; Kelly et al., *Irreducible Mind*.

20. B. Hagerty, *Fingerprints of God: The Search for the Science of Spirituality* (New York: Riverhead Books, 2010), 200.

21. Ibid.; M. Sabom, *Light and Death* (Grand Rapids, MI: Zondervan, 1998), EPub Edition, 2011.

22. Hagerty, *Fingerprints of God*, 200.

23. Ibid., 201.

24. Ibid.

25. Sabom, *Light and Death*, chap. 3.

26. Ibid.

27. Ibid.

28. Ibid.

29. Ibid.

30. Ibid.

31. Ibid.

32. Lommel et al., "Near-Death Experience in Survivors of Cardiac Arrest," 2039–45.

33. Hagerty, *Fingerprints of God*, 205.

34. Ibid., 205–6.

35. Ibid., 210.

36. J. E. Geshwiler, "Obituary for Pam Reynolds," *Atlanta Journal,* May 28, 2010.

37. B. Peyton, personal communication with author, January 23, 2014.

38. Ibid.

39. Ibid.

40. Ibid.

41. Ibid.

42. Ibid.

43. Ibid.

44. Ibid.

45. Ibid.

46. Ibid.

47. Ibid.

8. FOLLOWING A NEAR-DEATH EXPERIENCE

1. P. van Lommel et al., "Near-Death Experience in Survivors of Cardiac Arrest: A Prospective Study in the Netherlands," *Lancet* 358, no. 9298 (2001): 2043.

2. P. van Lommel, "Pim van Lommel: Consciousness Beyond Life," pts. 1 and 2, interview with M. Van Dusen, *Present!* KMVT 15, Mountain Valley, CA, uploaded Oct. 28, 2010, accessed January 24, 2015, pt. 1 www.youtube.com/watch?v=YOeLJCdHojU, pt. 2 www.youtube.com/watch?v=N1k4fwWZMwI.

3. Ibid.

4. B. Peyton, personal communication with author, January 23, 2014.

5. Ibid.

6. Ibid.

7. Ibid.

8. Ibid.

9. Ibid.

10. Ibid.

11. Ibid.

12. Ibid.

13. Ibid.

14. Ibid.

15. M. Shermer, "Proof of Hallucination," *Scientific American* 308, no. 4 (2013): 86; L. Dittrich, "The Prophet," *Esquire Magazine*, August 2013.

16. R. Mays, "Esquire Magazine Article on Eben Alexander Distorts the Facts," *International Association for Near-Death Studies*, uploaded August 21,

2013, accessed December 2014, http://iands.org/news/news/ndes-in-the-news/970-esquire-article-on-eben-alexander-distorts-the-facts.html.

17. Dittrich, "The Prophet."

18. E. Alexander, *Proof of Heaven: A Neurosurgeon's Journey in the After-life* (New York: Simon and Schuster, 2012).

19. Ibid., 143–44.

20. Ibid., 71.

21. Ibid., 157–58.

22. Ibid., 81.

23. Ibid., 84.

24. E. F. Kelly et al., *Irreducible Mind: Toward a Psychology for the 21st Century* (Lanham, MD: Rowman & Littlefield, 2010).

25. Ibid., 385.

26. Ibid.

27. Ibid., 387.

28. R. Trustman, S. Dubovsky, and R. Titley, "Auditory Perception during General Anesthesia—Myth or Fact?" *The International Journal of Clinical and Experimental Hypnosis* 25, no. 2 (1977): 88–105; M. M. Ghoneim and R. I. Block, "Learning and Memory during General Anesthesia: An Update," *Anesthesiology* 87 (1997): 387–410; Kelly et al., *Irreducible Mind*.

29. M. Sabom, *Light and Death* (Grand Rapids, MI: Zondervan, 1998), EPub Edition, 2011.

30. Kelly et al., *Irreducible Mind*.

31. Ibid., 364.

32. W. James, *The Varieties of Religious Experience: A Study in Human Nature* (New York: Simon & Schuster, 1997), first published 1902; E. D. Starbuck, *The Psychology of Religion* (New York: Walter Scott, 1906).

9. CONSCIOUSNESS AFTER DEATH

1. I. Stevenson, "Some of My Journeys in Medicine" (Flora Levy Lecture in the Humanities, 1989), in *Science, the Self and Survival after Death: Selected Writings of Ian Stevenson*, ed. E. W. Kelly (Plymouth, UK: Rowman & Littlefield, 2013a), 11–28.

2. Ibid., 25.

3. E. Haraldsson, "Personality and Abilities of Children Claiming Previous-Life Memories," *Journal of Nervous and Mental Disease* 183 (1995): 445–51; J. B. Tucker, "Children's Reports of Past-Life Memories: A Review," *Explore : The Journal of Science and Healing* 4, no. 4 (2008): 244–48; A. Mills, "A Replication Study: Three Cases of Children in Northern India Who Are

Said to Remember a Previous Life," *Journal of Scientific Exploration* 3, no. 2 (1989): 133–84; J. Keil and I. Stevenson, "Do Cases of the Reincarnation Type Show Similar Features over Many Years? A Study of Turkish Cases a Generation Apart," *Journal of Scientific Exploration,* 13, no. 2 (1999): 189–198.

4. L. S. King, "Reincarnation," *Journal of the American Medical Association* 234 (1975): 978.

5. I. Stevenson, "The Explanatory Value of the Idea of Reincarnation," *The Journal of Nervous and Mental Disease* 164, no. 5 (1977a): 324–25.

6. I. Stevenson, "Reincarnation: Field Studies and Theoretical Issues," in *Science, the Self and Survival after Death: Selected Writings of Ian Stevenson,* ed. E. W. Kelly (Plymouth, UK: Rowman & Littlefield, 2013b), 201.

7. Ibid.

8. E. W. Kelly, "Research on the Question of Survival after Death: Reviews and Representative Case Reports," in *Science, the Self and Survival after Death: Selected Writings of Ian Stevenson,* ed. E. W. Kelly (Plymouth, UK: Rowman & Littlefield, 2013), 145–49.

9. Stevenson, "Reincarnation," 201–27.

10. I. Stevenson and G. Samararatne, "Three New Cases of the Reincarnation Type in Sri Lanka with Written Records Made before Verification," *Journal of Scientific Exploration* 2 (1988): 217–38; Stevenson, "Reincarnation," 201–27.

11. Stevenson, "Reincarnation," 207.

12. Ibid.

13. Ibid., 208.

14. I. Stevenson, "American Children Who Claim to Remember Previous Lives," *The Journal of Nervous and Mental Disease* 171, no. 12 (1983): 742–48.

15. Stevenson, "Reincarnation," 201–27.

16. J. B. Tucker, *Return to Life: Extraordinary Cases of Children Who Remember Past Lives* (New York: St. Martin's Press, 2013), Kindle edition.

17. Ibid.

18. Ibid.

19. Ibid., chapter 4.

20. Ibid.

21. Ibid.

22. Ibid.

23. Ibid.

24. Ibid.

25. Ibid.

26. Ibid.

27. Ibid.

28. Ibid.

29. Ibid.

30. Ibid.

31. Ibid.

32. I. Stevenson, "Birthmarks and Birth Defects Corresponding to Wounds on Deceased Persons," *Journal of Scientific Exploration* 7 (1993): 403–10.

33. Mills, "A Replication Study," 133–84.

34. Ibid., 157.

35. Ibid., 157–58.

36. Ibid., 158.

37. Ibid., 159.

38. Ibid, 168.

39. Ibid., 170.

40. Ibid., 172.

41. Ibid., 175.

42. Ibid., 179.

43. Ibid., 181.

44. I. Stevenson, "Survival after Death: Evidence and Issues," in *Psychical Research: A Guide to Its History, Principles and Practices,* ed. I. Grattan-Guinness (Wellingborough, UK: Aquarian, 1982), 120; Kelly, "Research on the Question of Survival after Death," 149.

10. AWARENESS AND HEALING

1. A. G. Shore, "Long-Term Effects of Energetic Healing on Symptoms of Psychological Depression and Self-Perceived Stress," *Alternative Therapies in Health and Medicine* 10, no. 3 (2004a): 42–48.

2. D. G. Finniss et al., "Biological, Clinical, and Ethical Advances of Placebo Effects," *Lancet* 375, no. 9715 (2010): 686–95.

3. Kelly et al., *Irreducible Mind: Toward a Psychology for the 21st Century* (Lanham: MD: Rowman & Littlefield, 2010), 139.

4. Ibid., 140; D. E. Moerman, "Cultural Variations in the Placebo Effect: Ulcers, Anxiety, and Blood Pressure," *Medical Anthropology Quarterly* 14, no. 1 (2000): 51–72.

5. B. Klopfer, "Psychological Variables in Human Cancer," *Journal of Projective Techniques* 21, no. 4 (1957), 337.

6. Ibid., 338.

7. Ibid., 339.

8. Kelly et al., *Irreducible Mind*, 140.

9. Ibid., 141.

10. T. D. Wager et al., "Placebo-Induced Changes in fMRI in the Anticipation and Experience of Pain," *Science* 303, no. 5661 (2004): 1162–67.

11. J-K. Zubieta et al., "Placebo Effects Mediated by Endogenous Opioid Activity on Mu-Opioid Receptors," *The Journal of Neuroscience* 25, no. 34 (2005): 7754–62; Kelly et al., *Irreducible Mind*.

12. L. A. Pratt, D. J. Brody, and Q. Gu, "Antidepressant Use in Persons Aged 12 and Over: United States, 2005–2008," *NCHS Data Brief*, no. 76 (2011): 1–8.

13. I. Kirsch, and G. Sapirstein, "Listening to Prozac but Hearing Placebo: A Meta-Analysis of Antidepressant Medication," *Prevention and Treatment* 1 (1999), http://journals.apa.org/prevention.

14. I. Kirsch, "Challenging Received Wisdom: Antidepressants and the Placebo Effect," *McGill Journal of Medicine* 11, no. 2 (2008): 219–22.

15. Kelly et al., *Irreducible Mind*; C. G. Goetz et al., "Objective Changes in Motor Function During Placebo Treatment in PD," *Neurology* 54 (2000): 710–14; R. de la Fuente-Fernandez et al., "Expectation and Dopamine Release: Mechanism of the Placebo Effect in Parkinson's Disease," *Science* 293 (2001): 1164–66.

16. T. J. Kaptchuk et al., "Components of Placebo Effect: Randomised Controlled Trial in Patients with Irritable Bowel Syndrome," *British Medical Journal* 336, no. 7651 (2008): 999–1003.

17. M. Amanzio et al., "Response Variability to Analgesics: A Role for Non-Specific Activation of Endogenous Opioids," *Pain* 90, no. 3 (2001): 205–15; Finniss et al., "Biological, Clinical, and Ethical Advances of Placebo Effects," 686–95.

18. Kelly et al., *Irreducible Mind*; L. A. Cobb et al., "An Evaluation of Internal-Mammary-Artery Ligation by a Double-Blind Technic," *New England Journal of Medicine* 260 (1959): 1115–18; E. G. Dimond, C. F. Kittle, and J. E. Crockett, "Evaluation of Internal Mammary Artery Libation and Sham Procedure in Angina Pectoris," *Circulation* 18 (1958): 712–13.

19. R. H. Gracely et al., "Clinicians' Expectations Influence Placebo Analgesia," *Lancet* 5 (1985): 43; Finniss et al., "Biological, Clinical, and Ethical Advances of Placebo Effects," 686–95.

20. Kirsch, "Challenging Received Wisdom," 220.

21. Kelly et al., *Irreducible Mind*, 147; I. Kirsch, "Conditioning, Expectancy, and the Placebo Effect: Comment on Stewart-Williams and Podd," *Psychological Bulletin* 130, no. 2 (2004): 341–43; H. L. Fields and D. D. Price, "Toward a Neurobiology of Placebo Analgesia," in *The Placebo Effect: An Interdisciplinary Exploration*, ed. A. Harrington (Cambridge, MA: Harvard University Press, 1997), 94.

22. A. Harrington, "Introduction," in *The Placebo Effect: An Interdisciplinary Exploration,* ed. A. Harrington (Cambridge, MA: Harvard University Press, 1977), 5; Kelly et al., *Irreducible Mind,* 148.

23. A. Gauld, *A History of Hypnotism* (Cambridge: Cambridge University Press, 1992).

24. Ibid.

25. E. R. Hilgard, "Hypnotic Susceptibility and Implications for Measurement," *International Journal of Clinical and Experimental Hypnosis* 30 (1982): 394–403.

26. D. R. Patterson and M. P. Jensen, "Hypnosis and Clinical Pain," *Psychological Bulletin* 129, no. 4 (2003): 495–521; T. H. Adachi et al., "A Meta-Analysis of Hypnosis for Chronic Pain Problems: A Comparison between Hypnosis, Standard Care, and Other Psychological Interventions," *International Journal of Clinical and Experimental Hypnosis* 62, no. 1 (2014): 1–28.

27. Patterson and Jensen, "Hypnosis and Clinical Pain," 495–521.

28. D. A. Oakley and P. W. Halligan, "Hypnotic Suggestion and Cognitive Neuroscience," *Trends in Cognitive Sciences* 13, no. 6 (2009): 264–70.

29. D. A. Burns, "'Warts and All'—The History and Folklore of Warts: A Review," *Journal of the Royal Society of Medicine* 85, no. 1 (1992): 37–40.

30. N. P. Spanos, V. Williams, and M. I. Gwynn, "Effects of Hypnotic, Placebo, and Salicylic Acid Treatments on Wart Regression," *Psychosomatic Medicine* 52 (1990): 109–14.

31. Ibid., 113.

32. R. Dreaper, "Recalcitrant Warts on the Hand Cured by Hypnosis," *Practitioner* 220 (1978): 305–10; Kelly et al., *Irreducible Mind.*

33. Dreaper, 308; Kelly et al., *Irreducible Mind,* 194–95.

34. A. A. Mason, "A Case of Congenital Ichthyosiform Erythroderma of Brocq Treated by Hypnosis," *British Medical Journal* 2 (1952): 422.

35. Ibid.

36. Ibid.; A. A. Mason, "Ichthyosis and Hypnosis [Letter]," *British Medical Journal* 2 (1955): 57–58.

37. Kelly et al., *Irreducible Mind,* 198.

38. C. B. Kidd, "Congenital Ichthyosiform Erythroderma Treated by Hypnosis," *The British Journal of Dermatology* 78, no. 2 (1966): 101–05; H. C. Bethune and C. B. Kidd, "Psychophysiological Mechanisms in Skin Diseases," *Lancet* 2 (1961): 1419–22.

39. Kidd, "Congenital Ichthyosiform Erythroderma Treated by Hypnosis"; Kelly et al., *Irreducible Mind.*

40. J. Wyler-Harper et al., "Hypnosis and the Allergic Response," *Schweizerische medizinische Wochenschrift. Supplementum* 62 (1994): 67–76.

41. Y. Ikemi and S. Nakagawa, "A Psychosomatic Study of Contagious Dermatitis," *Kyushu Journal of Medical Science* 13 (1962): 335–50.

42. Kelly et al., *Irreducible Mind*, 200.

43. Ibid.

44. Ibid., 211.

11. THE HEALING INTENTION

1. R. G. Jahn et al., "Correlations of Random Binary Sequences with Pre-stated Operator Intention: A Review of a 12-Year Program," *Journal of Scientific Exploration* 11 (1997): 345–67.

2. D. I. Radin and R. Nelson, "Evidence for Consciousness-Related Anomalies in Random Physical Systems," *Foundations of Physics* 19 (1989): 1500–14; D. Radin and J. Utts. "Experiments Investigating the Influence of Intention on Random and Pseudorandom Events," *Journal of Scientific Exploration* 3, no. 1 (1989): 65–79; D. Radin et al., "Consciousness and the Double-Slit Interference Pattern: Six Experiments," *Physics Essays* 25 (2012): 156–71.

3. D. I. Radin and R. D. Nelson, "Research on Mind-Matter Interactions (Mmi): Individual Intention," in *Healing, Intention and Energy Medicine: Science, Research Methods and Clinical Implications,* ed. W. B. Jonas and C. Crawford (London: Churchill Livingstone, 2003), 39–48.

4. Jahn et al., "Correlations of Random Binary Sequences with Pre-stated Operator Intention," 345–67.

5. Ibid.; National Research Council, "Enhancing Human Performance: Issues, Theories, and Techniques," *Report of the Committee on Techniques for the Enhancement of Human Performance, Commission on Behavioral and Social Sciences and Education* (Washington, DC: National Academy Press, 1988).

6. B. Carey, "A Princeton Lab on ESP Plans to Close Its Door," *New York Times*, February 10, 2007, accessed January 27, 2015.

7. D. Kronmiller, *PhDTutor.com*, accessed January 27, 2015, phdtutor.com/young_double_slit_experiment.aspx.

8. D. Radin et al., "Consciousness and the Double-Slit Interference Pattern: Six Experiments," 158; N. D. Mermin, *Boojums All the Way Through: Communicating Science in a Prosaic Age* (Cambridge: Cambridge University Press, 1990).

9. Radin et al., "Consciousness and the Double-Slit Interference Pattern."

10. Ibid.

11. Ibid., 170.

12. Ibid.

13. E. Targ, "Evaluating Distant Healing: A Research Review," *Alternative Therapies in Health and Medicine* 3, no. 6 (1997): 74–78.

14. C. B. Nash, "Psychokinetic Control of Bacterial Growth," *Journal of the Society for Psychical Research* 51 (1982): 217–21.

15. S. R. Schmidt et al., "Distant Intentionality and the Feeling of Being Stared At: Two Meta-Analyses," *British Journal of Psychology* 95 (2004): 235–47.

16. S. Schmidt, "Can We Help Just by Good Intentions? A Meta-Analysis of Experiments on Distant Intention Effects," *Journal of Alternative and Complementary Medicine* 18, no. 6 (2012): 529–33.

17. Ibid., 533.

18. Targ, "Evaluating Distant Healing: A Research Review," 74; Kelly et al., *Irreducible Mind: Toward a Psychology for the 21st Century* (Lanham, MD: Rowman & Littlefield), 132.

19. J. A. Astin, E. Harkness, and E. Ernst, "The Efficacy of 'Distant Healing': A Systematic Review of Randomized Trials," *Annals of Internal Medicine* 132 (2000): 903; D. Benor, "Survey of Spiritual Healing Research," *Complementary Medicine Research* 4 (1990): 9–33.

20. J. Achterberg et al., "Evidence for Correlations between Distant Intentionality and Brain Function in Recipients: A Functional Magnetic Resonance Imaging Analysis," *Journal of Alternative and Complementary Medicine* 11, no. 6 (2005): 965–71.

21. Ibid.

22. Ibid.

23. A. G. Shore, "Long-Term Effects of Energetic Healing on Symptoms of Psychological Depression and Self-Perceived Stress," *Alternative Therapies in Health and Medicine* 10, no. 3 (2004a): 42–48.

24. Ibid.

25. A. G. Shore, "A Qualitative Analysis of the Long-Term Effects of Energetic Healing on Symptoms of Psychological Depression and Self-Perceived Stress," *The International Journal of Healing and Caring*, 4 (2004b): 1–11.

26. Ibid., 6.

27. Ibid.

28. Ibid., 1–11.

29. Ibid., 7.

30. Ibid.

31. Ibid.

32. R. S. Friedman et al., "Effects of Reiki on Autonomic Activity Early after Acute Coronary Syndrome," *Journal of the American College of Cardiology* 56, no. 12 (2010): 995–96.

33. Ibid., 996.

34. S. VanderVaart et al., "A Systematic Review of the Therapeutic Effects of Reiki," *Journal of Alternative and Complementary Medicine* 15, no. 11 (2009): 1157–69.

35. Shore, "Long-Term Effects of Energetic Healing on Symptoms of Psychological Depression and Self-Perceived Stress," 42–48.

12. RESEARCH INTO CONSCIOUSNESS

1. E. F. Kelly et al., *Irreducible Mind: Toward a Psychology for the 21st Century* (Lanham, MD: Rowman & Littlefield, 2010).

2. E. F. Kelly, personal communication with author, May 22–23, 2014.

3. Ibid.

4. Ibid.

5. Ibid.

6. Ibid.

7. Ibid.

8. Ibid.

9. Ibid.

10. B. Greyson, personal communication with author, May 23, 2014.

11. Ibid.

12. Ibid.

13. Ibid.

14. Ibid.

15. Ibid.

16. Ibid.

17. K. Clark, "Clinical Interventions with Near-Death Experiencers," in *The Near-Death Experience: Problems, Prospects, Perspectives*, ed. B. Greyson and C. P. Flynn (Springfield, IL: Charles C. Thomas, 1984), 242–55.

18. B. Greyson, personal communication.

19. Ibid.

20. M. Grosso, personal communication with author, May 23, 2014.

21. Ibid.

22. Ibid.

23. Ibid.

24. J. Tucker, personal communication with author, May 23, 2014.

25. Ibid.

26. Ibid.

27. J. B. Tucker, *Return to Life: Extraordinary Cases of Children Who Remember Past Lives* (New York: St. Martin's Press, 2013), Kindle edition, chapter 9.

13. THE CONSCIOUSNESS–BRAIN INTERFACE

1. W. James, *Human Immortality: Two Supposed Objections to the Doctrine* (The Ingersoll Lectureship) (Boston and New York: Houghton, Mifflin, 1898).

2. E. F. Kelly and D. Presti, "A Psychobiological Perspective on 'Transmission' Models," in *Beyond Physicalism: Toward Reconciliation of Science and Spirituality,* ed. E. F. Kelly, A. Crabtree, and P. Marshall (Lanham, MD: Rowman & Littlefield, 2015), chapter 4.

3. Kelly et al., *Irreducible Mind*, 28.

4. T. S. Kuhn, *The Structure of Scientific Revolutions*, 2nd ed. (Chicago: University of Chicago Press, 1970), 78.

5. H. Bergson, *Matter and Memory*, trans. N. M. Paul and W. Scott Palmer (London: George Allen, 1911); P. Marshall, *Mystical Encounters with the Natural World* (Oxford: Oxford University Press, 2005).

6. A. Huxley, *The Doors of Perception* (New York: Perennial Library, 1954/1991); M. Grosso, "The 'Transmission' Model of Mind and Body: A Brief History," in *Science-Based Spirituality: Why Physicalism Must Be Abandoned,* ed. E. F. Kelly, A. Crabtree, and P. Marshall (Lanham, MD: Rowman & Littlefield, 2015), 122.

7. Kelly et al., *Irreducible Mind*, 28.

8. D. Broadbent, *Perception and Communication* (London: Pergamon Press, 1958).

9. Grosso, "The 'Transmission' Model of Mind and Body: A Brief History."

10. Kelly and Presti, "A Psychobiological Perspective on 'Transmission' Models"; Kelly et al., *Irreducible Mind*.

11. P. Marshall, personal communication with author, July 30, 2014.

12. Ibid.

13. Marshall, *Mystical Encounters with the Natural World*, 32.

14. Ibid., 244.

15. Ibid., 237.

16. Ibid.

17. Ibid.

18. Ibid., 240.

19. Ibid., 244.

20. Ibid.

21. Ibid., 246.

22. E. F. Kelly, "Toward a Worldview Grounded in Science and Spirituality," in *Beyond Physicalism: Toward Reconciliation of Science and Spirituality,* ed. E. F. Kelly, A. Crabtree, and P. Marshall (Lanham, MD: Rowman & Littlefield, 2015).

23. Ibid.

24. Kshemaraja, *The Svacchanda Tantra with Commentary*, ed. M. K. Shastri (Bombay: Nirnaya Saga, 1935).

25. Kelly et al., *Irreducible Mind*, 569; W. James, "A Pluralistic Universe," in *Essays in Radical Empiricism and A Pluralistic Universe* (New York: E. P. Dutton, 1971 (first published 1909), 268.

26. Kelly, "Toward a Worldview Grounded in Science and Spirituality."

27. Ibid.; C. Hartshorne and W. L. Reese, eds. *Philosophers Speak of God* (Chicago: University of Chicago Press, 1976), first published 1953.

28. Kelly, "Toward a Worldview Grounded in Science and Spirituality," 560.

29. T. L. S. Sprigge, *The Vindication of Absolute Idealism* (Edinburgh: Edinburgh University Press, 1983).

30. Marshall, *Mystical Encounters with the Natural World*, 251.

31. Ibid.

32. Ibid., 264–5.

33. Sw. Shantananda, *The Splendor of Recognition* (South Fallsburg, NY: SYDA Foundation, 2003), 69.

34. P. Marshall, *Mystical Encounters with the Natural World*, 267.

35. Kelly et al., *Irreducible Mind*; Kelly, "Toward a Worldview Grounded in Science and Spirituality."

36. Kelly and Presti, "A Psychobiological Perspective on 'Transmission' Models," 152.

37. Ibid.

38. E. Carpenter, *The Drama of Love and Death* (New York: Allen, 1912), 79; Kelly, "Toward a Worldview Grounded in Science and Spirituality," 556.

39. G. Feuerstein, *The Yoga Sutra of Patañjali: A New Translation and Commentary* (Rochester, VT: Inner Traditions, 1989).

40. Kelly, "Toward a Worldview Grounded in Science and Spirituality"; Kelly et al., *Irreducible Mind*.

41. Kelly et al., *Irreducible Mind*, 593.

42. J. Tyndall, *Address Delivered Before the British Association at Belfast, with Additions* (London: Longmans, Green, 1874), 59; H. Stapp,"A Quantum Mechanical Theory of the Mind/Brain Connection," in *Beyond Physicalism: Toward Reconciliation of Science and Spirituality*, ed. E. F. Kelly, A. Crabtree, and P. Marshall (Lanham, MD: Rowman & Littlefield, 2015), 191–92.

43. Stapp, "A Quantum Mechanical Theory of the Mind/Brain Connection."

44. Ibid., 190.

45. Ibid., 191.

46. Ibid., 193, 195.

47. Ibid., 195.

48. Ibid., 208–9.

49. Ibid., 198.

50. Ibid.

51. Ibid., 197–98.

52. Ibid., 199–200.

53. Ibid., 201.

54. Ibid., 206.

55. Ibid., 221

56. J. Nemec, *The Ubiquitous Śiva: Somananda's Śivadrsti and His Tantric Interlocutors* (Oxford: Oxford University Press, 2011).

57. F. Crick and C. Koch, "A Framework for Consciousness," *Nature Neuroscience* 6 (2003): 119–26.

58. C. Koch, "Qualia," *Current Biology* 14, no. 13 (2004): R496.

59. C. Koch, *Consciousness: Confessions of a Romantic Reductionist* (Cambridge, MA: MIT Press, 2012), 113.

60. Ibid., 114.

61. Ibid.

62. Ibid., 119.

63. Ibid.

64. Ibid., 132.

BIBLIOGRAPHY

Achterberg, J., K. Cooke, T. Richards, L. J. Standish, L. Kozak, and J. Lake. "Evidence for Correlations between Distant Intentionality and Brain Function in Recipients: A Functional Magnetic Resonance Imaging Analysis." *Journal of Alternative and Complementary Medicine* 11, no. 6 (2005): 965–71.

Adachi, T., H. Fujino, A. Nakae, T. Mashimo, and J. Sasaki. "A Meta-Analysis of Hypnosis for Chronic Pain Problems: A Comparison between Hypnosis, Standard Care, and Other Psychological Interventions." *International Journal of Clinical and Experimental Hypnosis* 62, no. 1 (2014): 1–28.

Alexander, E. *Proof of Heaven: A Neurosurgeon's Journey in the Afterlife*. New York: Simon and Schuster, 2012.

Amanzio, M., A. Pollo, G. Maggi, and F. Benedetti. "Response Variability to Analgesics: A Role for Non-Specific Activation of Endogenous Opioids." *Pain* 90, no. 3 (2001): 205–15.

Angell, M. "Disease as a Reflection of the Psyche (Editorial)." *New England Journal of Medicine* 312 (1985): 1570–72.

Astin, J. A., E. Harkness, and E. Ernst. "The Efficacy of 'Distant Healing': A Systematic Review of Randomized Trials." *Annals of Internal Medicine* 132 (2000): 903–10.

Barber, T. X. "Changing 'Unchangeable' Bodily Processes by (Hypnotic) Suggestions: A New Look at Hypnosis, Cognitions, Imagining, and the Mind-Body Problem." In *Imagination and Healing*, edited by A. A. Sheikh, 69–127. New York: Baywood Publishing, 1984.

Barnes, P. M., B. Bloom, and R. Nahin. "Complementary and Alternative Medicine Use Among Adults and Children." *CDC National Health Statistics Report* no. 12. United States, 2007, accessed January 31, 2015, https://nccih.nih.gov/news/2008/nhsr12.pdf.

Bazner, H., and M. G. Hennerici. "Painting after Right-Hemisphere Stroke—Case Studies of Professional Artists." In *Neurological Disorders in Famous Artists*, pt. 2, edited by J. Bogousslavsky and M. G. Hennerici, *Frontiers of Neurology and Neuroscience*. Basel: Karger, 22 (2007): 1–13.

Beck, F., and J. C. Eccles. "Quantum Aspects of Brain Activity and the Role of Consciousness." *Proceedings of the National Academy of Sciences of the United States of America* 89, no. 23 (1992): 11357–61.

Bellini, M. A. "Hypnosis in Dermatology." *Clinical Dermatology* 16 (1998): 725–26.

Benedetti, F., M. Amanzio, and G. Maggi. "Potentiation of Placebo Analgesia by Proglumide." *Lancet* 346, no. 8984 (1995): 1231.

Benor, D. "Survey of Spiritual Healing Research." *Complementary Medicine Research* 4 (1990): 9–33.

Bergson, H. *Matter and Memory*. Translated by N. M. Paul and W. Scott Palmer. London: George Allen, 1911.

Bethune, H. C., and C. B. Kidd. "Psychophysiological Mechanisms in Skin Diseases." *Lancet* 2 (1961): 1419–22.

Bohm, D. *Wholeness and the Implicate Order*. London: Routledge & Kegan Paul, 1980.

Britton, W. "Why a Neuroscientist Would Study Meditation." *TEDx Talk*. Accessed January 27, 2014. http://www.tedxtalks.ted.com/video/TEDxBrownUniversity-Willoughby.

Broadbent, D. *Perception and Communication*. London: Pergamon Press, 1958.

Brown, F. *Reynold Brown: Fine Art Paintings* (website). Accessed January 23, 2015. http://www.franzbrown.com/reynoldbrownart/reynoldbrown/reynold0501_Fine-art_1970-1976.htm.

Burns, D. A. "'Warts and All'—The History and Folklore of Warts: A Review." *Journal of the Royal Society of Medicine* 85, no. 1 (1992): 37–40.

Carey, B. "Scientists Bridle at Lecture Plan for Dalai Lama." *New York Times*, October 19, 2005. Accessed December 27, 2014. http://www.nytimes.com/2005/10/19/national/19meditate.html?pagewanted=all&_r=0.

———. "A Princeton Lab on ESP Plans to Close Its Door." *New York Times*, February 10, 2007. Accessed January 27, 2015. http://www.nytimes.com/2007/02/10/science/10princeton.html?pagewanted=all.

Carpenter, E. *The Drama of Love and Death*. New York: Allen, 1912.

Chalmers, D. J. *The Conscious Mind*. New York: Oxford University Press, 1996.

Chalmers, D. "Facing Up to the Problem of Consciousness." *Journal of Consciousness Studies* 2, no. 3 (1995): 200–19.

Chan, D., and M. H. Woollacott. "Effects of Level of Meditation Experience on Attentional Focus: Is the Efficiency of Executive or Orientation Networks Improved?" *Journal of Alternative and Complementary Medicine* 13 (2007): 651–57.

Clark, K. "Clinical Interventions with Near-Death Experiencers." In *The Near-Death Experience: Problems, Prospects, Perspectives*, edited by B. Greyson and C. P. Flynn, 242–55. Springfield, IL: Charles C. Thomas, 1984.

Cobb, L. A., G. I. Thomas, D. H. Dillard, K. A. Merendino, and R. A. Bruce. "An Evaluation of Internal-Mammary-Artery Ligation by a Double-Blind Technic." *New England Journal of Medicine* 260 (1959): 1115–18.

Crick, F., and C. Koch. "Toward a Neurobiological Theory of Consciousness." *Seminars in the Neurosciences* 2 (1990): 263–75.

———. "A Framework for Consciousness." *Nature Neuroscience* 6 (2003): 119–26.

Dennett, D. *Consciousness Explained*. London: Penguin Books, 1991.

Dimond, E. G., C. F. Kittle, and J. E. Crockett. "Evaluation of Internal Mammary Artery Libation and Sham Procedure in Angina Pectoris." *Circulation* 18 (1958): 712–13.

Dittrich, L. "The Prophet." *Esquire Magazine*, August 2013.

Dreaper, R. "Recalcitrant Warts on the Hand Cured by Hypnosis." *Practitioner* 220 (1978): 305–10.

Dunbar, H. F. *Emotions and Bodily Changes*. 4th ed. New York: Columbia University Press, 1954.

Eccles, J. C. *How the Self Controls Its Brain*. Berlin: Springer-Verlag, 1994.

Feuerstein, G. *The Yoga Sutra of Patañjali: A New Translation and Commentary*. Rochester, VT: Inner Traditions, 1989.

Fields, H. L., and D. D. Price. "Toward a Neurobiology of Placebo Analgesia." In *The Placebo Effect: An Interdisciplinary Exploration*. Edited by A. Harrington, 93–116. Cambridge, MA: Harvard University Press, 1997.

Finniss, D. G., T. J. Kaptchuk, F. Miller, and F. Benedetti. "Biological, Clinical, and Ethical Advances of Placebo Effects." *Lancet* 375, no. 9715 (2010): 686–95.

Freeman, L. *Mosby's Complementary and Alternative Medicine*. 3rd ed. St. Louis, MO: Mosby, 2008.

Friedman, R. S., M. M. Burg, P. Miles, F. Lee, and R. Lampert. "Effects of Reiki on Autonomic Activity Early after Acute Coronary Syndrome." *Journal of the American College of Cardiology* 56, no. 12 (2010): 995–96.

Fuente-Fernandez R. de la, T. J. Ruth, V. Sossi, M. Schulzer, D. B. Calne, and A. J. Stoessl. "Expectation and Dopamine Release: Mechanism of the Placebo Effect in Parkinson's Disease." *Science* 293 (2001): 1164–66.

Gauld, A. *A History of Hypnotism*. Cambridge: Cambridge University Press, 1992.

Gazzaniga, M. *The Bisected Brain*. New York: Appleton-Century-Crofts, 1970.

Geshwiler, J. E. "Obituary for Pam Reynolds." *Atlanta Journal*, May 28, 2010.

Ghoneim, M. M., and R. I. Block. "Learning and Memory during General Anesthesia: An Update." *Anesthesiology* 87 (1997): 387–410.

Goetz, C. G., S. Leurgans, R. Raman, and G. T. Stebbins. "Objective Changes in Motor Function During Placebo Treatment in PD." *Neurology* 54 (2000): 710–14.

Gracely, R. H., R. Dubner, W. D. Deeter, and P. J. Wolskee. "Clinicians' Expectations Influence Placebo Analgesia." *Lancet* 5 (1985): 43.

Gregoriou, G. G., S. J. Gotts, H. Zhou, and R. Desimone. "Long-Range Neural Coupling through Synchronization with Attention." *Progress in Brain Research* 176 (2009): 35–45. doi: 10.1016/S0079-6123(09)17603-3.

Greyson. B. "Biological Aspects of Near-Death Experiences." *Perspectives in Biology and Medicine* 42 (1998): 14.

———. "Incidence and Correlates of Near-Death Experiences in a Cardiac Care Unit." *General Hospital Psychiatry* 25 (2003): 269–75.

Grosso, M. "The 'Transmission' Model of Mind and Body: A Brief History." In *Science-Based Spirituality: Why Physicalism Must Be Abandoned*, edited by E. F. Kelly, A. Crabtree, and P. Marshall. Lanham, MD: Rowman & Littlefield, 2015.

Hadfield, J. A. "The Influence of Hypnotic Suggestion on Inflammatory Conditions." *Lancet* 2 (1917): 678–79.

Hagerty, B. *Fingerprints of God: The Search for the Science of Spirituality*. New York: Riverhead Books, 2010.

Hansen, G. *Ugeskrift for laeger* ["Schizophrenia or Spiritual Crisis? On 'Raising the Kundalini' and Its Diagnostic Classification"] [Article in Danish]. *Weekly Journal of the Danish Medical Association* 157, no. 31 (1995): 4360–62.

Haraldsson, E. "Children Claiming Past-Life Memories: Four Cases in Sri Lanka." *Journal of Scientific Exploration* 5 (1991): 233–61.

———. "Personality and Abilities of Children Claiming Previous-Life Memories." *Journal of Nervous and Mental Disease* 183 (1995): 445–51.

Hariharananda Aranya, Sw. *Yoga Philosophy of Patanjali*. Albany: State University of New York Press, 1981.

Harrington, A. "Introduction." In *The Placebo Effect: An Interdisciplinary Exploration*, edited by A. Harrington, 1–11. Cambridge, MA: Harvard University Press, 1977.

Hartshorne, C., and W. L. Reese, eds. *Philosophers Speak of God*. Chicago: University of Chicago Press. 1976. First published 1953.

Hawkes, T. D., W. Manselle, and M. H. Woollacott. "Cross-Sectional Comparison of Executive Attention Function in Normally Aging Long-Term T'ai Chi, Meditation, and Aerobic Fitness Practitioners versus Sedentary Adults." *Journal of Alternative and Complementary Medicine* 20 (2014a): 178–84.

———. "Tai Chi and Meditation-Plus-Exercise Benefit Neural Substrates of Executive Function: A Cross-Sectional, Controlled Study." *Journal of Complementary and Integrative Medicine* 11 (2014b): 279–88.

Hawkins, H. L., A. F. Kramer, and D. Capaldi. "Aging, Exercise, and Attention." *Psychology and Aging* 7, no. 4 (1992): 643–53.

Hilgard, E. R. "Hypnotic Susceptibility and Implications for Measurement." *International Journal of Clinical and Experimental Hypnosis* 30 (1982): 394–403.

Huxley, A. *The Doors of Perception*. New York: Perennial Library, 1954/1991.

Ikemi, Y., and S. Nakagawa. "A Psychosomatic Study of Contagious Dermatitis." *Kyushu Journal of Medical Science* 13 (1962): 335–50.

Jahn, R. G., B. J. Dunne, R. D. Nelson, Y. H. Dobyns, and G. J. Bradish. "Correlations of Random Binary Sequences with Pre-stated Operator Intention: A Review of a 12-Year Program." *Journal of Scientific Exploration* 11 (1997): 345–67.

James, W. *Human Immortality: Two Supposed Objections to the Doctrine* (The Ingersoll Lectureship). Boston and New York: Houghton, Mifflin, 1898.

———. "A Pluralistic Universe." In *Essays in Radical Empiricism and a Pluralistic Universe,* 121–284. New York: E. P. Dutton, 1971. 1909.

———. *The Varieties of Religious Experience: A Study in Human Nature.* New York: Simon & Schuster, Inc., 1997. First published 1902.

James, W. *The Heart of William James.* Edited by R. Richardson. Cambridge, MA: Harvard University Press, 2010.

Jeans, J. "In the Mind of Some Eternal Spirit." In *Quantum Questions: Mystical Writings of the World's Great Physicists,* edited by K. Wilber. Boston: Shambhala, 2001.

Kandel, E., J. Schwartz, and T. Jessell. *Principles of Neuroscience.* 4th ed. New York: McGraw-Hill, 2000.

Kandel, E., J. Schwartz, T. Jessel, A. Siegelbaum, and A. J. Hudspeth. *Principles of Neuroscience.* 5th ed. New York: McGraw-Hill, 2013.

Kaptchuk, T. J., J. M. Kelley, L. A. Conboy, R. B. Davis, C. E. Kerr, E. E. Jacobson, I. Kirsch, et al. "Components of Placebo Effect: Randomised Controlled Trial in Patients with Irritable Bowel Syndrome." *British Medical Journal* 336, no. 7651 (2008): 999–1003.

Keil J., and I. Stevenson. "Do Cases of the Reincarnation Type Show Similar Features over Many Years? A Study of Turkish Cases a Generation Apart." *Journal of Scientific Exploration* 13, no. 2 (1999): 189–98.

Kellehear, A. *Experiences Near Death: Beyond Medicine and Religion.* New York: Oxford University Press, 1996.

Kelly, E. F. "Toward a Worldview Grounded in Science and Spirituality." In *Beyond Physicalism: Toward Reconciliation of Science and Spirituality,* edited by E. F. Kelly, A. Crabtree, and P. Marshall. Lanham, MD: Rowman & Littlefield, 2015.

Kelly, E. F., and D. Presti. "A Psychobiological Perspective on 'Transmission' Models." In *Beyond Physicalism: Toward Reconciliation of Science and Spirituality,* edited by E. F. Kelly, A. Crabtree, and P. Marshall. Lanham, MD: Rowman & Littlefield, 2015.

Kelly, E. F., E. W. Kelly, A. Crabtree, A. Gauld, M. Grosso, and B. Greyson. *Irreducible Mind: Toward a Psychology for the 21st Century.* Lanham, MD: Rowman & Littlefield, 2010.

Kelly, E. W. "Research on the Question of Survival after Death: Reviews and Representative Case Reports." In *Science, the Self and Survival after Death: Selected Writings of Ian Stevenson,* edited by E. Kelly, 145–49. Plymouth, UK: Rowman & Littlefield, 2013.

Kidd, C. B. "Congenital Ichthyosiform Erythroderma Treated by Hypnosis." *The British Journal of Dermatology* 78, no. 2 (1966): 101–5.

Kihlstrom, J. F. "Discussion." In *Experimental and Theoretical Studies of Consciousness,* edited by G. R. Bock and J. Marsh. Chichester, UK: John Wiley, 1993.

Killingsworth, M. A., and D. T. Gilbert. "A Wandering Mind Is an Unhappy Mind." *Science* 330, no. 6006 (2010): 932.

King, L. S. "Reincarnation." *Journal of the American Medical Association* 234 (1975): 978.

Kirsch, I. "Challenging Received Wisdom: Antidepressants and the Placebo Effect." *McGill Journal of Medicine* 11, no. 2 (2008): 219–22.

———. "Conditioning, Expectancy, and the Placebo Effect: Comment on Stewart-Williams and Podd." *Psychological Bulletin* 130, no. 2 (2004): 341–43.

Kirsch, I., and G. Sapirstein. "Listening to Prozac but Hearing Placebo: A Meta-Analysis of Antidepressant Medication." *Prevention and Treatment* 1 (1999). http://journals.apa.org/prevention.

Klopfer, B., "Psychological Variables in Human Cancer." *Journal of Projective Techniques* 21, no. 4 (1957): 331–40.

Koch, C. "Qualia." *Current Biology* 14, no. 13 (2004): R496.

———. *Consciousness: Confessions of a Romantic Reductionist.* Cambridge, MA: MIT Press, 2012.

Krishna, G. *Kundalini: The Evolutionary Energy in Man.* Berkeley: Shambhala, 1971.

———. *Living with Kundalini.* Boston: Shambhala, 1993.

Kronmiller D. *PhDTutor.com*. Accessed January 27, 2015. phdtutor.com/young_double_slit_experiment.aspx.

Kshemaraja. *The Svacchanda Tantra with Commentary*, edited by M. K. Shastri. Bombay: Nirnaya Saga, 1935.

Kuhn, T. S. *The Structure of Scientific Revolutions*. 2nd ed. Chicago: University of Chicago Press, 1970.

Kuijpers, H. J. H., F. M. van der Heijden, S. Tuinier, and W. M. Verhoeven. "Meditation-Induced Psychosis." *Psychopathology* 40, no. 6 (2007): 461–64.

Laidlaw, T. M., R. J. Booth, and R. G. Large. "Reduction in Skin Reactions to Histamine after a Hypnotic Procedure." *Psychosomatic Medicine* 58, no. 3 (1996): 242–48.

Lazar, S. W. "How Meditation Can Reshape Our Brains." *Ted-Talk*, March 14, 2012. Accessed February 1, 2014. http://tedxtalks.ted.com/video/TEDxCambridge-Sara-Lazar-on-how.

Lazar, S. W., C. E. Kerr, R. H. Wasserman, J. R. Gray, D. N. Greve, M. T. Treadway, M. McGarvey, B. T. Quinn, J. A. Dusek, H. Benson, S. L. Rauch, C. I. Moore, and B. Fisch. "Meditation Experience Is Associated with Increased Cortical Thickness." *Neuroreport* 16, no. 17 (2005): 1893–97.

LeDoux, J. E., D. H. Wilson, and M. S. Gazzaniga. "A Divided Mind: Observations on the Conscious Properties of the Separated Hemispheres." *Annals of Neurology* 2, no. 5 (1977): 417–21.

Leininger, B., and A. Leininger. *Soul Survivor: The Reincarnation of a World War II Fighter Pilot*. New York: Grant Central Publishing, 2009.

Leuchter, A. F., I. A. Cook, E. A. Witte, M. Morgan, and M. Abrams. "Changes in Brain Function of Depressed Subjects During Treatment with Placebo." *The American Journal of Psychiatry* 159, no. 1 (2002): 122–29.

Levine, J. D., N. C. Gordon, and H. L. Fields. "The Mechanism of Placebo Analgesia." *Lancet* 2, no. 8091 (1978): 654–57.

Libet, B. "Cerebral Physiology of Conscious Experience: Experimental Studies in Human Subjects." In *Neural Basis of Consciousness*, edited by N. Osaka, 57–84. Amsterdam: John Benjamins, 2003.

———. "Do We Have Free Will?" *Journal of Consciousness Studies* 6 (1999): 47–57.

Libet, B., C. A. Gleason, E. W. Wright, and D. K. Pearl. "Time of Conscious Intention to Act in Relation to Onset of Cerebral Activity (Readiness-Potential): The Unconscious Initiation of a Freely Voluntary Act." *Brain* 106 (1983): 623–42.

Libet, B., E. W. Wright, and C. A. Gleason. "Readiness-Potentials Preceding Unrestricted Spontaneous Pre-planned Voluntary Acts." *Electroencephalography and Clinical Neurophysiology* 54, no. 3 (1982): 322–35.

Lommel, P. van. *Consciousness Beyond Life: The Science of the Near-Death Experience*. New York: HarperOne, 2010.

———. "Pim van Lommel: Consciousness Beyond Life." Interview, pts. 1 and 2 with M. Van Dusen, *Present!* KMVT 15, Mountain Valley, CA. Uploaded Oct. 28, 2010. Accessed January 24, 2015. Pt. 1: www.youtube.com/ watch?v=YOeLJCdHojU. Pt. 2: www.youtube.com/watch?v=N1k4fwWZMwI.

Lommel, P. van, R. van Wees, V. Meyers, and I. Elfferich. "Near-Death Experience in Survivors of Cardiac Arrest: A Prospective Study in the Netherlands." *Lancet* 358, no. 9298 (2001): 2039–45.

Marshall, P. *Mystical Encounters with the Natural World*. Oxford: Oxford University Press, 2005.

Mason, A. A. "A Case of Congenital Ichthyosiform Erythroderma of Brocq Treated by Hypnosis." *British Medical Journal* 2 (1952): 422–23.

———. "Ichthyosis and Hypnosis [Letter]." *British Medical Journal* 2 (1955): 57–58.

Mays, R. "Esquire Magazine Article on Eben Alexander Distorts the Facts." *International Association for Near-Death Studies*. Uploaded August 21, 2013. Accessed December 2014. http://iands.org/news/news/ndes-in-the-news/970-esquire-article-on-eben-alexander-distorts-the-facts.html.

Mermin, N. D. *Boojums All the Way Through: Communicating Science in a Prosaic Age.* Cambridge: Cambridge University Press, 1990.

Miller, B. *Yoga: Discipline of Freedom: The Yoga Sutra Attributed to Patanjali.* New York: Bantam, 1995.

Mills, A. "A Replication Study: Three Cases of Children in Northern India Who Are Said to Remember a Previous Life." *Journal of Scientific Exploration* 3, no. 2 (1989): 133–84.

Moerman, D. E. "Cultural Variations in the Placebo Effect: Ulcers, Anxiety, and Blood Pressure." *Medical Anthropology Quarterly* 14, no. 1 (2000): 51–72.

Moody, R. *Life after Life: The Investigation of a Phenomenon—Survival of Bodily Death.* Covington, GA: Mockingbird Books, 1975.

Moran, J., and R. Desimone. "Selective Attention Gates Visual Processing in the Extrastriate Cortex." *Science* 229, no. 4715 (1985): 782–84.

Muller-Ortega, P. Author's notes from class at yoga institute. (2000).

Nash, C. B. "Psychokinetic Control of Bacterial Growth." *Journal of the Society for Psychical Research* 51 (1982): 217–21.

National Research Council. "Enhancing Human Performance: Issues, Theories, and Techniques." *Report of the Committee on Techniques for the Enhancement of Human Performance, Commission on Behavioral and Social Sciences and Education.* Washington, DC: National Academy Press, 1988.

Nemec, J. *The Ubiquitous Śiva: Somananda's Śivadrsti and His Tantric Interlocutors.* Oxford: Oxford University Press, 2011.

Oakley, D. A., and P. W. Halligan. "Hypnotic Suggestion and Cognitive Neuroscience." *Trends in Cognitive Sciences* 13, no. 6 (2009): 264–70.

Orchin, M., R. S. Macomber, A. Pinhas, and R. M. Wilson. "Atomic Orbital Theory." *Wiley Online Library* 27 Jan DOI 10.1002/0471713740.ch1 (2005).

Parnia, S., and P. Fenwick. "Near Death Experiences in Cardiac Arrest: Visions of a Dying Brain or Visions of a New Science of Consciousness." *Resuscitation* 52 (2002): 5–11.

Parnia, S., K. Spearpoint, and P. B. Fenwick. "Near Death Experiences, Cognitive Function and Psychological Outcomes of Surviving Cardiac Arrest." *Resuscitation* 74, no. 2 (2007): 215–21.

Parnia, S., K. Spearpoint, G. de Vos, P. Fenwick, D. Goldberg, J. Yang, J. Zhu, et al. "Aware—Awareness During Resuscitation—A Prospective Study." *Resuscitation* 85, no. 12 (2014): 1799–805. doi: 10.1016/j.resuscitation.2014.09.004. Epub 2014 Oct 7.

Parnia, S., D. G. Waller, R. Yeates, and P. Fenwick. "A Qualitative and Quantitative Study of the Incidence, Features and Aetiology of Near Death Experiences in Cardiac Arrest Survivors." *Resuscitation* 48, no. 2 (2001): 149–56.

Patterson, D. R., and M. P. Jensen. "Hypnosis and Clinical Pain." *Psychological Bulletin* 129, no. 4 (2003): 495–521.

Peyton, B. Personal communication with author, January 23, 2014.

Prabhavananda, Sw., and C. Isherwood. *How to Know God.* Hollywood: Vedanta Press, 1953.

Pratt, D. "David Bohm and the Implicate Order." *Sunrise Magazine*, February/March, 1993. Theosophical University Press. Accessed January 31, 2015. http://www.theosophy-nw.org/theosnw/science/prat-boh.htm.

Pratt, L. A., D. J. Brody, and Q. Gu. "Antidepressant Use in Persons Aged 12 and Over: United States, 2005–2008." *NCHS Data Brief*, no. 76 (2011): 1–8.

Radin, D. I., and R. D. Nelson. "Evidence for Consciousness-Related Anomalies in Random Physical Systems." *Foundations of Physics* 19 (1989): 1500–14.

———. "Research on Mind-Matter Interactions (Mmi): Individual Intention." In *Healing, Intention and Energy Medicine: Science, Research Methods and Clinical Implications*, edited by W. B. Jonas and C. C. Crawford, 39–48. London: Churchill Livingstone, 2003.

Radin, D., L. Michel, K. Galdamez, P. Wendland, R. Rickenbach, and A. Delorme. "Consciousness and the Double-Slit Interference Pattern: Six Experiments." *Physics Essays* 25 (2012): 156–71.

Radin, D., and J. Utts. "Experiments Investigating the Influence of Intention on Random and Pseudorandom Events." *Journal of Scientific Exploration* 3, no. 1 (1989): 65–79.

Ring, K., and M. Lawrence. "Further Evidence for Veridical Perception During Near-Death Experiences." *Journal of Near-Death Studies* 11 (1993): 223–29.

Roberts-Wolfe, D., M. D. Sacchet, E. Hastings, H. Roth, and W. Britton. "Mindfulness Training Alters Emotional Memory Recall Compared to Active Controls: Support for an Emotional Information Processing Model of Mindfulness." *Frontiers in Human Neuroscience* 6 (2012): 15. doi: 10.3389/fnhum.2012.00015. eCollection 2012.

Robinson, D. N. "Preface." In *Significant Contributions to the History of Psychology 1750–1920*, edited by D. N. Robinson, (vol. 10, xxi–xxxvi). Washington, DC: University Publications of America, 1977.

Sabom, M. *Light and Death*. Grand Rapids, MI: Zondervan, 1998. EPub Edition, 2011.

Sacks, O. *The Man Who Mistook His Wife for a Hat*. New York: Touchstone Books, 1998.

Sannella, L. *The Kundalini Experience: Psychosis or Transcendence?* Lower Lake, CA: Integral Publishing, 1987. First published in 1976.

Schaechter, J. D., E. Kraft, T. S. Hilliard, R. M. Dijkhuizen, T. Benner, S. P. Finklestein, B. R. Rosen, and S. C. Cramer. "Motor Recovery and Cortical Reorganization after Constraint-Induced Movement Therapy in Stroke Patients: A Preliminary Study." *Neurorehabilitation and Neural Repair* 16, no. 4 (2002): 326–38.

Schechter, E. "The Switch Model of Split-Brain Consciousness." *Philosophical Psychology* 25 (2012): 203–26.

Schmidt, S. "Can We Help Just by Good Intentions? A Meta-Analysis of Experiments on Distant Intention Effects." *Journal of Alternative and Complementary Medicine* 18, no. 6 (2012): 529–33.

Schmidt, S., R. Schneider, J. Utts, and H. Walach. "Distant Intentionality and the Feeling of Being Stared At: Two Meta-Analyses." *British Journal of Psychology* 95 (2004): 235–47.

Schroedinger, E. "Why Not Talk Physics?" In *Quantum Questions: Mystical Writings of the World's Great Physicists*, edited by K. Wilber. Boston: Shambhala, 2001.

Schwartz, J. M., H. P. Stapp, and M. Beauregard. "Quantum Physics in Neuroscience and Psychology: A Neurophysical Model of Mind-Brain Interaction." *Philosophical Transactions of the Royal Society of London. Series B, Biological Sciences* 360, no. 1458 (2005): 1309–27.

Sethi, S., and S. C. Bhargava. "Relationship of Meditation and Psychosis: Case Studies." *The Australian and New Zealand Journal of Psychiatry* 37, no. 3 (2003): 382.

Shantananda, Sw. *The Splendor of Recognition*. South Fallsburg, NY: SYDA Foundation, 2003.

Shermer, M. "Proof of Hallucination." *Scientific American* 308, no. 4 (2013): 86.

Shore, A. G. "Long-Term Effects of Energetic Healing on Symptoms of Psychological Depression and Self-Perceived Stress." *Alternative Therapies in Health and Medicine* 10, no. 3 (2004a): 42–48.

———. "A Qualitative Analysis of the Long-Term Effects of Energetic Healing on Symptoms of Psychological Depression and Self-Perceived Stress." *The International Journal of Healing and Caring* 4 (2004b): 1–11.

Singh, J. *Siva Sutras: The Yoga of Supreme Identity*. Delhi: Motilal Banarsidass, 1979.

———. *Pratyabhijnahrdayam. The Secret of Self-Recognition*. Delhi: Motilal Banarsidass, 1991.

Smith, C. U. M. "The 'Hard Problem' and the Quantum Physicists. Part 2: Modern Times." *Brain and Cognition* 71 (2009): 54–63.

Society for Neuroscience. "Dalai Lama Urges That Ethics Be a Guide in the Application of New Scientific Knowledge." NR-05-08 (11/12/05). Accessed December 20, 2014. http://www.sfn.org/Press-Room/News-Release-Archives/2005/Dalai-Lama-Urges?returnId={0C16364F-DB22-424A-849A-B7CF6FDCFE35}.

Spanos, N. P., and J. F. Chaves. "Hypnotic Analgesia and Surgery: In Defence of the Social-Psychological Position." *British Journal of Experimental and Clinical Hypnosis* 6 (1989): 131–39.

Spanos, N. P., V. Williams, and M. I. Gwynn. "Effects of Hypnotic, Placebo, and Salicylic Acid Treatments on Wart Regression." *Psychosomatic Medicine* 52 (1990): 109–14.

Sperry, R. W. *Science and Moral Priority: Merging Mind, Brain and Human Values.* New York: Columbia University Press, 1983.

———. "Changing Priorities." *Annual Review of Neuroscience* 4 (1981): 1–15.

———. "Mind-Brain Interaction: Mentalism, Yes; Dualism, No." *Neuroscience* 5, no. 2 (1980): 195–206.

Spiro, H. M. "A Contribution to the Debate." *Advances in Mind-Body Medicine* 16, no. 1 (2000): 26–27.

Sprigge, T. L. S. *The Vindication of Absolute Idealism.* Edinburgh: Edinburgh University Press, 1983.

Stapp, H. P. *Mindful Universe: Quantum Mechanics and the Participating Observer.* Heidelberg: Springer, 2007.

———. "A Quantum Mechanical Theory of the Mind/Brain Connection." In *Beyond Physicalism: Toward Reconciliation of Science and Spirituality*, edited by E. F. Kelly, A. Crabtree, and P. Marshall. Lanham, MD: Rowman & Littlefield, 2015.

Starbuck, E. D. *The Psychology of Religion.* New York: Walter Scott, 1906.

Stevenson, I. "The Explanatory Value of the Idea of Reincarnation." *The Journal of Nervous and Mental Disease* 164, no. 5 (1977a): 305–26.

———. "Survival after Death: Evidence and Issues." In *Psychical Research: A Guide to Its History, Principles and Practices*, edited by I. Grattan-Guinness, 109–122. Wellingborough, UK: Aquarian, 1982.

———. "American Children Who Claim to Remember Previous Lives." *The Journal of Nervous and Mental Disease* 171, no. 12 (1983): 742–48.

———. "Birthmarks and Birth Defects Corresponding to Wounds on Deceased Persons." *Journal of Scientific Exploration* 7 (1993): 403–10.

———. "Some of My Journeys in Medicine." (The Flora Levy Lecture in the Humanities, 1989). In *Science, the Self and Survival after Death: Selected Writings of Ian Stevenson*, edited by E. W. Kelly, 11–28. Plymouth, UK: Rowman & Littlefield, 2013a.

———. "Reincarnation: Field Studies and Theoretical Issues." In *Science, the Self and Survival after Death: Selected Writings of Ian Stevenson*, edited by E. W. Kelly, 201–27. Plymouth, UK: Rowman & Littlefield, 2013b.

Stevenson, I., and G. Samararatne. "Three New Cases of the Reincarnation Type in Sri Lanka with Written Records Made before Verification." *Journal of Scientific Exploration* 2 (1988): 217–38.

Tang, Y-Y., Y. Ma, J. Wang, Y. Fan, S. Feng, Q. Lu, Q. Yu, D. Sui, M. K. Rothbart, and M. I. Posner. "Short-Term Meditation Training Improves Attention and Self-Regulation." *Proceedings of the National Academy of Sciences of the United States of America* 104, no. 43 (2007): 17152–56.

Tang, Y-Y., and M. I. Posner. "Training Brain Networks and States." *Trends in Cognitive Sciences* 18, no. 7 (2014): 345–50. doi: 10.1016/j.tics.2014.04.002. Epub 2014 May 7.

Targ, E. "Evaluating Distant Healing: A Research Review." *Alternative Therapies in Health and Medicine* 3, no. 6 (1997): 74–78.

Tirtha, Sw. V. *Devatma Shakti (Kundalini): Divine Power.* Varanasi, India: Swami Shivom Tirth, 1962.

Travis, F. "Autonomic and EEG Patterns Distinguish Transcending from Other Experiences During Transcendental Meditation Practice." *International Journal of Psychophysiology* 42 (2001): 1–9.

Travis, F., J. Tecce, A. Arenander, and R. K. Wallace. "Patterns of EEG Coherence, Power, and Contingent Negative Variation Characterize the Integration of Transcendental and Waking States." *Biological Psychology* 61, no. 3 (2002): 293–319.

Trustman, R., S. Dubovsky, and R. Titley. "Auditory Perception During General Anesthesia—Myth or Fact?" *The International Journal of Clinical and Experimental Hypnosis* 25, no. 2 (1977): 88–105.

Tucker, J. B. "Children's Reports of Past-Life Memories: A Review." *Explore: The Journal of Science and Healing* 4, no. 4 (2008): 244–48.

———. *Return to Life: Extraordinary Cases of Children Who Remember Past Lives.* New York: St. Martin's Press, 2013. Kindle edition.

Tweedie, I. *Chasm of Fire*. Shaftesbury, UK: Element Books, 1979.

Tyndall, J. *Address Delivered Before the British Association at Belfast, with Additions*. London: Longmans, Green, 1874.

VanderVaart, S., V. M. Gijsen, S. N. de Wildt, and G. Koren. "A Systematic Review of the Therapeutic Effects of Reiki." *Journal of Alternative and Complementary Medicine* 15, no. 11 (2009): 1157–69.

Verrier, L., J. Langan, A. Shumway-Cook, and M. Woollacott. "An Intensive Massed-Practice Approach to Retraining Balance Post-Stroke." *Gait and Posture* 22 (2005): 154–63.

Vøllestad, J., M. B. Nielsen, and G. H. Nielsen. "Mindfulness- and Acceptance-Based Interventions for Anxiety Disorders: A Systematic Review and Meta-Analysis." *The British Journal of Clinical Psychology* 51, no. 3 (2012): 239–60.

Voss, H. U., A. M. Uluç, J. P. Dyke, R. Watts, E. J. Kobylarz, B. D. McCandliss, L. A. Heier, B. J. Beattie, K. A. Hamacher, S. Vallabhajosula, S. J. Goldsmith, D. Ballon, J. T. Giancino, and N. D. Schiff. "Possible Axonal Regrowth in Late Recovery from the Minimally Conscious State." *The Journal of Clinical Investigation* 116, no. 7 (2006): 2005–11.

Wager, T. D., J. K. Rilling, E. E. Smith, A. Sokolik, K. L. Casey, R. J. Davidson, S. M. Kosslyn, R. M. Rose, and J. D. Cohen. "Placebo-Induced Changes in fMRI in the Anticipation and Experience of Pain." *Science* 303, no. 5661 (2004): 1162–67.

Wijdicks, E. F. M. "Minimally Conscious State vs. Persistent Vegetative State: The Case of Terry (Wallis) vs. the Case of Terri (Schiavo)." *Mayo Clinic Proceedings* 81, no. 9 (2006): 1155–58.

Wyler-Harper, J., A. J. Bircher, W. Langewitz, and A. Kiss. "Hypnosis and the Allergic Response." *Schweizerische medizinische Wochenschrift. Supplementum* 62 (1994): 67–76.

Zubieta, J-K., J. A. Bueller, L. R. Jackson, D. J. Scott, Y. Xu, R. A. Koeppe, T. E. Nichols, and C. S. Stohler. "Placebo Effects Mediated by Endogenous Opioid Activity on Mu-Opioid Receptors." *The Journal of Neuroscience* 25, no. 34 (2005): 7754–62.

INDEX

ABOUT THE AUTHOR

Marjorie Hines Woollacott, PhD, has been a neuroscience professor at the University of Oregon for more than three decades and a meditator for almost four. She also has a master's degree in Asian studies, which she began on a teaching sabbatical and completed at the UO while a full-time professor. Her master's thesis was the foundation for her latest book, *Infinite Awareness: The Awakening of a Scientific Mind*, which is both a scientist's memoir and a research survey on human consciousness. Woollacott's own research has been funded by the National Institutes of Health and the National Science Foundation, and includes both research in neuroscience and testing the efficacy of alternative forms of therapy such as tai chi and meditation for improving both attention and balance in adults. She also has ongoing studies on sensory contributions to music performance, in collaboration with Steven Pologe, professor of cello performance in the UO School of Music, and studies on attentional network changes associated with meditation practice. With Dr. Anne Shumway-Cooke, Woollacott has coauthored a popular textbook for health professionals, *Motor Control: Theory and Practical Applications*, in its fifth edition, and she has written more than 180 peer-reviewed research articles. She has been the keynote speaker at conferences in North and South America, Europe, Australia, and Asia, and has taught courses not only in neuroscience and rehabilitation medicine but also in meditation, hatha yoga, and alternative and complementary medicine. Her undergraduate work and doctoral studies were in neuroscience at the University of Southern California.